Postwar Fertility Trends and Differentials in the United States

STUDIES IN POPULATION

Under the Editorship of: H. H. WINSBOROUGH

Department of Sociology
University of Wisconsin
Madison, Wisconsin

Samuel H. Preston, Nathan Keyfitz, and Robert Schoen. Causes of Death: *Life Tables for National Populations.*

Otis Dudley Duncan, David L. Featherman, and Beverly Duncan. Socioeconomic Background and Achievement.

James A. Sweet. Women in the Labor Force.

Tertius Chandler and Gerald Fox. 3000 Years of Urban Growth.

William H. Sewell and Robert M. Hauser. Education, Occupation, and Earnings: *Achievement in the Early Career.*

Otis Dudley Duncan. Introduction to Structural Equation Models.

William H. Sewell, Robert M. Hauser, and David L. Featherman (Eds.). Schooling and Achievement in American Society.

Henry Shryock, Jacob S. Siegel, and Associates. The Methods and Materials of Demography. *Condensed Edition by Edward Stockwell.*

Samuel H. Preston. Mortality Patterns in National Populations: *With Special Reference to Recorded Causes of Death.*

Robert M. Hauser and David L. Featherman. The Process of Stratification: *Trends and Analyses.*

Ronald R. Rindfuss and James A. Sweet. Postwar Fertility Trends and Differentials in the United States.

Postwar Fertility Trends and Differentials in the United States

Ronald R. Rindfuss

Department of Sociology
University of North Carolina
Chapel Hill, North Carolina

James A. Sweet

Center for Demography and Ecology
Department of Sociology
University of Wisconsin—Madison
Madison, Wisconsin

ACADEMIC PRESS   New York, San Francisco, London

A Subsidiary of Harcourt Brace Jovanovich, Publishers

ACADEMIC PRESS, INC.
111 Fifth Avenue, New York, New York 10003

United Kingdom Edition published by
ACADEMIC PRESS, INC. (LONDON) LTD.
24/28 Oval Road, London NW1

Library of Congress Cataloging in Publication Data

Rindfuss, Ronald R   Date
  Postwar fertility trends and differentials in the
United States.

  (Studies in population)
  Bibliography: p.
  Includes index.
  1. Fertility, Human—United States. 2. United
States—Statistics, Vital. I. Sweet, James A., joint
author. II. Title. III. Series.
HB915.R56   301.36'1'0973   76-50403
ISBN 0−12−589250−0

Contents

Preface   ix

1   INTRODUCTION   1

Historical and Contemporary Perspective   2
Methodological Perspective   5
Overview of the Study   6

2   MEASUREMENT: SOURCES, OPPORTUNITIES,
AND LIMITATIONS   9

Own-Children Data   9
Data Requirements   11
Comparisons with Vital Registration Data   13
Comparisons with Birth History Data   25
Individual and Aggregate Measures   29
Summary   31

3   TRENDS IN FERTILITY: 1945–1969   33

Education and the Estimation of Annual Fertility Rates   33
Pervasiveness   38
Trends within Education Groups   38
Trends within Racial and Education Groups   44
Fertility Patterns: Concept and Measurement   49
Trends in Fertility Patterns   51
Summary   58

4   DIFFERENTIALS: PERSISTENCE AND CHANGE   61

Poverty and Fertility   62
Differentials within the Total Population   63
Differentials in Trends: Urban Whites   86
Summary   87

5   FERTILITY TRENDS AMONG MINORITY GROUPS   89

Aggregate Trends: 1955–1969   89
Annual Rates and Recent Marital Fertility   97
Changing Status and Own-Children Trend Estimates   100
Fertility Declines within Two High-Fertility Groups   103
Fertility Declines within the Southern Urban Black and
the Non-Southern Black Population   110
Minority Status and Fertility   112
Summary   115

6   FERTILITY DIFFERENTIALS WITHIN MINORITY GROUPS   117

Differentials within Three High-Fertility Groups   117
Differentials within the Urban Black Population   126
Differentials within Two Low-Fertility Populations   133
Differentials within the Puerto Rican Population   137
Differences in the Timing of Fertility   139
Summary   148

7   RURAL FERTILITY TRENDS AND DIFFERENTIALS   151

Definitions of "Rural" and "Urban"   151
Migration and Fertility Rate Estimates   154
Aggregate Trends   155
Differential Fertility Declines within the Farm Population:
1960–1970   160
Trends in the Pattern of Fertility   164
Current Differentials   166
Rural/Urban Differences in the Age Patterns of Fertility   169
Summary   172

8   FERTILITY AND MIGRATION:
     THE CASE OF PUERTO RICO   173

Measuring Migration Status   175
Other Methodological Concerns   176
Migration and Current Fertility   177

Migration and Children Ever Born   180
Knowledge of English and Current Fertility   182
Summary   183

9   SIMILARITY AND DIVERSITY:
     SOME EXTENSIONS AND IMPLICATIONS   185
     Similarity and Diversity in the 1970s   186
     Some Implications   191

Appendix A   Urban White Recent Marital Fertility Differentials   195
Appendix B   Stability of Racial Estimates of Annual Fertility Rates 199
Appendix C   Differentials in Recent Marital Fertility within
              Various Racial and Ethnic Groups: 1960   203
Appendix D   Post-1970 Fertility Trends and Differentials within
              the Black Population   209
References   213
Index   221

Preface

This book is about fertility trends and differentials within the United States. Our interest is in examining and describing fertility trends and levels within social and economic subgroups; and the focus is on period rather than cohort fertility. Knowledge of such subgroup differences facilitates the understanding of the composition of aggregate fertility rates as well as of the dynamics of changes in those rates. The major portion of the book deals with the time period 1945–1969; the last chapter extends the findings through the first half of the 1970s.

The study is based on data made available by the release of the 1-in-a-100 Public Use Samples from the 1960 and 1970 United States Censuses. This book is the first comprehensive study of socioeconomic fertility trends and differentials to use these Public Use Samples. The availability of individual records (with appropriate safeguards to protect confidentiality), very large sample sizes, and a range of social and economic characteristics permits more extensive and detailed analyses of fertility trends and differentials than had been possible with existing tabulations.

A major, and somewhat unexpected, finding of the study is that the dominant fertility trends of the past three decades—the "baby boom" of the late 1940s and the 1950s, and the decline in fertility that has occurred since the late 1950s—are found within virtually every social and economic subgroup examined. Of course, there are some differences across groups and these differences are examined in the book, but the principle features of the fertility trends within the United States since World War II are found within almost every major subgroup.

Yet, along with this pervasiveness of trends, there is a persistence of subgroup differentials in fertility levels in any given cross section; and these cross-sectional differentials are examined in detail. For some of the social and economic variables considered, differentials are smaller in later periods than in earlier periods; for other social and economic variables, the reverse is true. Contrary to what many social scientists had expected, there has not been an extensive and pervasive diminishing of social and economic differentials in cross-sectional fertility levels.

This research was supported by a grant to James A. Sweet from the Center for Population Research of the National Institute of Child Health and Human Development (Grant No. HD-07682). Additional support for this project came from the Institute for Research on Poverty of the University of Wisconsin under funds granted by the Economic Opportunity Act of 1964 and administered by the Department of Health, Education, and Welfare. In addition, this study benefited from a Population Research Center's Grant from the Center for Population Research of NICHD (Grant No. HD-05876). Needless to say, we are very grateful for this research support. Any opinions, findings, conclusions, or recommendations are those of the authors and do not necessarily reflect the views of the funding agencies.

The authors collaborated fully in this research; the order of authorship is alphabetical. To the extent that there was a division of labor, Sweet concentrated more on the analysis of the recent marital fertility rates, and Rindfuss on the annual age-specific fertility rates.

Portions of this monograph have appeared, in somewhat different form, in *Demography, Family Planning Perspectives,* and *International Migration Review.* We thank these journals for permission to use that material in this book.

Drafts of various parts of this book have been read by Larry Bumpass, Dennis Hogan, and Maurice MacDonald. Their comments are deeply appreciated.

Part of this research is based on a set of annual age-specific fertility rates that were constructed for various subgroups from data from the 1960 and 1970 United States Censuses. For reasons of economy, these actual rates are not included here. Readers desiring these rates, either to gain a better understanding of the research reported here or to pursue further research with them, can obtain a copy of these rates by writing to either of the authors and asking for a copy of "Fertility Rates for Racial and Social Subpopulations within the United States: 1945–1969."

Finally, special thanks and credit are due to Margaret Knoll and Barbara Witt. Without their skilled assistance in tasks ranging from computer programming to keeping track of bits and pieces of the research results, it is doubtful that we ever would have finished the analysis reported in this monograph.

1

Introduction

Fertility history in the United States since World War II has been dominated by two important trends: a rise in fertility beginning during the late 1940s and lasting through 1957 and a decline in fertility beginning in the late 1950s and continuing through the time of this writing. It is possible to determine the demographic components of this rise and subsequent decline with existing data, but our ability to examine the social components of the rise and decline in fertility has been severely hampered by the failure of published vital statistics to provide relevant data.

It is not enough to know national trends in fertility and their demographic components, because individual fertility behavior is not simply a function of country of residence or of demographic characteristics. Rather, fertility behavior is a complex function of social and biological factors mediated by individual characteristics. Social differences—whether they be educational, residential, religious, or racial differences—have consistently been found to be strong determinants of fertility behavior. In this volume, we examine the social and economic components of postwar fertility trends, as well as the cross-sectional relationship between social characteristics and fertility levels.

Ours is primarily a "descriptive" study of reproductive trends and differentials. The emphasis throughout the monograph will be on investigating *what* has been occurring; as such, the study should sharpen the focus of the question of *why* recent fertility trends have occurred the way they have. Although we will occasionally speculate about why certain trends have occurred, an explanation for all of the patterns found is clearly beyond the scope of the present study. The remainder of this chapter will provide some background and perspective on the fertility trends that are the subject of this monograph, provide some

methodological perspective on the present study, and provide an overview of the
chapters that follow.

HISTORICAL AND CONTEMPORARY PERSPECTIVE

The time period under consideration for this research is from World War II to
the present. The first decade or so following the war witnessed a sustained
increase in fertility. Subsequent years witnessed a steady decline in fertility
rates, followed by the more recent precipitous decline (Figure 1-1). The current
total fertility rate is at a historic low. The 1973 rate of 1900 births per 1000
women represents a reduction of almost 50% since 1957. The fluctuations in
period fertility rates are reflected in the sizes of annual birth cohorts that pass
through our educational institutions, the job market, the marriage market, and
other societal institutions. In 1945, there were 2.7 million babies born. By 1957,
this number had increased to 4.3 million; by 1973, it had declined to 3.1 million
births.

A different perspective is obtained if a longer time frame is used. From
colonial times to the 1940s, fertility levels declined almost continuously and,
indeed, the substantial postwar rise was completely unexpected. The length,

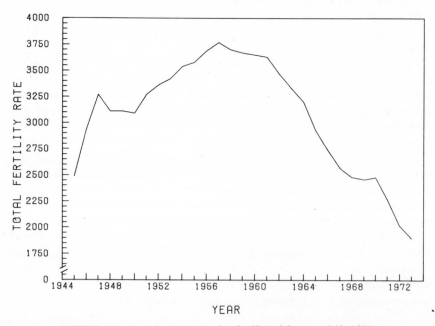

YEAR

FIGURE 1-1   *Total fertility rates for the United States: 1945–1973.*

constancy, and extent of the historic fertility decline suggest that the postwar period represents a new era.

Various estimates of fertility before the Revolutionary War indicate that fertility was very high (see Grabill, Kiser, and Whelpton, 1958: Ch. 2). At the completion of childbearing, the average woman had probably borne eight children. The crude birth rate was over 50 births per 1000 population—compared to the current rate of less than 15 per 1000. This level of fertility was accomplished by early marriage and high rates of marital fertility (see Taeuber and Taeuber, 1971). Reliable information on trends in fertility is not available until the beginning of the nineteenth century. Through the nineteenth century and during the first third of the twentieth century, fertility persistently declined, by more than four children per woman on the average.

The effect of social characteristics on fertility in the United States has been evident ever since demographers have had relevant data. Whelpton (1928) examined rural/urban fertility differentials for the period from 1800 to 1920 and found that rural areas had considerably higher fertility over the entire period. Notestein (1936) and his colleagues (Sydenstriker and Notestein, 1930; Sallume and Notestein, 1932), using data from the 1910 census on children ever born, examined residential and occupational differentials in the latter part of the nineteenth century. The rural rate was 63% higher than the urban rate; and the fertility rate of unskilled laborers was 73% higher than that of professional workers. More recent studies have shown the persistence and, in some cases, the narrowing of socioeconomic, residential, and racial differentials (Grabill, Kiser, and Whelpton, 1958; Kiser, Grabill, and Campbell, 1968; and Cho, Grabill, and Bogue, 1970). This study is a descendant and an extension of that tradition.

The trends and group variations in actual fertility behavior, with which we are concerned, are brought about by changes and differences in a large number of intermediate factors affecting exposure to intercourse, exposure to conception, and the probability of conception resulting in a live birth (see Davis and Blake, 1956). In the past several decades, significant shifts have occurred in a number of these intermediate factors.

There is suggestive, but not conclusive, evidence that age at entry into premarital sexual liaisons has declined (Zelnik and Kantner, 1972); and there is evidence that age at first marriage, that is, entry into a permanent sexual union, has increased since the 1950s (Glick and Norton, 1973). Increases in rates of separation and divorce have also characterized the decade of the 1960s and, thus, have reduced the time spent in permanent sexual unions.

One of the most dramatic changes during the 1960s was the increase in contraceptive technological capability and usage (Westoff, 1976). There has been a significant shift toward the use of contraception earlier in the reproductive career and a shift toward the use of more effective methods by those who used contraception for childspacing purposes (Rindfuss and Westoff, 1974).

Technologically, the most significant change has been the introduction of methods that do not require attention at the time of sexual intercourse. The pill was introduced in the early 1960s and quickly became the most popular method of contraception; the modern IUD was introduced in the mid-1960s and was diffusing rapidly in the latter part of the decade (Ryder, 1972). The use of contraceptive sterilization as a terminal method of contraception increased dramatically during the latter part of the 1960s (Westoff, 1972, 1976; Presser and Bumpass, 1972). Thus, not only is the act of contraception separate from the act of coitus for many contemporary couples, but also, for some couples, contraception has become permanent as well.

There has also been a fundamental change with respect to the availability of abortion as a means of birth control. Prior to 1967, all states in the United States had statutes prohibiting abortions with the exception of certain medical situations—generally only to save the mother's life (Sarvis and Rodman, 1974). Beginning in 1967, some states began passing liberalized abortion laws. The process of liberalizing abortion laws was completed by the 1973 Supreme Court decisions in *Roe* v. *Wade* and *Doe* v. *Bolton,* which struck down restrictive abortion laws. Abortion is now legal throughout the United States.

Even though there is considerable diversity within developed nations with respect to those intermediate factors affecting exposure to intercourse, exposure to conception, and the probability of conception resulting in a live birth (see Glass, 1969; Berent, 1974), many of the trends in actual fertility levels that have occurred within the United States have occurred in other developed societies as well. In general, those countries that had comparatively low levels of fertility during the 1930s experienced a sustained postwar surge in fertility, followed by declining fertility rates in the 1960s (Teitelbaum, 1973; Campbell, 1974; Westoff, 1974). In the United States, Canada, Australia, and New Zealand, the so-called "baby boom" was most pronounced. In Northern and Western European countries, the fertility rate declined after the immediate postwar rise and then gradually increased again through the 1950s. The Eastern European countries and Japan began the period with comparatively high rates of fertility and have experienced fertility reductions during the 1950s and 1960s.

Responses to questions about the number of children that couples expect to have suggest that period fertility will remain low, at least in the near future. Whether the measure is wanted fertility, desired family size, ideal family size, fertility intentions, or childbearing expectations, in the United States there has been a significant reduction in overall means and a large increase in the proportion responding "two" (see Ryder and Westoff, 1972; Blake, 1974; U.S. Bureau of the Census, 1975). To use expected family size as an example, American married women expected 3.1 children in 1967; by 1975, this number had declined to 2.6. For younger women (18–24 years old), expected family size declined from 2.9 children in 1967 to about 2.2 in 1974 (U.S. Bureau of the Census, 1975).

METHODOLOGICAL PERSPECTIVE

Because demographers have found no one method, data source, or framework to be suitable for all substantive questions, they have developed a multitude of techniques and approaches—each with its own strengths and weaknesses. In our research, we rely on data gathered by the census, we use the own-children technique, and the emphasis is on period fertility. Although Chapter 2 is devoted to a detailed exposition of methodological issues, it may be helpful to provide an overview here.

One of the fundamental distinctions made by demographers is between period and cohort perspectives. With respect to fertility, the cohort perspective refers to the lifetime childbearing of an aggregate of women born or first married during the same time period. Period fertility derives from the childbearing of a number of contiguous cohorts during a specific time period. As such, period fertility has an inherent ambiguity because changes in period fertility may be due to changes in the timing of fertility in the absence of changes in the actual level of fertility achieved by each cohort. Cohort fertility, on the other hand, while conceptually more pure, requires the analyst to suspend final judgment until the cohort has finished the childbearing period—a period that spans over 30 years. Our decision to focus on period fertility reflects our desire to investigate contemporary fertility trends and differentials, particularly the declines in fertility during the 1960s.

There are also other reasons for examining differentials in period fertility besides the fact that they are current. Period levels of fertility have important consequences in that they determine the sizes of future cohorts; and given the likelihood of future fluctuations in period fertility (Campbell, 1974; Lee, 1974; Sklar and Berkov, 1975), it is necessary to examine the extent to which various subgroups are differentially responsible for such period fluctuations. The examination of differentials in period fertility is also necessary because some statuses, such as income and occupation, change over time; comparisons of differentials in completed fertility would be inappropriate because of such changes.

When studying fertility, there are three principal sources of information: vital registration systems, censuses, and fertility surveys. In the present study of group differences in fertility, we rely primarily on census data, which, for our purposes, have a number of advantages. The decennial censuses are very close to being replications of one another and thus are well suited to the analysis of social change. The census data for 1960 and 1970 are now available on magnetic tape in the form of individual records of sample households in the United States (with appropriate safeguards to protect the confidentiality of the individual respondents). Since we are not dependent on published tabulations, we can retabulate in the ways most appropriate to our own problem, and we can also utilize techniques of multivariate analysis in order to better understand patterns of differential fertility. The large samples available from the census permit the reconstruction of previous period fertility by disaggregating the cumulative reproductive experience of women enumerated in the census. The large samples also permit detailed analysis of fertility differentials within small subpopulations. Finally, the census, in comparison with the vital registration system, provides a fairly wide array of socioeconomic characteristics.

However, there are also disadvantages in using census data for analysis of fertility trends and differentials. First, many important characteristics simply are not available in the census. The most obvious are measures of religion and religiosity. We do not have such data on the United States census; thus, variation by religion is necessarily undocumented and uncontrolled in our comparisons. Second, census data do not provide details on many important variables affecting fertility. We do not have any information on contraception, for example. Third, only past fertility experience can be analyzed with data from the decennial census; no measure of reproductive intentions is available.

Finally, this research relies almost entirely on data generated by the own-children method. This is just one of a number of techniques available for obtaining fertility measures from census data. Others include stable population techniques and questions on children ever born. The primary advantage of the own-children method is the fine detail it makes possible. The drawback of the own-children technique is that assumptions are required regarding children living with their parents, coverage of the census, mortality, and the correct reporting of ages. These assumptions and the effect of departures from them on our own-children-derived fertility rates are discussed in detail in Chapter 2.

OVERVIEW OF THE STUDY

Chapter 3 begins our examination of the social and economic components of postwar fertility change. Annual age-specific birth rates since 1945 are aggregated to total fertility rates, which are examined for education groups and for several racial and ethnic minority groups. In Chapter 3, as in later chapters, a good deal of attention is devoted to examining differences in the pattern of fertility change. However, the reader will be struck, as we were, by the pervasiveness of fertility trends in the postwar period among all social and economic groups. Fertility increased during the 1950s and decreased during the 1960s for virtually every group. Indeed, the principal finding of Chapter 3 is the remarkable pervasiveness of fertility change. The chapter concludes with an examination of the age pattern of fertility within various education and racial groups over the period 1945–1965. Again, the pattern of change pervaded all groups within the population, with fertility becoming concentrated within a smaller age range and the mean shifting toward younger ages.

Chapter 4 shifts attention from fertility trends to fertility differentials. Marital fertility, rather than total fertility, is examined. Differentials in relation to education, race and ethnic status, husband's occupation, age at first marriage, type of place of residence, and husband's income are examined for births occurring in the period immediately preceding the 1960 and 1970 censuses. One important conclusion is a corollary of the pervasiveness of fertility trends: That is, differentials that existed in the late 1950s have tended to persist in the late 1960s. Net of other factors, women with high levels of education have lower fertility than women with lower levels of education. Fertility of the black and Spanish-surname populations remains higher than that for the white population, although the black/white difference has diminished considerably. Women who marry in their teens have higher fertility than those who marry in their early twenties, and those who marry beyond their mid-twenties have the lowest levels of fertility. Persons living on farms and persons living in more remote areas in the United States tend to have somewhat higher fertility than those living in urban, metropolitan areas. A somewhat surprising and persisting positive relationship between husband's income and recent fertility was found and is investigated in some detail. We conclude that it may be a phenomenon of the timing of births in relation to anticipated changes in the husband's income.

Chapters 5 and 6 examine fertility trends and differentials among minority groups. Chapter 5 compares fertility trends between 1955 and 1969 among Mexican Americans, American Indians, Chinese Americans, Japanese Americans, blacks, and whites in the aggregate, and for various social and economic subgroups within the ethnic groups. In general, all groups studied have experienced considerable absolute declines in fertility, but the relative levels among the groups have remained similar throughout the period. Differentials in marital fertility within the racial and ethnic groups are examined in detail in Chapter 6. The focus of this discussion is on the late 1960s, with data from the late 1950s included as Appendix C. All groups studied exhibited a negative relationship between education and fertility, and between age at first marriage and fertility, but the magnitude of these effects varies widely. The positive income effect found for the total population is also found for most minority groups, with the exception of three high-fertility groups: the Spanish-surname, American Indian, and Southern rural black populations.

Chapter 7 devotes special attention to the fertility trends and differentials in the rural and the rural farm populations. These groups warrant special attention because of their traditionally higher than average levels of fertility. We find that rural women experienced a fertility decline during the 1960s similar to that of the urban population. However, during the 1950s, rural women had experienced a much smaller increase in fertility than urban women; and among older, less educated rural women, there was actually a decrease in fertility during the 1950s. This constitutes the only discovered exception to the pervasiveness of the fertility increase in the 1950s. In spite of this difference in trend, a farm/nonfarm fertility differential persists. Fertility differentials within the rural population also parallel those within the population at large.

In some of the work reported in these earlier chapters, the population of persons of Puerto Rican origin living in the United States is examined. In Chapter 8, we use data from the Census of Puerto Rico in conjunction with data on the Puerto Rican Americans enumerated in the Census of the United States, thus obtaining a sample of all Puerto Ricans. The focus of the chapter is on the relationship between migration and fertility. We find no difference between the current fertility level of Puerto Ricans living in urban areas on the island and those living in the United States. However, we do find that rural island residents have higher fertility than the urban residents. In addition, fertility differentials among island residents, in relation to the ability to speak English, are examined and discussed.

Finally, in the concluding chapter, we discuss some of the implications of this pervasive pattern of fertility decline and the persisting pattern of fertility differentials. In addition, using data from the Current Population Survey (CPS), we attempt to determine whether or not the rapid fertility change observed in the aggregate population in the early 1970s occurred throughout the population and whether or not patterns of differential fertility have changed in any significant manner. We again find a pervasive pattern of decline and persisting differentials in the period 1970–1975.

2

Measurement: Sources, Opportunities, and Limitations

The study of subgroup differences in fertility is essential to the understanding of the composition of aggregate fertility rates, as well as to the understanding of changes in those rates. Typically, in industrialized nations, vital registration systems supply insufficient detail, and limitations on sample sizes in national surveys prevent detailed examination of numerous fertility differentials. For many developing nations, vital registration systems are either inadequate or simply do not exist.

One method that has been developed to remedy this deficit is the use of information on own children from national censuses (Grabill and Cho, 1965). Since many censuses are recorded in a manner that permits linking the records of children to the records of their mothers, "own-children" data can be used to examine a wide variety of fertility differentials. Since own-children data are obtained from national censuses, sufficient numbers of cases are available to examine most groups that are of theoretical interest. It is these data on own children for the United States that are analyzed throughout this monograph. This chapter describes own-children data and the dependent variables that are used based on that data, indicates some of the assumptions and requirements of the data, and presents a series of comparisons between own-children-derived fertility estimates and estimates obtained from other sources.

OWN-CHILDREN DATA

Standard census procedure is to enumerate households and ascertain the age of each member of that household and his or her relationship to the head of the household. If the data are coded such that the record for the child can be matched with the record for the mother, then the series of child records becomes analogous to a birth history of the woman and can be used for the analysis of recent fertility.

Since the use of own-children data has been described elsewhere (Grabill and Cho, 1965; Cho, 1968; Cho, Grabill, and Bogue, 1970; Cho, 1971; Retherford and Cho, 1974; Cho, 1974), a lengthy exposition is unnecessary here. In brief, own children are defined as all children who can be identified as residing with their mothers; thus, this category includes some adopted children or stepchildren and excludes any offspring that may have died or moved away. If a child cannot be matched to a "mother" residing in the same household, it is not defined as an own child and is thus excluded.

In the United States, prior to the release of the 1-in-a-100 Public Use Sample tapes, analysis of own-children data had to rely on published census tabulations or special tabulations provided by the Bureau of the Census. Such tabulations are available from the censuses of 1910, 1940, 1950, and 1960, and they generally show number of own children under 5 years (or in some cases, under 1 year or 5–9 years) by various characteristics of age of mother. These data have been ably analyzed by Cho, Grabill, and Bogue (1970).

However, the analysis of differential change in fertility is hampered by the discontinuous nature of the tabulations. Generally, it is possible to compute fertility rates only for an average of a 5-year time period. Furthermore, without the actual micro data, multivariate analysis of recent fertility is impossible. With the release of the 1-in-a-100 Public Use Sample tapes for the 1960 and 1970 censuses, it is now possible to analyze own-children data both by computing annual age-specific fertility rates and by using various multivariate techniques. There is one 1% sample available for the 1960 census and there are six 1% samples available for the 1970 census. By combining the 1970 samples, it is possible to obtain a 6% sample for 1970.

In order to exploit these data for the analysis of differential fertility, two types of dependent variables are constructed using own-children data: annual age-specific fertility rates for all women irrespective of marital status, and the number of own children under 3 years for women currently married and under age 40 at the time of census. The annual fertility rates are aggregate measures and will be used to examine differentials in fertility trends for the period 1945–1969. The number of own children under 3 years is an individual measure and will be used in the multivariate examination of fertility differentials as well as in the more detailed examination of differentials in fertility trends. For ease of communication, we will refer to this latter type of measurement as a measure of recent fertility. The relative strengths and weaknesses of these two types of measures will be discussed in a later section of this chapter. Both the annual rates and the recent fertility measure are period fertility measures.

The construction of the measure of recent fertility is straightforward: The records of currently married women are scanned for own children under 3 years. The construction of the annual rates is somewhat more complex. Before the annual age-specific fertility rates are constructed, it is necessary to recode ages of women and children, because the censuses are taken as of April 1, 1970, or April 1, 1960. With age appropriately recoded, age of child and age of mother are used to determine the numerators of annual age-specific fertility rates; age of woman is used to determine the denominators. The rates calculated are central rates, where exposure is estimated by the mid-year population. (See Retherford and Cho, 1974, for the calculation of other types of annual rates from own-children data.)

DATA REQUIREMENTS

If own-children data were used as recorded by the census, four implicit assumptions would be involved (Grabill and Cho, 1965; Cho, Grabill, and Bogue, 1970; Retherford and Cho, 1974): (*1*) that ages of children and women are correctly reported; (*2*) that all children reside with their mothers; (*3*) that mortality is negligible for women and children; and (*4*) that all women and children are covered by the census. These four basic requirements and departures from them for the United States are discussed below.

The effect of systematic age misstatement on estimated annual fertility rates can be described as follows: (*a*) If the ages of children are misreported, then all of the estimates for some years will be artificially inflated and all of the estimates for other years will be artifically depressed; (*b*) if the ages of women are misstated, then some age-specific estimates for every year will be over- or underestimated accordingly. The effect on number of own children under 3 years depends on whether ages 0, 1, and 2 are over- or underreported. Within the United States, age misstatement among the white population has shown a linear decline between 1880 and 1950 (Coale and Zelnik, 1963); and Shryock and Siegel (1973) report that the age distribution for the 1960 census is less subject to digit preference than its predecessors.

If children do not reside with their mothers, it is impossible to include them in any fertility measure except the simplest—such as a crude birth rate or a general fertility rate. This difficulty, unlike the others described, only affects the numerator of an estimated rate and thus consistently produces a downward bias.

Estimates of the proportion of children living with their mothers can be obtained from census data by classifying children according to whether or not they live in the same household with their mother. (This, of course, presupposes that net census undercount is unrelated to whether or not children reside with their mother.) The average proportion of children living in the same household as their mothers—"mothers" is being used here in the social, rather than biological, sense—for children aged 0–14 is 96% in 1960 and 95% in 1970 (see Table 2-1). This percentage is higher for whites than for nonwhites.

For the purposes of constructing annual age-specific rates, the relationship between the proportion residing with their mothers and age of child is critical, because each age group of children is used to obtain fertility estimates for a single calendar year. It is necessary to choose an upper age limit that minimizes the amount of deterioration in the proportion living with their mothers and maximizes the time interval over which annual fertility rates can be estimated.

TABLE 2-1

Proportion (per 1000) of Children Living in the Same Household as Their Mothers, by Race and Age of Child: 1960 and 1970 Census.

Age of Child*	1960 Census			1970 Census		
	Total	White	Non-white	Total	White	Non-white
0	965	981	870	957	970	876
1	961	980	861	954	966	886
2	963	980	866	957	973	867
3	960	975	866	958	971	890
4	959	975	870	957	968	900
5	960	975	874	952	967	875
6	966	979	885	950	961	892
7	962	975	883	955	962	914
8	958	973	856	952	963	891
9	953	971	829	946	961	883
10	946	964	835	946	958	877
11	948	964	845	942	956	869
12	945	962	812	946	958	882
13	949	961	851	937	947	880
14	926	941	825	927	939	849
15	917	931	800	916	927	852
16	899	919	763	892	910	790
17	815	829	716	862	877	769
Average, all ages	942	958	839	939	952	869
Average, 0-14	955	970	855	949	961	882

* Age as of December 30, 1969 or December 31, 1959.
Source: 1960 from a 1-in-10 sample of the 1-in-a-100 sample. 1970 from a 1-in-10 sample of the 5 percent state 1-in-a-100 sample.

The proportion living with their mothers begins to deteriorate slightly at about ages 9 or 10; for the total population, it changes from about 96% to about 95%. The decline accelerates at about ages 14 or 15. Only 92% of all 15-year-olds live with their mothers; by age 17, this percentage declines to the low 80s. We have chosen age 14 as the cutoff because (a) it allows estimation of annual age-specific fertility rates for each of the 15 years preceding the census, and (b) when two decennial censuses are used, there is a 5-year overlap in the estimates—thus providing an internal check when there is not an external source with which to compare the results.

Since mortality can affect both women and children, it can lead to either over- or underestimates of fertility, depending on which of the two is higher. If the proportion of births that survive to the time of enumeration were approximately the same as the proportion of women who survive from the year for which the estimate is being made to time of enumeration, then the two factors would tend to offset one another. However, this is not the case. With the exception of estimating annual age-specific fertility rates for older women for distant years, the proportion of births surviving is smaller than the proportion of women surviving. Because of the effect of infant mortality, census estimates of fertility will be biased downward unless numbers of children and women are adjusted for mortality.

The effect of census underenumeration on the estimated fertility rates is similar to the effect of mortality: Both children and women can be missed by the census. The estimates of net undercount prepared by Siegel (1974) for the 1960 and 1970 censuses show that the net undercount rates for adult females decreased between 1960 and 1970, while the undercount rates for children under 10 years, and particularly for children under 5 years, have increased (see Siegel, 1974: Table 6). This means that, in the absence of adjustment for underenumeration, there will be a greater downward effect on the fertility estimates from the 1970 census than from the 1960 census.

COMPARISONS WITH VITAL REGISTRATION DATA

Using census data on own children available from the 1960 and 1970 Public Use Samples, annual age-specific fertility rates and total fertility rates can be calculated for the period 1945–1969, separately for whites and nonwhites. These rates are in a form comparable to those available from vital registration data. In order to examine the validity of the own-children data, we have compared the two sets of rates. To construct the census rates, a 1-in-a-1000 sample was used for whites and a 1-in-a-100 sample was used for blacks.

Two types of comparisons are presented. First, the correspondence between the recorded fertility statistics for the United States and a set of "adjusted" own-children-derived rates is examined. These comparisons focus on the validity and limitations of the own-children estimation technique. Second, the correspondence between recorded rates and a set of "unadjusted" own-children-derived rates is examined. The second set of own-children-derived rates uses census data without adjusting for such factors as mortality or underenumeration; that set is the equivalent of what Grabill and Cho (1965) term "child/woman ratios." This comparison is of importance because, typically, a complete set of accurate adjustment factors is unavailable; thus, it is necessary to know the effects of departures from the requirements of own-children data.

Adjusted Estimates

A set of fertility rate estimates from census data was prepared adjusting for mortality, proportion of children not living with their mothers, and net census undercount (see Cho, 1971; Retherford and Cho, 1974). These adjusted estimates (as described below) were then compared with the recorded vital statistics rates.

Explicit adjustments for age misreporting and census underenumeration were not used. Rather, net under- or overcount adjustments were used, which combine the effect of coverage error and age-reporting error. It should be noted that the use of broad age groups means that age misstatement within an age group will not be captured. To adjust for the fact that some children do not live with their mothers, the numbers of children have been multiplied by the inverse of the proportion of children living with their mothers. Unfortunately, for children not living with their mothers, the age of their mothers is not known. Thus, it is necessary to use the same adjustment factor for every age of woman—in effect, to assume that the probability of a child not living with its mother is unrelated to the age of that child's mother. (It should be noted that the adjustment factors are slightly too small, because some children are living with "social" mothers who are too old or too young to have been their "biological" mothers.)

Adjustments were also made for mortality of women and children by means of reverse-survival techniques. Children were reverse survived to birth, and women were projected back to the midpoint of each year for which estimates were made. The life tables of 1967, 1962, 1957, 1952, and 1947 were used. Although annual life tables were available, their use would have made little numerical difference in the results.

This adjustment procedure makes the implicit assumption that the mortality of mothers and nonmothers is the same. Kitagawa and Hauser (1973) found a J-shaped relationship between number of children ever born and mortality for white women 45–64 years old. However, because mortality among white women 15–59 years old is very low at all but the highest ages, any difference between

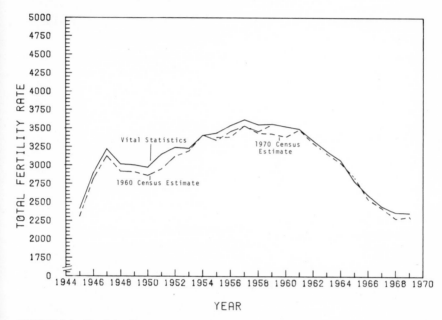

FIGURE 2-1 *Total fertility rates for whites, from recorded vital statistics and estimated from the 1960 and 1970 censuses. Census estimates are adjusted for mortality, proportion of children not living with their mothers, and net census undercount.*

the mortality of mothers and nonmothers would have a minor effect on the census estimates. The effect on the estimates for nonwhites is unknown.

Figures 2-1 and 2-2 show the adjusted estimated total fertility rates and the recorded total fertility rates for whites and nonwhites, respectively.[1] For whites, the two sets of total fertility rates are remarkably close. The average difference between the estimates from the census and the recorded rates is less than 3% for both the 1960 census estimates and the 1970 census estimates (Table 2-2). The estimated total fertility rates for nonwhites do not provide as close a match with the recorded rates as was obtained for whites (Table 2-3).

One reason—indeed, a principal reason—for the consistently lower census estimates is that the denominators of the census estimates have been adjusted for net census undercount, but the recorded vital statistics have not been adjusted. In order to illustrate this, a second set of "adjusted" or "partially adjusted" rates has been constructed that is identical to those rates previously described, with the exception that there was no adjustment for the underenumeration of

[1] In 1959, two sets of birth rates were published in the United States: (*1*) birth rates adjusted for underregistration of births and (*2*) birth rates unadjusted for underregistration of births. Throughout we have used the former set of rates.

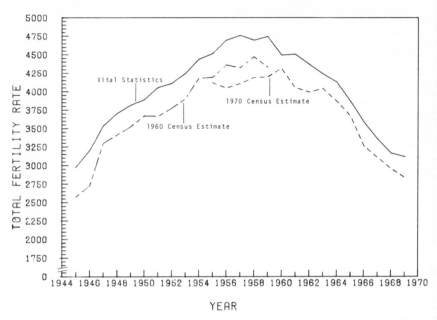

YEAR

FIGURE 2-2 *Total fertility rates for nonwhites, from recorded vital statistics and esti-mated from the 1960 and 1970 censuses. Census estimates are adjusted for mortality, proportion of children not living with their mothers, and net census undercount.*

women. For whites, the average difference between the partially adjusted rates and the recorded rates is reduced to less than 1% and 2% for the 1970 and 1960 census estimates, respectively. For nonwhites, the average difference is reduced to 4% and 3% respectively. Thus, the fact that the original estimates adjusted for the underenumeration of women, and the recorded rates did not, accounts for a substantial share of the difference between the two sets of rates.[2]

A possibility for the remaining differences between the two sets of total fertility rates has already been alluded to: The adjustment factors for children

[2] Not adjusting for the underenumeration of women does not completely remove the underenumeration differences between the two sets of rates. To see this, it is necessary to realize that the denominators for the vital statistics rates and for the own-children rates are not based on the same census. For a given year, the denominator for the published vital statistics rate is obtained by forward projection from the previous census; the denominator for the own-children rate is calculated by reverse projection from the subsequent census. Since there have been declines in the underenumeration of women in the past four censuses, the denominators for the vital statistics rates are too small vis-à-vis the own-children rates. There is an additional slight difference in the same direction because, when the denomi-nators for the own-children method are obtained by reverse survival, all immigrants are reverse survived, including some who were not United States residents at the time. This does not happen for the recorded vital statistics rates.

Ratio of 1970 and 1960 Census Adjusted Estimates to Recorded Vital Statistics Rates: Whites.

| | 1970 Estimates/Vital Statistics | | | | | | | 1960 Estimates/Vital Statistics | | | | | | |
| | Total Fertility Rate Comparisons | Age Specific Fertility Rates Comparisons | | | | | | Total Fertility Rate Comparisons | Age Specific Fertility Rates Comparisons | | | | | |
Year	parisons	15-19	20-24	25-29	30-34	35-39	40-44	parisons	15-19	20-24	25-29	30-34	35-39	40-44
1969	.978	.819	.978	.953	1.053	1.133	1.247	...	...	...	...	...	...	...
1968	.965	.794	.942	1.011	.944	1.009	1.326	...	...	...	...	...	...	...
1967	.911	.864	.955	.991	1.048	1.041	1.041	...	...	...	...	...	...	...
1966	.978	.908	.953	.928	1.111	1.028	1.278	...	...	...	...	...	...	...
1965	1.019	.987	.987	.974	1.058	1.228	1.250	...	...	...	...	...	...	...
1964	.989	.949	.984	.972	1.032	1.023	1.023	...	...	...	...	...	...	...
1963	.989	.924	.939	.985	1.051	1.119	1.276	...	...	...	...	...	...	...
1962	.989	.886	.955	1.002	1.058	1.077	1.113	...	...	...	...	...	...	...
1961	.998	.966	.952	1.023	1.026	1.077	1.101	...	...	...	...	...	...	...
1960	.961	.941	.909	.969	1.007	1.024	1.252	...	...	...	...	...	...	...
1959	.969	.860	.904	1.002	1.063	1.007	1.061	1.004	.929	.964	1.028	1.015	1.050	1.196
1958	.967	.960	.915	1.008	.997	.968	1.095	.973	.889	.949	.969	1.049	.995	1.243
1957	.978	.811	.915	.968	1.071	1.209	1.117	.977	.907	.944	.965	1.009	1.061	1.506
1956	.957	.916	.912	.967	1.012	1.047	1.045	.978	.886	.956	.999	1.011	1.042	1.078
1955	.983	.958	.929	1.017	1.039	1.116	1.175	.971	.927	.910	.974	1.085	1.016	1.065
1954	...	...	...	...	...	...	...	1.002	.863	.949	1.015	1.088	1.164	1.117
1953	...	...	...	...	...	...	...	.990	.867	.922	.951	1.061	1.109	1.173
1952	...	...	...	...	...	...	...	.962	.883	.948	.953	1.028	1.013	1.000
1951	...	...	...	...	...	...	...	.937	.901	.868	.992	.997	.977	.849
1950	...	...	...	...	...	...	...	.963	.811	.933	.970	1.019	1.012	1.069
1949	...	...	...	...	...	...	...	.969	.874	.895	1.021	1.068	.969	1.164
1948	...	...	...	...	...	...	...	.967	1.010	.932	.990	.986	.908	1.053
1947	...	...	...	...	...	...	...	.971	.933	.942	.951	1.064	.921	1.242
1946	...	...	...	...	...	...	...	.973	.994	.932	.943	1.000	1.029	1.227
1945	...	...	...	...	...	...	...	.956	.869	.910	.975	.980	1.035	1.125
Average	.975	.908	.942	.985	1.038	1.073	1.160	.973	.908	.930	.980	1.031	1.020	1.144

17

TABLE 2-3

Ratio of 1970 and 1960 Census Adjusted Estimates to Recorded Vital Statistics Rates: Nonwhites.

	1970 Estimates/Vital Statistics							1960 Estimates/Vital Statistics						
	Total Fertility Rate Comparisons	Age Specific Fertility Rates Comparisons						Total Fertility Rate Comparisons	Age Specific Fertility Rates Comparisons					
Year	parisons	15-19	20-24	25-29	30-34	35-39	40-44	parisons	15-19	20-24	25-29	30-34	35-39	40-44
1969	.909	.649	.879	1.000	.992	1.148	1.590	...	...	...	...	...	...	...
1968	.933	.731	.925	.963	.988	1.183	1.407	...	...	...	...	...	...	...
1967	.925	.766	.944	.908	.894	1.179	1.522	...	...	...	...	...	...	...
1966	.910	.828	.887	.913	.931	1.005	1.359	...	...	...	...	...	...	...
1965	.950	.857	.951	.935	.972	1.002	1.422	...	...	...	...	...	...	...
1964	.938	.824	.899	.910	1.042	1.080	1.344	...	...	...	...	...	...	...
1963	.953	.863	.855	.929	1.075	1.234	1.405	...	...	...	...	...	...	...
1962	.914	.811	.870	.914	.973	1.061	1.309	...	...	...	...	...	...	...
1961	.899	.834	.834	.932	.960	.962	1.305	...	...	...	...	...	...	...
1960	.962	.838	.857	1.005	1.091	1.119	1.455	...	...	...	...	...	...	...
1959	.855	.828	.821	.893	.957	.926	1.502	.913	.596	.836	1.023	1.024	1.152	1.661
1958	.892	.900	.815	.857	.951	1.011	1.472	.952	.683	.866	1.003	1.170	1.153	1.564
1957	.863	.784	.816	.884	.900	.987	1.162	.908	.689	.834	.948	1.060	1.051	1.643
1956	.861	.792	.799	.879	.951	.931	1.220	.928	.739	.895	.925	1.052	1.110	1.415
1955	.912	.800	.872	.916	.966	1.090	1.348	.929	.726	.881	.908	1.108	1.160	1.448
1954	...	...	...	...	...	...	...	.943	.762	.889	.936	1.109	1.108	1.533
1953	...	...	...	...	...	...	...	.919	.705	.876	.924	1.021	1.204	1.365
1952	...	...	...	...	...	...	...	.918	.752	.863	.938	1.062	1.102	1.279
1951	...	...	...	...	...	...	...	.905	.803	.841	.940	.972	1.083	1.221
1950	...	...	...	...	...	...	...	.944	.783	.871	.997	1.075	1.062	1.533
1949	...	...	...	...	...	...	...	.924	.816	.956	.928	1.050	1.111	1.294
1948	...	...	...	...	...	...	...	.922	.770	.878	1.029	1.003	.981	1.191
1947	...	...	...	...	...	...	...	.934	.757	.846	.987	1.075	1.159	1.346
1946	...	...	...	...	...	...	...	.852	.747	.751	.925	.981	.943	1.032
1945	...	...	...	...	...	...	...	.865	.710	.804	.959	.943	.853	1.309

not living with their mothers are too small, because some children have social mothers who could not have been their biological mothers. Unfortunately, we do not have the appropriate data to adequately test this possibility.

Table 2-2 also shows the comparison between the adjusted (as originally described) estimated age-specific fertility rates and the recorded age-specific rates. For each of the six 5-year age groups, the estimated trend closely parallels the recorded trend; that is, the ratios do not vary consistently within a given column.[3] However, there is a persistent pattern in the discrepancies between the estimated and recorded rates. The estimated rates for the younger age groups are consistently lower than the recorded rates (the ratio is less than one), and the estimated rates for the older age groups are consistently higher than the recorded rates (the ratio is greater than one). The probable reason for this apparent transference of children from younger biological mothers to older social mothers is the pattern of adoption—adoption in the broad, rather than the legal, sense. Presumably, it is younger biological mothers who, for various reasons, "give up" their children; it is older women who receive these children. Unfortunately, data on adoptions—in the broad, rather than the legal, sense—are not available to prove this supposition. Census data provide information only on social mothers and not on biological mothers. Furthermore, recorded adoption data do not cross-tabulate age of biological mother with age of social mother. Even if such a tabulation were available, legal adoptions represent an unknown proportion of all children transferred. Whatever the cause, this discrepancy pattern by age should be taken into account when analyzing age-specific own-children-derived fertility rates. However, it should also be realized that, although the discrepancy is large in relative terms at the older ages, the corresponding discrepancy in absolute number of births is quite small because of the very low birth rates at these ages.

The discrepancies between the estimated and recorded nonwhite rates (Table 2-3) are substantially larger, in comparison with the white rates. The estimated rates for the 15—19-year age group are about one-fourth lower than the recorded rates; for the 40—44-year age group, the estimated rates are about one-third higher than those recorded by the vital statistics system.

Unadjusted Estimates

The accuracy of the estimates presented in the preceding section is partly the result of adjustments having been made for mortality, net undercount, and children not living with mothers. However, to extend the method to the study of differential fertility in the United States, it would be necessary either to assume

[3] Note that the fluctuations within columns in Table 2-2 are the result of sampling error and generally are larger in those columns that represent the lowest fertility rates.

that the adjustments needed for various subgroups are identical or to have exact adjustment factors for each subgroup under consideration. This latter possibility is not feasible: The appropriate adjustment factors simply are not available for each subgroup of interest. For example, it is not possible to obtain information on the proportion of children of farm women who are not living with their mothers.

It is only necessary to examine studies of differential mortality to see that the same adjustments cannot be used for all subgroups. Kitagawa and Hauser (1973) found that, among females 25–64 years old, mortality was related to such factors as education, income, and ethnicity. Data from the National Natality and National Infant Mortality Surveys of 1964–1966 (National Center for Health Statistics, 1972) suggest that infant mortality rates are inversely associated with socioeconomic status.

Much less is known about the variability of levels of age misstatement, census underenumeration, and children not living with their mothers; but, most likely, there is variation across groups. If, in the situation in which there is variation across groups in these factors, the same adjustment factors are used for all groups (or all white groups), then the average or expected error in the estimates of fertility *levels* will be reduced. However, the error in the estimates of fertility *differences* between various groups will remain. Thus, it would be unknown whether differences between groups are the result of differences in fertility behavior or the result of differences in other behaviors that, in turn, affect the quality of the basic own-children data. In order to explore the effect of not adjusting for these factors, we have prepared a series of unadjusted census estimates for whites and nonwhites.

Figure 2-3 shows the unadjusted census estimates and recorded total fertility rates for whites. The unadjusted estimates are, on the average, about 8% lower than the recorded total fertility rates (Table 2-4). However, although the census estimates are uniformly lower than the recorded total fertility rates, the trends displayed by both sets of rates are virtually identical. This can be seen by multiplying the census estimates by a scalar factor (the inverse of the average ratio between the census estimate and the recorded rate) and comparing the scalar adjusted rates with the recorded rates (Figure 2-4). There is a slight and irregular tendency for the unadjusted estimates to deteriorate over time (see Table 2-4). The white unadjusted *age-specific* fertility estimates also show a trend identical to that of the recorded rates.

The unadjusted census estimates and recorded total fertility rates for non-whites are shown in Figure 2-5. Although the census unadjusted estimates are more than 25% lower than the recorded rates (Table 2-5), the trends displayed by both sets of rates are similar. The nonwhite unadjusted age-specific estimates also indicate a trend similar to that of the recorded rates, but (*a*) the estimates fluctuate more than the recorded rates, and (*b*) the estimates for younger

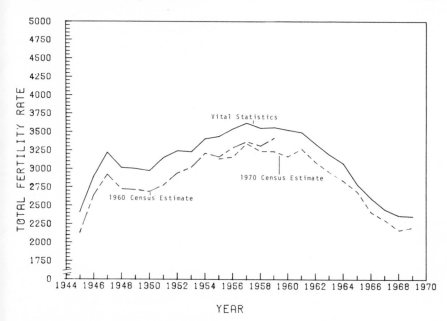

FIGURE 2-3 *Total fertility rates for whites, from recorded vital statistics and unadjusted estimates from the 1960 and 1970 censuses.*

women tend to be too low and the estimates for older women tend to be too high (see Table 2-5).

The unadjusted estimates accurately replicate the recorded trends, even though the levels were underestimated, because the amount of error introduced by not adjusting for mortality, children not living with their mothers, age misstatement, and underenumeration is approximately the same for each of the 25 years. These results suggest that own-children data, unadjusted, can be used to accurately estimate fertility trends for various social, racial, and economic subgroups, provided that the sources of error remain constant over time. If the constancy assumption is not met for a particular subgroup, then the trend estimate for that group will correspondingly be misspecified. Unfortunately, little is known about the stability of these confounding factors for the various subgroups of interest. However, because estimates for 15 calendar years can be obtained from a single census, and because, for the United States, it is possible to make estimates for two censuses, there is a 5-year overlap for the two sets of estimates. Appreciable changes in some of the confounding factors should be discernible by comparing the two sets of estimates for the same 5-year period.

It should not be assumed that all total fertility estimates for subgroups will underestimate the actual rates, for the same reason that some age-specific estimates are greater than the recorded rates. Mortality and net census under-

TABLE 2-4

Ratio of 1970 and 1960 Census Unadjusted Estimates to Recorded Vital Statistics Rates: Whites.

| | 1970 Estimates/Vital Statistics | | | | | | | 1960 Estimates/Vital Statistics | | | | | | |
| | Total Fertility Rate Comparisons | Age Specific Fertility Rates Comparisons | | | | | | Total Fertility Rate Comparisons | Age Specific Fertility Rates Comparisons | | | | | |
Year		15-19	20-24	25-29	30-34	35-39	40-44		15-19	20-24	25-29	30-34	35-39	40-44
1969	.936	.775	.932	.918	1.014	1.076	1.185	...	...	...	...	...	...	...
1968	.917	.747	.893	.967	.948	.947	1.247	...	...	...	...	...	...	...
1967	.941	.813	.943	.948	.995	.978	.990	...	...	...	...	...	...	...
1966	.927	.854	.907	.883	1.048	.968	1.204	...	...	...	...	...	...	...
1965	.965	.928	.938	.927	.992	1.152	1.175	...	...	...	...	...	...	...
1964	.923	.891	.932	.921	.908	.958	.962	...	...	...	...	...	...	...
1963	.925	.860	.883	.922	.974	1.041	1.194	...	...	...	...	...	...	...
1962	.925	.828	.899	.935	.983	.994	1.043	...	...	...	...	...	...	...
1961	.936	.906	.898	.955	.957	1.008	1.041	...	...	...	...	...	...	...
1960	.899	.883	.856	.899	.938	.957	1.190	...	...	...	...	...	...	...
1959	.915	.822	.863	.944	1.006	.967	1.027	.965	.909	.940	.990	.978	1.005	1.143
1958	.911	.911	.864	.943	.938	.918	1.061	.932	.860	.914	.925	.998	.939	1.182
1957	.924	.837	.864	.910	1.012	1.153	1.091	.931	.877	.899	.920	.959	1.003	1.442
1956	.894	.859	.847	.899	.947	.991	1.026	.928	.851	.910	.949	.952	.981	1.039
1955	.912	.894	.854	.939	.895	1.055	1.156	.920	.889	.863	.923	1.019	.956	1.032
1954	...	...	...	...	...	...	...	.942	.822	.893	.954	1.015	1.091	1.084
1953	...	...	...	...	...	...	...	.935	.825	.869	.896	.996	1.053	1.147
1952	...	...	...	...	...	...	...	.906	.836	.893	.894	.962	.967	.973
1951	...	...	...	...	...	...	...	.882	.851	.817	.928	.934	.939	.836
1950	...	...	...	...	...	...	...	.905	.829	.877	.904	.954	.979	1.055
1949	...	...	...	...	...	...	...	.904	.811	.831	.943	.995	.937	1.144
1948	...	...	...	...	...	...	...	.903	.937	.864	.915	.927	.880	1.046
1947	...	...	...	...	...	...	...	.907	.862	.871	.878	1.005	.896	1.236
1946	...	...	...	...	...	...	...	.913	.921	.859	.873	.953	1.005	1.277
1945	...	...	...	...	...	...	...	.883	.791	.821	.886	.922	.994	1.106

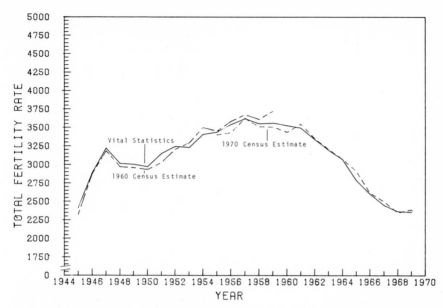

FIGURE 2-4 *Total fertility rates for whites, from recorded vital statistics and scalar adjusted estimates from the 1960 and 1970 censuses.*

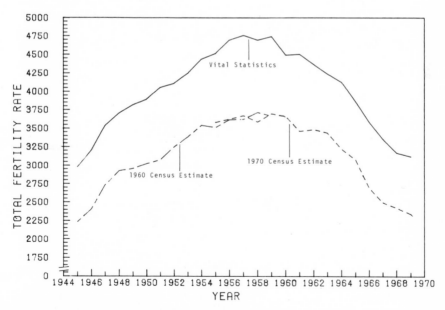

FIGURE 2-5 *Total fertility rates for nonwhites, from recorded vital statistics and unadjusted estimates from the 1960 and 1970 censuses.*

23

TABLE 2-5

Ratio of 1970 and 1960 Census Unadjusted Estimates to Recorded Vital Statistics Rates: Nonwhites.

	1970 Estimates/Vital Statistics							1960 Estimates/Vital Statistics						
	Total Fertility Rate Comparisons	Age Specific Fertility Rates Comparisons						Total Fertility Rate Comparisons	Age Specific Fertility Rates Comparisons					
Year		15-19	20-24	25-29	30-34	35-39	40-44		15-19	20-24	25-29	30-34	35-39	40-44
1969	.750	.525	.723	.834	.830	.935	1.295	...	...	...	...	...	...	...
1968	.764	.590	.758	.799	.816	.961	1.147	...	...	...	...	...	...	...
1967	.744	.606	.760	.738	.719	.939	1.244	...	...	...	...	...	...	...
1966	.751	.673	.734	.761	.766	.825	1.130	...	...	...	...	...	...	...
1965	.796	.708	.800	.791	.808	.835	1.214	...	...	...	...	...	...	...
1964	.781	.679	.752	.763	.860	.899	1.148	...	...	...	...	...	...	...
1963	.811	.727	.730	.791	.908	1.057	1.229	...	...	...	...	...	...	...
1962	.798	.702	.762	.796	.845	.939	1.184	...	...	...	...	...	...	...
1961	.768	.707	.714	.789	.817	.838	1.161	...	...	...	...	...	...	...
1960	.815	.706	.728	.842	.926	.976	1.300	...	...	...	...	...	...	...
1959	.810	.751	.747	.800	.877	.885	1.566	.804	.535	.745	.886	.904	.988	1.500
1958	.764	.674	.707	.741	.840	.926	1.408	.791	.580	.728	.828	.961	.934	1.289
1957	.771	.691	.717	.779	.815	.928	1.153	.761	.588	.704	.791	.876	.860	1.383
1956	.772	.698	.700	.778	.869	.883	1.237	.770	.626	.745	.766	.860	.906	1.208
1955	.793	.682	.735	.786	.860	1.011	1.348	.778	.621	.737	.761	.912	.960	1.267
1954	...	...	...	...	...	...	...	.798	.655	.749	.791	.924	.936	1.378
1953	...	...	...	...	...	...	...	.797	.616	.756	.797	.874	1.057	1.270
1952	...	...	...	...	...	...	...	.790	.648	.738	.799	.904	.976	1.192
1951	...	...	...	...	...	...	...	.759	.669	.700	.776	.807	.949	1.119
1950	...	...	...	...	...	...	...	.776	.636	.710	.803	.878	.927	1.392
1949	...	...	...	...	...	...	...	.774	.671	.708	.759	.880	1.003	1.222
1948	...	...	...	...	...	...	...	.789	.645	.736	.860	.869	.912	1.172
1947	...	...	...	...	...	...	...	.772	.608	.677	.793	.907	1.043	1.294
1946	...	...	...	...	...	...	...	.752	.637	.637	.792	.896	.913	1.078
1945	...	...	...	...	...	...	...	.750	.589	.662	.803	.854	.814	1.363
Average	.779	.675	.738	.786	.837	.922	1.251	.777	.622	.716	.800	.887	.945	1.275

count will always tend to have a downward biasing effect, but some subgroups might be "net receivers" of children to such an extent as to offset the effect of mortality and underenumeration.

In using own-children data for constructing annual fertility rates for various subgroups, an additional assumption is necessary because the method uses the characteristics of the woman at the time of the census to project back 15 years: The person's status at the time of the census is applicable (or adjustable) to each of the 15 years preceding the census. This problem will be treated in greater detail in Chapters 3 and 7. The point to be made here is that, if the status under consideration is subject to considerable change over time, then the estimates may be misleading. Change in status will also cause the two overlapping sets of estimates to diverge, provided there is variation in the dependent variable.

COMPARISONS WITH BIRTH HISTORY DATA

The measure of recent fertility minimizes some of the limitations of unadjusted own-children data by restricting the children considered to those under 3 years of age and by examining only currently married women. In order to examine the effect of mortality, children not living with their mothers, and age misstatement on the measure of recent fertility for various subgroups, we examined a data set that contained both own-children data and birth history data: the 1967 Survey of Economic Opportunity (SEO).

The 1967 SEO, conducted by the Bureau of the Census for the Office of Economic Opportunity, began with the conventional household listing: head of household and all other household members related to the head by blood, marriage, or adoption. For each listed member, the following information was determined: relationship to head, month of birth, and age at last birthday. Data thus obtained are comparable to the census data on own children used in this monograph. Subsequently, in the interview schedule, for each ever-married female household member, the respondent was asked:

Q. 58: *How many babies has _____ had, not counting stillbirths?*

There followed questions to determine the birth date (year and month) for the firstborn child, the second, the next to last, and the last child born. Thus, for women with four or fewer children, there is a complete birth history. This birth history information represents the dependent variable we are actually concerned with—that is, the recent fertility of women, regardless of where those children currently are.[4]

---

[4] This, of course, assumes that the birth history information is accurately reported. Undoubtedly, there is some misreporting on the birth history.

For a number of reasons, the SEO does not allow the precise comparison of data on own children and data on recent fertility that we would ideally like to make. In the first place, birth history records are only complete for women having four or fewer live births; for other women, the birth record is incomplete. However, the effect of incomplete birth records on the comparisons presented here should be minimal, because the comparisons are limited to fertility occurring in the 3 years preceding the interview. Secondly, the household listing form asked for "age last birthday" rather than following the recent census practice of asking for "age last birthday" and "year of birth." Just asking for "age last birthday" probably increases the amount of age misreporting (cf. Coale and Zelnik, 1963:93, fn. 11; Seltzer, 1973: Ch. 2). Also, these two sources of information on recent fertility are not independent: Both items are obtained from the same informant in a fixed order, with the household record preceding the birth record. Finally, the respondent reporting the birth record information is not necessarily the woman who had the births, introducing a source of error not usually found in survey birth record data.

Nevertheless, these SEO data provide the only opportunity for comparing, on an individual basis, information on recent fertility gathered from household records and birth records. As such, these data address the issue of children not living with their mothers, misstatement of age of child, and child mortality. They do not address the issues of underenumeration, misstatement of age of mother, or mortality of mother.

Table 2-6 shows the percentage giving the same number of children under 3 years of age on the household record and the birth record, and the direction of the discrepancy when the two records do not agree. The table is restricted to currently married women who have at least one child under 3 years on either or both records. Overall, the same number of children under 3 years is obtained by both types of records for 94% of the whites and 91% of the blacks. When the number of children under 3 years differs, the occurrence of a greater number of children on the birth record than on the household record is more common than the reverse. Thus, the use of own-children data underestimates the level of recent fertility. This is to be expected, given the known effects of infant mortality and children not living with their mothers. Examination of the detailed cross-tabulations (not shown) indicates that, when there is a discrepancy between the birth record and the household record, in approximately 60% of the cases, there is disagreement regarding whether or not there is a child under 3 years; in the remaining cases, there is disagreement regarding the number of children under 3 years. Also, if the table were not restricted to women who have at least one child under 3 years on either or both records, then the percentage agreeing would increase. For example, there is agreement for 98% of the whites and 96% of the blacks when all currently married women under age 40 are included.

TABLE 2-6

Comparison of Number of Children under 3 Years Obtained from Birth Record (BR) Data and Household Record (HR) Data for Currently Married, Spouse Present, Women under 40 Who Indicate at Least One Child under 3 on Either or Both Questioning Procedures, by Race, Marriage Duration, Education, and Husband's Income: 1967 SEO.

Characteristic	White					Black				
	HR<BR	HR=BR	HR>BR	Total Percent[1]	Number of Women[2]	HR<BR	HR=BR	HR>BR	Total Percent[1]	Number of Women[2]
Total	4%	94%	2%	100%	2307	5%	91%	4%	100%	1056
Marriage Duration										
<5 years	4	95	1	100	866	6	90	3	100	435
5-9 years	3	93	3	100	830	2	93	5	100	287
10-14 years	4	95	1	100	398	4	91	4	100	192
15-19 years	4	92	4	100	163	3	92	5	100	104
20-24 years	11	89	0	100	36	15	74	12	100	26
25+ years	*	*	*	*	3	*	*	*	*	5
Education										
0-8 years	5	94	1	100	244	8	88	4	100	199
9-11 years	5	93	2	100	523	4	92	4	100	422
12 years	4	94	2	100	1094	5	89	6	100	336
13-15 years	4	93	3	100	274	3	97	0	100	71
16+ years	1	99	1	100	172	3	95	1	100	28
Husband's Income										
<$3,000	5	93	2	100	230	8	87	5	100	351
$3,000-4,999	3	96	1	100	447	3	94	3	100	345
$5,000-5,999	4	95	2	100	326	1	92	7	100	149
$6,000-7,999	6	92	2	100	626	6	90	4	100	153
$8,000-9,999	2	95	3	100	367	2	98	0	100	35
$10,000-14,999	3	95	2	100	249	5	92	3	100	22
$15,000+	2	94	4	100	62	*	*	*	*	1

[1] Percents may not add to 100 because of rounding errors.

[2] The 1967 SEO survey oversampled in areas with large nonwhite populations. The percents shown have been weighted appropriately, and the columns labeled "number of women" show the unweighted numbers of respondents.

* N less than 20.

Of more concern to this study than the fact that own-children data slightly underestimate levels of recent fertility is whether or not the amount of this underestimate varies among subgroups of the population. For both blacks and whites, the relationship between the household-record/birth-record discrepancy and marriage duration, education, or husband's income is not strong. But we do note a slight and irregular tendency for the discrepancy to be somewhat larger among those with the longest marriage duration, the least education, and the lowest income. This should be kept in mind when interpreting our results.

Finally, it should be noted that this comparison has been limited to currently married women. If all women had been included, undoubtedly the overall agreement would have declined and there would have been larger differentials. Unfortunately, the required data are not available for single women. Data are available for postmarried women, but there are not a sufficient number of postmarried women to examine differentials. Among whites, the percentage of those agreeing drops from 94 among currently married women to 93 for postmarried women; among blacks, the percentage agreeing declines from 91 among currently married women to 85 among the postmarried. For this reason, the measure of recent fertility used in this volume has been restricted to currently married women. This is particularly necessary when differentials in levels of fertility are being examined.

Unfortunately, the 1967 Survey of Economic Opportunity is not suitable for examining the extent to which the own-children underestimate varies among racial and ethnic subgroups. To consider this issue, we examined, with census

TABLE 2-7

Proportion of Married Women with the Same Number of Own Children under 18 as Children Ever Born, by Marriage Duration, for Selected Racial and Ethnic Groups: 1970.

Racial and Ethnic Group	Marriage Duration	
	0-4 years	5-9 years
Urban White	96	90
Black	83	81
Mexican Origin	94	88
Puerto Rican Origin	90	85
American Indian	84	77
Japanese	97	92
Chinese	95	91

data, the degree of correspondence between children ever born and the number of own children in the household for currently married women under age 40. To minimize the possibility of including children who have grown up and left the parental household, the analysis has been limited to women whose first marriage occurred less than 10 years before the census. However, this restriction does not eliminate the problem. Furthermore, it should be remembered that data on children ever born are subject to error (Grabill, Kiser, and Whelpton, 1958: Appendix A). For these reasons, differences in the degree of correspondence should be interpreted cautiously.

The proportion of married women with the same number of own children under 18 years as children ever born is shown in Table 2-7 for various racial and ethnic groups. Blacks, American Indians, and, to a lesser extent, Puerto Rican residents of the mainland tend to have a lower level of correspondence than the other groups. Since these groups tend to have the highest levels of fertility, the amount of the fertility differentials estimated in subsequent chapters will tend to be conservatively estimated.

INDIVIDUAL AND AGGREGATE MEASURES

As noted earlier, own-children data will be used to construct two types of fertility measures: annual age-specific fertility rates and number of own children under 3 years (recent fertility). The two measures are designed to address different questions. The recent fertility measure is used to examine socioeconomic differentials in fertility in the very recent past and to investigate change in patterns of differential fertility over a decade during which there was a rapid rate of fertility decline. The annual fertility rates are designed to examine time trends in fertility for major subgroups in the population for the period 1945–1969. Each measure has its own strengths and weaknesses; these will be discussed in the present section.

Many of the individual characteristics that are presumed to affect fertility can be difficult to examine because the characteristics may change over time. Certain characteristics are also reversible (see Schnore, 1961). Income would be such a variable, as would occupation. Because the recent fertility measure is almost contemporaneous with data collection and because it is restricted to currently married women, such variables as husband's income and husband's occupation can be examined with only slight misclassification. They cannot, however, be used when annual rates are presented, because the annual rates are based on all women and extend too far back in time. Thus, a more detailed examination of differentials in fertility trends is possible with the recent fertility measure than with the annual fertility rates. The decision to use number of own children under 3 years (rather than 5 years or 1 year) was made in order to obtain, as much as possible, contemporaneous measurement of independent and dependent variables, while at the same time maximizing the reliability of the estimates. We experimented with the number of own children under 1 year and found that the sampling variability was too high.

For any given year, the annual fertility rates for that year are based on a single-year age group of children, whereas the recent fertility measure is based on 3-year age groups of children. For this reason, the annual rates require larger samples for reliable estimates than the recent fertility measure, particularly since the annual rates are being estimated for single-year ages of women.

Both measures have advantages. The recent fertility measure provides a convenient dependent variable for multivariate analysis, whereas the annual fertility rates do not. And since the recent fertility measure is restricted to currently married women, the error introduced because own children do not correspond to number of children born is minimized. The annual fertility rates, on the other hand, provide a fertility measure that is more traditional and in a more readily interpretable metric than is the recent fertility measure. Thus, it is easier for the reader accustomed to demographic measures to comprehend. Furthermore, the annual fertility rates extend back to the late 1940s, whereas the recent fertility measure is available only for the periods 1957–1960 and 1967–1970. Thus, with annual rates, it is possible to examine both the postwar increase in fertility and the subsequent decline; but the detailed trend examination made possible by the recent fertility measure is available only for the decline in fertility. Also, the annual fertility rates make it possible to document and contrast the location of turning points in fertility.

The annual fertility rates measure the fertility of all women, and the recent fertility measure describes the fertility of currently married women. Therefore, the annual fertility rates can be affected by two factors not included in the recent fertility measure: nonmarital fertility and the proportion currently married. Since subgroups may differ in both the level of nonmarital fertility and the proportion currently married, it is possible that the annual rates may show results somewhat different from those shown by the recent fertility measure. When such differences occur, it will be possible to attribute them to differences in nonmarital fertility and/or differences in the proportion married; it will not be possible, however, to determine the exact influence of each component.

When the annual fertility rates are used in this monograph, they will be used either to graphically show trends or to compute rates of change. The actual rates themselves and the numbers of women on which they are based will not be shown. Space considerations were the primary reason for this omission. These rates and the numbers of women on which they are based are available in a separate publication (Rindfuss, 1976).

SUMMARY

The data to be used for the analysis of fertility trends and differentials presented in this monograph are own-children data from the 1960 and 1970 U.S. censuses. With these data, it is possible to compute annual age-specific fertility rates for various subgroups, which permits examination of fertility trends for the period 1945–1969. It is also possible to compute measures of recent fertility for the periods immediately preceding the two censuses. With this individual-level measure of fertility, the multivariate analysis of fertility differentials is possible, as is the detailed analysis of the fertility decline in the 1960s.

The major portion of this chapter was concerned with the validity and limitations of fertility rates based on own-children data. When the correspondence between the recorded vital statistics and a set of adjusted own-children derived rates was examined, remarkable agreement was found for total fertility rates. The agreement improved when own-children rates were not adjusted for underenumeration of women by the census. It was also found that the estimated, adjusted age-specific rates for the younger age groups were consistently lower than the recorded rates, and the estimated rates for the older age groups were consistently higher than the recorded rates. The probable explanation for this pattern of discrepancies involves adoption practices. When the biological and social mother are not the same, it is likely that the biological mother is the younger of the two.

Also examined was the correspondence between the recorded vital statistics and a set of own-children rates estimated without benefit of a complete set of adjustment factors—a fairly typical situation. It was seen that census data on own children can be used to accurately estimate past fertility *trends* (for both summary indices, such as total fertility rates, and for age-specific rates), but that such data can be misleading regarding *levels*. Even though the level may be over- or underestimated, the use of own-children data provides a powerful tool for examining fertility *trends* when comparable vital statistics data do not exist. It is these unadjusted annual fertility rates that will be used throughout this monograph.

Finally, own-children data were compared with birth history data, both of which were obtained in the 1967 SEO. As expected, own-children data underestimate the level of recent fertility; but, when the comparison is restricted to currently married women, the amount of the underestimate shows comparatively little variation across subgroups, and the variation is typically in the direction of minimizing expected differentials.

3

Trends in Fertility: 1945–1969

This chapter presents annual estimates of age-specific fertility rates by educational attainment of women and by race for the period 1945–1969. These annual age-specific fertility rates will be utilized in two different ways. First, they will be aggregated into total fertility rates in order to examine trends in the level of fertility. These total fertility estimates allow, for the first time, examination on an annual basis of the extent to which various education subgroups participated in the baby boom and in the subsequent fertility decline. Second, the age-specific fertility rates will be left unaggregated, and the fertility schedules themselves will be examined. The emphasis throughout will be on describing differentials in the trends.

EDUCATION AND THE ESTIMATION OF ANNUAL FERTILITY RATES

Estimating annual fertility rates from own-children data for education groups requires the assumption that the education of women at the time of the census is applicable to the years for which estimates are made. Annual fertility rates have been estimated for each education group for 15 years preceding the census. Since two successive decennial censuses are being used, there is a 5-year period (1955–1959) for which two estimates are available, thus providing an internal check for consistency of the estimates. It should be noted that the comparison of these two estimates addresses the effect of compositional changes, but it does not guarantee accuracy. The estimates are independent in that they are obtained from two different censuses, but both sets of estimates are obtained by use of the same methodology.

TABLE 3-1

Ratio of 1960 Census Estimates to 1970 Census Estimates for Five-Year Overlap (1955 to 1959): Total.

Education Group and Years Being Compared	Age-Specific Fertility Rate Comparisons						Total Fertility Rate Comparisons
	15-19	20-24	25-29	30-34	35-39	40-44	
5-8 years							
1959	.68	1.05	1.04	1.07	1.04	.88	.96
1958	.93	1.06	1.08	1.08	1.02	1.04	1.04
1957	.99	1.06	.99	1.00	.95	1.09	1.01
1956	1.08	1.12	1.00	.98	.98	.95	1.05
1955	1.13	1.06	1.03	1.03	.92	.83	1.04
9-11 years							
1959	.44	1.01	1.10	.97	1.03	1.01	.90
1958	.51	1.08	1.06	1.08	1.01	1.01	.94
1957	.61	1.04	1.04	1.00	1.02	1.03	.94
1956	.82	1.06	1.05	1.02	.96	1.07	.99
1955	.93	.99	.95	1.08	.97	.92	.98
12 years							
1959	1.65	1.04	1.02	1.05	1.05	.96	1.09
1958	1.23	1.04	1.04	1.07	1.05	.95	1.06
1957	1.02	1.05	1.00	1.00	.97	.97	1.01
1956	.87	1.04	1.02	1.02	1.00	.88	1.00
1955	.88	1.06	1.04	1.05	1.00	1.15	1.03
13-15 years							
1959	1.23	.78	1.02	.99	1.05	1.07	.94
1958	.91	.87	.95	1.01	1.02	.93	.94
1957	.65	.96	1.04	1.02	.99	.80	.98
1956	.57	.95	1.04	1.04	1.02	.86	.98
1955	.43	1.00	.93	.95	1.03	1.06	.95
16+ years							
1959	8.92	1.37	1.08	1.13	1.26	.83	1.27
1958	2.78	1.17	1.07	1.07	1.04	1.09	1.11
1957	1.56	.97	1.06	1.06	1.02	.88	1.04
1956	.73	.98	1.04	.97	1.00	1.32	1.01
1955	.50	.85	.98	1.05	1.02	1.02	.97

Table 3-1 shows the ratio of the 1960 census estimates to the 1970 census estimates for the 5-year overlap period for each education group for all women. Tables 3-2 and 3-3 show similar ratios for whites and blacks, respectively.[1]

[1] Rates for black women with 13–15 and 16+ years of education have not been computed because the numbers of women involved are too small to produce reliable rates. Also, rates have not been computed for women with 0–4 years of education; the rationale for this will be discussed later.

TABLE 3-2

Ratio of 1960 Census Estimates to 1970 Census Estimates for Five-Year Overlap (1955 to 1959):   Whites.

Education Group and Years Being Compared	Age-Specific Fertility Rate Comparisons						Total Fertility Rate Comparisons
	15-19	20-24	25-29	30-34	35-39	40-44	
5-8 years							
1959	.77	1.09	1.04	1.06	1.00	.84	.99
1958	1.02	1.06	1.06	1.06	1.04	1.10	1.05
1957	1.06	1.08	.98	.93	.98	1.06	1.02
1956	1.12	1.13	1.01	1.01	.96	.98	1.06
1955	1.15	1.05	1.04	.99	.93	.83	1.04
9-11 years							
1959	.44	1.02	1.08	.98	1.04	1.05	.90
1958	.51	1.11	1.06	1.09	1.07	1.06	.96
1957	.61	1.05	1.04	1.00	1.06	.95	.94
1956	.85	1.07	1.06	1.04	1.00	1.05	1.01
1955	.97	1.01	.98	1.08	.96	.92	1.00
12 years							
1959	1.78	1.04	1.02	1.05	1.05	.97	1.10
1958	1.24	1.05	1.04	1.06	1.03	.96	1.06
1957	1.03	1.06	1.01	1.01	.96	.97	1.02
1956	.88	1.01	1.03	1.02	1.00	.91	1.00
1955	.90	1.07	1.04	1.06	1.00	1.19	1.04
13-15 years							
1959	1.35	.78	1.00	1.00	1.03	1.05	.94
1958	.97	.88	.94	1.01	1.00	.95	.94
1957	.69	.95	1.04	1.02	.98	.79	.98
1956	.58	.96	1.07	1.03	1.01	.85	.99
1955	.45	.99	.94	.95	1.01	1.02	.95
16+ years							
1959	10.36	1.39	1.07	1.15	1.24	.79	1.27
1958	3.35	1.17	1.07	1.06	1.07	1.02	1.11
1957	1.66	1.00	1.06	1.08	1.01	.91	1.05
1956	.69	.97	1.03	.99	1.00	1.17	1.00
1955	.51	.86	.98	1.05	1.00	.97	.97

Overall, the two sets of estimates are remarkably close. Generally, the two estimates are within 10% of one another; typically, they are within 5%. The major exceptions are the fertility of women 15–19 years old and, to a lesser extent, that of women 20–24 years old. For the less-educated groups, the ratio of the 1960 census estimates to the 1970 census estimates for women 15–19 years old decreases from 1955 to 1959. For the better-educated groups, the pattern is reversed.

TABLE 3-3

Ratio of 1960 Census Estimates to 1970 Census Estimates for Five-Year Overlap (1955 to 1959):   Blacks.

Education Group and Years Being Compared	Age-Specific Fertility Rate Comparisons						Total Fertility Rate Comparisons
	15-19	20-24	25-29	30-34	35-39	40-44	
5-8 years							
1959	.42	.87	.99	1.08	1.10	.95	.84
1958	.69	1.02	1.08	1.12	.95	.93	.96
1957	.78	.98	1.01	1.22	.79	1.22	.97
1956	.89	1.06	.95	.86	1.00	.86	.95
1955	1.04	1.05	.96	1.14	.88	.84	1.01
9-11 years							
1959	.50	.99	1.22	1.00	1.00	.82	.92
1958	.54	.97	1.07	1.09	.82	.86	.89
1957	.63	.97	1.05	1.03	.84	1.34	.92
1956	.71	.99	1.01	.91	.83	1.22	.91
1955	.78	.90	.86	1.09	1.01	.94	.90
12 years							
1959	.83	.98	.98	.99	.96	.75	.95
1958	1.12	1.01	1.15	1.22	1.23	.75	1.10
1957	.93	.84	.92	.89	.96	.95	.90
1956	.88	1.07	.96	1.21	1.18	.73	1.03
1955	.76	.92	1.00	.83	.94	.94	.91

The primary reason for the lack of agreement among the rates of the 15–19-year-old group is that, for most women, educational attainment is changing at ages 15–19, thus violating our assumption. For example, the rates for 1959 from the 1960 census are based on women approximately $15\frac{3}{4}$ to $19\frac{3}{4}$ years old at time of census; thus, many of these women have not yet completed their education. The rates for 1959 from the 1970 census are based on women approximately $25\frac{3}{4}$ to $29\frac{3}{4}$ years old; thus, their educational attainment is comparatively fixed. For the less-educated group, the estimates from the 1960 census for the years closest to the census are based on two types of women: (*1*) women who are not in school and who will remain in the given education classification, and (*2*) women who are in school and who will eventually be in a higher education classification. Since women in the latter group have lower fertility at ages 15–19 than women in the former group, their inclusion has the effect of depressing the estimates from the 1960 census. Similarly, for the better-educated group, the estimates from the years closest to the 1960 census are based on a subset of all women who will eventually be in that category: women who complete a given amount of education at a comparatively early age.

Presumably, these women also begin childbearing at a comparatively early age; therefore, the estimates for the 15–19-year-old group from the 1960 census are somewhat inflated. If it is ultimate, rather than current, educational attainment that is important with respect to fertility, then the somewhat paradoxical conclusion is reached that the estimates for fertility rates of the 15–19-year-old group are more accurate for the years more distant from the census than for the years closer to the census.

In order to minimize these biases, whenever fertility rates for education groups for women 15–19 or 20–24 years old are being examined in their own right or as a component of a summary measure, the following steps have been taken: (1) The rates for the two years closest to the census (1968–1969 for the 1970 census and 1958–1959 for the 1960 census) have been eliminated; (2) for the 3-year period for which two estimates are available (1955–1957), the estimates from the 1960 and 1970 censuses have been averaged. The two years closest to the census have been eliminated because they are the years for which the ratio of the 1960 to 1970 census estimates for young women departs most radically from unity (see Tables 3-1, 3-2, and 3-3). This procedure has the unfortunate disadvantage of truncating the series at 1967 instead of at 1969. Whenever fertility rates for women 15–19 and 20–24 years old are not being used, the series has been extended to the full 25 years and the two estimates for the 5-year overlap period have been averaged.

It should also be noted that, in Tables 3-1, 3-2, and 3-3, the ratios, more often than not, tend to be greater than unity. In other words, there is a tendency for the estimates from the 1960 census to be slightly larger than the estimates from the 1970 census. The principal reason probably is children leaving the household. The 1960 estimates for the overlap period are based on children 0–4 years old; the 1970 estimates are based on children 10–14 years old. Children 10–14 years old are slightly less likely to reside in the maternal household than children 0–4 years old (see Chapter 2).

Women with 0–4 years of education have been eliminated from the analysis for a number of reasons. First, they constitute a very small proportion of women in the childbearing ages—approximately 2% in 1970. Second, a non-negligible proportion are institutionalized and therefore are presumably not exposed to the whole range of fertility decisions and actions. For example, in 1970, 0.2% of all women 25–34 years old resided in institutions. However, 6% of the women with 0–4 years of education who were 25–34 years old resided in institutions. Finally, we suspect that census data on own children would be most deficient for women with 0–4 years of education.

It should also be noted that the education classification used here for women may not be the educational attainment of these women when they were having their children. For the most part, the education classification used here is probably best thought of as "permanent education." This statement is qualified because undoubtedly some of the women will go on to attain more education (see Davis and Bumpass, 1976).

PERVASIVENESS

This chapter examines differential trends in period fertility rates by education from 1945 through 1969—and indeed there are some. However, before getting lost in the differentials, it should be emphasized that, for virtually every education, racial, and age group examined, fertility rates increased during the 1950s and decreased during the 1960s. There are differences in the levels, the slopes, and the timing of the peaks; but the dominant picture is that of a rise followed by a decline. The only major exception found is among older, less-educated, rural women. For these women, there was an actual decrease in fertility during the 1950s; this decline continued throughout the 1960s. This exception will be discussed in Chapter 7.

We do not claim to know what factors caused the rise and the subsequent decline in fertility, nor do we claim that the same factors were operating on each education group. The possibilities are numerous: postponement of births because of the depression and World War II; the relative prosperity of the 1950s; the glorification of children by the media; the so-called religious revival; the upward, then downward, pressure of military draft regulations; the introduction of the pill, IUD, and other contraceptive methods; increased media concern about the effects of population growth; the entry of "baby boom" cohorts into the job market; the women's movement; and the expansion of organized delivery of family-planning services. However, the fertility trend estimates presented in this chapter clearly indicate the pervasiveness of these basic trends. In the concluding chapter, we address the importance and implications of the pervasiveness of postwar fertility fluctuations.

TRENDS WITHIN EDUCATION GROUPS

Total fertility rates for the period 1945–1967 are shown in Figure 3-1 for five education groups. It can be seen that the same trend—an initial postwar rise, followed by a brief decline, followed by a sustained increase during the 1950s, then followed by a decline during the 1960s—is found for each education group. The first difference of note is that the decline in fertility began earlier for the better-educated women. Those who finished high school and those who attended college tended to have their highest fertility around 1957. Women who did not complete high school had their peak fertility about 2 to 3 years later.

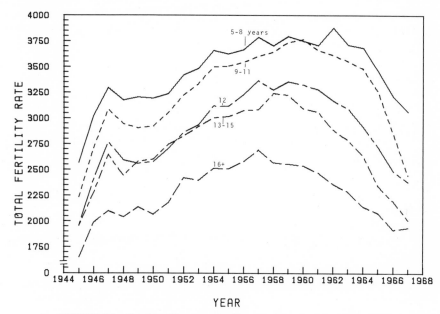

FIGURE 3-1 *Total fertility rates for five education groups: 1945–1967.*

Figures 3-2 and 3-3 show total fertility rate analogs for women 15–29 and 30–44 years old, respectively. These rates are calculated in a manner similar to a conventional total fertility rate, except that the age limits are 15–29 or 30–44 years old instead of 15–44. The sum of the fertility rate for women 15–29 and the fertility rate for women 30–44 is equal to the conventional total fertility rate. The tendency for the peak period fertility to occur later for less-educated women than for better-educated women is found for both older and younger women. Women with only a grade school education consistently are the latest to begin a sustained decline in fertility.

With respect to the rise in fertility from 1945 through the late 1950s, the largest relative (and absolute) increase in the total fertility rate was experienced by high school graduates—an increase of approximately 70%. The smallest increase (48%) was recorded for women who never attended high school. A similar pattern was displayed by younger women. The largest increase was recorded for high school graduates, whose fertility more than doubled (an increase of 102%). The fertility rates of women with 9–11, 13–15, and 16+ years of education increased 84%, 87%, and 87%, respectively; the smallest increase (64%) was found among women who did not attend high school. Among older women, the size of the relative increase tended to be directly

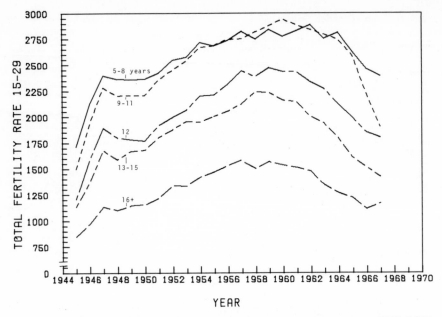

FIGURE 3-2 Fertility rates for women age 15–29 for five education groups: 1945–1967.

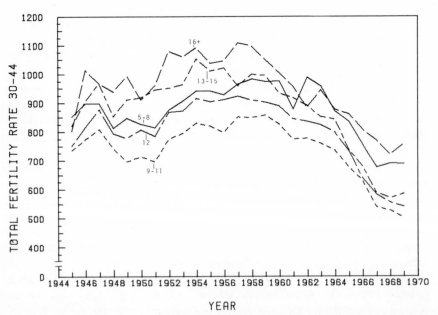

FIGURE 3-3 Fertility rates for women age 30–44 for five education groups: 1945–1969.

related to level of educational attainment, ranging from 13% for women who did not complete high school to 38% for college graduates. In every education group, the amount of the relative increase was substantially larger among younger women than among older women, generally about three times as great. Furthermore, the absolute amount of the increase tended to decrease with age (not shown). Thus, the substantial rise in fertility during the 1950s was most noticeable among younger women and better-educated women. The large increases among the better-educated women reinforce the perspective that the baby boom was essentially voluntary and that its explanations are necessarily social.

For the more recent decline in fertility, 1957 has been chosen (somewhat arbitrarily) as the beginning of the decline; this decline will be examined for the period 1957–1967. The decline in the total fertility rate shows a somewhat curious pattern: The decline was largest for high school dropouts and college dropouts (see Table 3-4). If the decline is separated into that occurring for younger women (under age 30) and that occurring for older women (aged 30–44), and is separated by time period (1957–1962 and 1962–1967), it can be seen that the pattern of the largest declines occurring among high school or college dropouts is found only among younger women and only in the 1962–1967 period. The rate of decline in this more recent period for high school and college dropouts was 5 to 12 percentage points greater than the decline for high school or college graduates. For younger women in the earlier period (1957–1962), the rate of decline tended to be directly related to educational attainment, and women with 5–8 and 9–11 years of education actually registered a slight increase in fertility. For older women in either period, there was no strong or consistent relationship between education and rate of decline.

Also, a sustained decline in fertility began substantially earlier among the better-educated women (see Figures 3-1, 3-2, and 3-3, and Table 3-4). Women with less than a high school education experienced very little change in level of fertility between 1957 and 1962. Among college-educated women, on the other hand, over 40% of the decline from 1957 to 1967 occurred in the first 5 years of the period. The fact that, in the 1957–1962 period, the rate of fertility decline was directly associated with education conforms in general to the concept of diffusion. Whether the deciding factors were changes in fertility preferences or in the ability to realize these preferences, the changes were apparently implemented "from the top down."

The pattern found in the recent period for younger women is more unusual. Even though this period (1962–1967) was characterized by increased availability and use of effective contraception (Ryder, 1972; Westoff, 1972; Rindfuss and Westoff, 1974), we suspect that the explanation for the greater decline in the dropout categories is not the result of changes in contraceptive technology or availability. There is no apparent reason for contraceptive improvements being

TABLE 3-4

Percent Decline in Total Fertility, Fertility 15-29, and Fertility 30-44 in Periods 1957-1967, 1957-1962, and 1962-1967, and Percent of the 1957-1967 Decline That Occurred in 1962-1967, by Education Group.

Fertility Rate and Education Group	Percent Decline in Fertility Rate			Percent of 1957-1967 Decline That Occurred in 1962-1967
	1957-1967	1957-1962	1962-1967	1962-1967
Total Fertility				
5-8 years	19	- 2[a]	21	112
9-11 years	32	0	32	101
12 years	29	6	25	80
13-15 years	35	6	30	83
16+ years	28	12	18	56
Fertility 15-29				
5-8 years	15	- 2	17	115
9-11 years	31	- 3	33	110
12 years	26	4	23	83
13-15 years	33	6	29	83
16+ years	26	7	21	75
Fertility 30-44				
5-8 years	30	- 2	32	108
9-11 years	37	9	31	76
12 years	37	9	30	75
13-15 years	39	7	34	81
16+ years	31	20	13	34

[a]Minus sign indicates an increase.

more readily adopted by, or having a greater impact on, the fertility of women who did not complete high school or college than on the fertility of those who did. The available evidence on the adoption of the pill and IUD suggests that their adoption was directly related to education (see Ryder, 1972; however, note that his education categories are not comparable to ours).

Why, then, was the change in tastes, perferences, or motivations of young people greater among those who left school? Of course, the answer is unknown, but we can, nevertheless, speculate. If, during this period, a number of social and economic factors exerted downward pressure on fertility, this "pressure" may have been greater on those who did not finish high school or college than on those who did. First, during this period (1962–1967), the so-called "marriage squeeze" was at its peak (Akers, 1967); that is, there were not a sufficient number of eligible males relative to the number of eligible females in the population. When competition for husbands is intensified, women who have not completed high school or college may be at a disadvantage vis-à-vis their contemporaries who have. In this case, one might expect a greater relative rise in age at marriage and a greater relative decline in the proportion marrying among high school and college dropouts; this would be accompanied by a greater relative decline in fertility. Second, among high school and college dropouts who did marry, we would expect a greater proportion (than among women who finished) to marry males who were themselves high school or college dropouts. During this period, there was an expansion of the armed forces. Men who did not complete high school or college would have been more likely to be drafted than men who did; the draft probably also produced a downward effect on period fertility rates. Finally, this period has been characterized as one in which men entering the labor market found conditions less favorable than they had been a few years before (Easterlin, 1973); presumably, this effect would be greatest on those who had not finished high school or college, compared to those who did. In short, the suggestion here is that some of the factors that might have been affecting fertility in the mid-1960s had their greatest effect on those who had not finished high school or college.

Before examining differentials by race and education, one further point remains to be made: Throughout the period, there was no consistent trend with respect to the expansion or contraction of fertility differentials by education. Perhaps the easiest way to see this is to examine Figure 3-1. At the beginning of the period, the fertility differential between women with 9–11 years of education and those with 12 years of education was comparatively small. This differential expanded in the early 1950s and was greatest in the early 1960s. The differential subsequently contracted to the point that, in 1967, the two groups were experiencing similar levels of fertility. Meanwhile, the fertility differential between women with 12 years of education and those with 13–15 years of education exhibited a substantially different pattern. The differential was quite small at the beginning of the period, remained small throughout most of the 1950s, and then began to increase; it reached its maximum at the end of the period.

The import of the fact that there is no consistent trend in fertility differentials derives from the place differentials hold within demographic transition theory (Kiser, 1969, addresses this issue). Simply put, the existence of fertility differentials has been described as a transitional phase of declining fertility. The theory is that the decline in fertility begins among better-educated women and spreads to less-educated women. As the transition begins, fertility differentials become wider; as the transition progresses toward its conclusion, fertility differentials become progressively narrower. The data presented here do not consistently support this theory in its most elementary form.

TRENDS WITHIN RACIAL AND EDUCATION GROUPS

This section further disaggregates fertility trends of the past 25 years by both race and education. We first describe differential trends for whites, then those for blacks, and finally contrast the two.

Figure 3-4 shows total fertility rates for whites for five education groups for the period 1945–1967. By comparing Figures 3-4 and 3-1, it can be seen that, as would be expected, the differential patterns for whites are quite similar to those displayed by all women. The increase in fertility during the late 1940s and 1950s was largest for high school graduates (71%) and smallest for women with 5–8 years of education (45%). Between 1957 and 1967, period fertility rates declined for every white education group; this decline was largest for high school and college dropouts (33% and 35%, respectively). When the rates for younger and older white women are examined (not shown), the trends and differentials are again similar to those displayed by the total population.

For blacks, the numbers of women were not sufficiently large to produce estimates for all five education groups for the period 1945–1969; for this period estimates have been produced for the following groups; 5–8, 9–11, and 12 years. Even for these three groups, the numbers of women are only minimally large enough to produce reliable estimates, as evidenced by the sawtooth patterns that

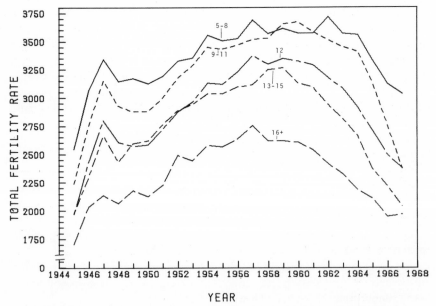

FIGURE 3-4   *Total fertility rates for five education groups: whites, 1945–1967.*

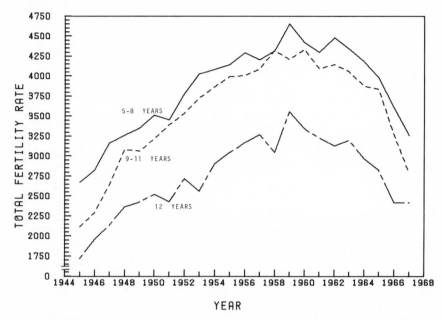

FIGURE 3-5 *Total fertility rates for three education groups: blacks, 1945–1967.*

result when the rates are plotted (for example, see Figure 3-5). For the more recent period (1955–1969), it is possible to combine all six 1-in-a-100 Public Use Samples of the 1970 census. This produces satisfactory trend estimates, as can be seen by the comparatively smooth lines in Figure 3-6.

For blacks, as for whites and for the total population, fertility increased during the 1950s and decreased during the 1960s for every education group (Figure 3-5). The largest relative increase from 1945 to 1957 (90%) was recorded for black high school graduates, followed by 79% for black women with 9–11 years of education and 57% for women with 5–8 years of education (Table 3-5).

TABLE 3-5

Percent Increase in Total Fertility, Fertility 15-29 and Fertility 30-44 during the Period 1945-1957, by Education Group and Race.

Education Group	Total Fertility		Fertility 15–29		Fertility 30–44	
	White	Black	White	Black	White	Black
5–8 years	45	57	64	69	8	34
9–11 years	57	79	80	108	10	63
12 years	71	90	102	128	22	36

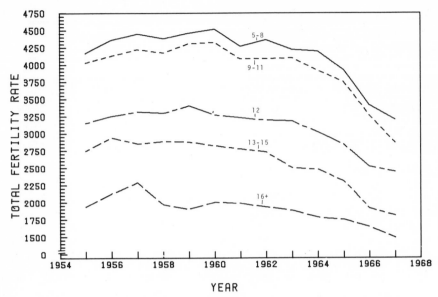

FIGURE 3-6 *Total fertility rates for five education groups: blacks, 1955–1967.*

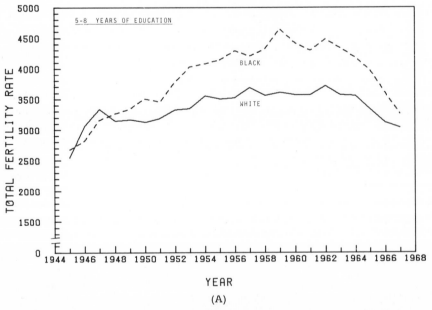

(A)

FIGURE 3-7 *Total fertility rates for whites and blacks by education: 1945–1967. Parts (B) and (C) are on facing page.*

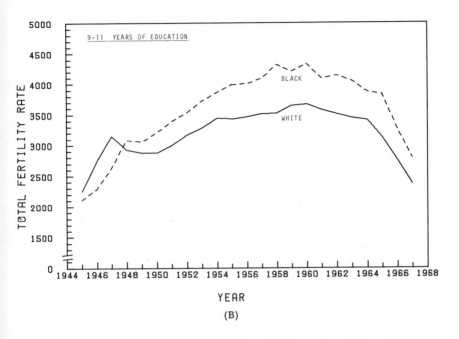

(B)

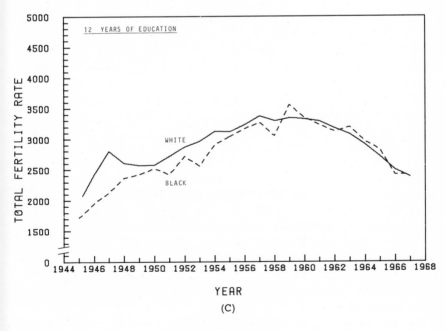

(C)

FIGURE 3-7 continued

47

For the decline in fertility since the late 1950s, we have relied solely on data from the 1970 census, combining all six 1-in-a-100 samples. This allows examination of all five education groups. Blacks do not precisely follow the pattern of largest relative declines for high school and college dropouts (Figure 3.6). The largest relative declines for the entire period were for college dropouts (37%) and college graduates (35%). High school dropouts had a decline of 32%. However, for younger women in the most recent period (1962–1967), the pattern found for whites and for the total population was also found for blacks (see Table 3-6). High school and college dropouts had larger relative declines (30% and 33%, respectively) than did women with a grade school education, high school graduates, or college graduates (25%, 22%, 24%, respectively).

In order to contrast the trends for blacks and whites by education, we have replotted the lines showing both racial groups for each education category (Figure 3-7). As before, we can examine the rise in fertility during the 1950s for only three education groups. The immediate postwar rise (1945–1947) in the total fertility rate was substantially larger for whites than for blacks in each education group. However, for the entire period 1945–1957, the increase in the black total fertility rate was greater than the increase in the white total fertility rate for each education group (Table 3-5).

For the two lowest education groups, with the exception of the late 1940s, the black total fertility rate tended to be higher than the white rate. For high school graduates, the levels of the two rates are similar. And during the period 1955–1967, black college dropouts and black college graduates had lower levels of fertility than their white counterparts (not shown). However, as noted in Chapter 2, differences in levels of own-children total fertility estimates should be interpreted with caution.

For the period 1945–1957, the rate of increase in the fertility of both younger and older women was greater among blacks than among whites. It can also be seen in Table 3-5 that the relative difference in rates of increase between whites and blacks was greater among older women than among younger women.

Table 3-6 shows rates of decline in the 1960s for white and black education groups. (The black rates of decline in this table are based on fertility rates obtained by combining all six 1-in-a-100 Public Use Samples of the 1970 census.) In general, the white and black trends are similar within each education group, overall and for the two 5-year periods. This can be seen by examining the top panel of Table 3-6. The major exception is for women with 5–8 years of education. For these women, there was a substantial contraction of the racial differential during the mid-1960s. Note that this contraction in the total fertility rate differential is primarily the result of the contraction among younger women (center panel of Table 3-6).

With few exceptions, the pattern of decline was also similar for blacks and whites for both younger and older women among the five education groups.

TABLE 3-6

Percent Decline in Total Fertility, Fertility 15-29, and Fertility 30-44 in Periods 1957-1967, 1957-1962, and 1962-1967, and Percent of the 1957-1967 Decline That Occurred in 1962-1967, by Education Group and Race.

| Fertility Rate and Education Group | Percent Decline in Fertility Rate | | | | | | Percent of 1957-1967 Decline That Occurred in 1962-1967 | |
| | 1957-1967 | | 1957-1962 | | 1962-1967 | | 1962-1967 | |
	White	Black	White	Black	White	Black	White	Black
Total Fertility								
5-8 years	18	28	1	2	18	27	105	93
9-11 years	33	32	0	3	32	30	100	90
12 years	30	26	6	4	25	23	78	86
13-15 years	35	37	6	4	31	34	84	89
16+ years	29	35	12	16	19	23	57	55
Fertility 15-29								
5-8 years	14	27	0	3	14	25	103	91
9-11 years	31	31	- 3[a]	2	33	30	110	94
12 years	27	25	5	3	23	22	82	88
13-15 years	32	39	5	8	29	33	85	78
16+ years	30	34	7	13	25	24	77	61
Fertility 30-44								
5-8 years	29	31	- 2	1	30	31	107	98
9-11 years	38	36	11	7	30	32	71	81
12 years	37	30	9	6	31	26	76	81
13-15 years	39	32	7	- 5	35	35	81	117
16+ years	28	36	20	19	10	21	28	47

[a]Minus sign indicates an increase.

Even though fertility differentials by education were changing during the mid-1960s, the racial differentials within each education group remained fairly constant.

FERTILITY PATTERNS: CONCEPT AND MEASUREMENT

The pace of family building has received considerable attention because it is related to the aggregate growth rate of a population, to individual fertility decisions and actions, and to the individual's social, economic, and health situation (Ryder, 1960; Coale and Tye, 1961; Coombs and Freedman, 1966, 1970; Coombs, Freedman, Friedman, and Pratt, 1970; Presser, 1971; Rindfuss and Bumpass, forthcoming). In the first part of this chapter, it was seen that changes in fertility since 1945 have not occurred at the same rate for all age groups. This, of course, suggests that the pace or tempo of childbearing has been changing. The remainder of this chapter examines the trend in the age pattern of childbearing within various education and racial groups over the period 1945–1960.

The basic data to be used here are the same as those used in the first part of the chapter: the set of annual age-specific fertility rates constructed from the 1960 and 1970 censuses by using own-children data. The first part of this chapter aggregated the age-specific rates into total fertility rates. The remainder of this chapter will leave them unaggregated and thus focus attention on the timing or pace of fertility.

Conceptually, the issue of the timing of fertility is essentially a cohort issue. Since the basic data used here are a series of annual, single-year, age-specific fertility rates, in theory, these rates could be used to construct cohort age patterns of fertility. Unfortunately, because the series spans only 25 years, it is not possible to construct a complete fertility schedule for any cohort, and, for most cohorts, the schedules so constructed would be highly truncated. For this reason, period fertility schedules have been employed and thus represent synthetic cohorts. Therefore, what is being examined is the proportionate contribution made to a period total fertility rate by women of various ages within the childbearing span; these schedules do not represent the experience of actual cohorts of women, and period changes need not reflect cohort changes.

It was shown in Chapter 2 that fertility rates from own-children data for younger women tend to be underestimated and that the rates for older women tend to be overestimated. This "tilting" is probably the result of prevailing patterns of adoption—adoption in the broad social, rather than the strict legal, sense. Because the new social mothers tend to be of childbearing age, albeit older than the biological mothers, the pattern of adoption does not have a significant impact on the total fertility rate. For the analysis of trends in the patterns of fertility, the tilting inherent in all of these fertility schedules is only problematic if there are significant changes over time in the age patterns of adoption or in the proportions of children adopted.

Unfortunately, satisfactory data are not available to evaluate either possibility. Trends have occurred in the numbers of children available at formal adoption agencies; but children placed through these agencies are an unknown fraction of all children not reared by their biological mothers. For the present analysis, it is necessary to make the assumption that there has been little change in adoption practices over the time span of interest. In subsequent chapters, when the fertility schedules of various groups are being compared, it will be necessary to make the additional assumption that there are no significant differences across groups with respect to adoption. This assumption is somewhat more doubtful than the previous one; but, again, the relevant data are not available to test it. A priori, it would be expected that those groups with the highest rates of fertility at ages 15–19 would also be the groups with the highest rates of placing children with adoptive mothers.[2]

In order to examine differences in the age pattern of fertility without the confounding effect of differences in levels of fertility, the fertility schedules to be graphically presented here have been constructed such that the total fertility rate of each group is equal to 1.0. Thus, differences that are shown reflect differences in the timing of fertility, and each plotted point represents the proportion of total fertility that occurs at that age.

TRENDS IN FERTILITY PATTERNS

The fertility schedules for the years 1945, 1950, 1955, 1960, and 1965 are shown in Figure 3-8 for each education group. It can be seen that there has been a tendency, within each education group, for the fertility schedule to become more concentrated or peaked. Simply put, an increased proportion of childbearing is now occurring during the prime years of childbearing. This can also be seen by examining, in Table 3-7, the standard deviations of the fertility schedules. There has also been a trend toward a younger pattern of fertility. During the entire time span under consideration, the percentage of fertility occurring before age 30 increased 12 percentage points for high school and college dropouts and increased 7–11 percentage points for the other three groups. Similarly, the mean age of fertility declined during the period.

The largest decline in the mean age of fertility occurred to women with 9–11 years of education. At the beginning of the postwar period, high school dropouts had approximately the same mean age of fertility as those who never attended high school. By 1965, however, the mean age of fertility of high school dropouts was more than half a year younger than the mean age for those with 5–8 years of education. At present, high school dropouts have the lowest mean age of fertility, the most skewed fertility schedule, and the steepest rise to peak fertility. In fact, the age pattern of fertility for high school dropouts suggests that, at present, the effects runs from fertility to educational attainment, rather than the reverse.

---

[2] We have sought information on the incidence of, and differentials in, the practice of adoption. Surprisingly little is available, and what is available is generally misleading.

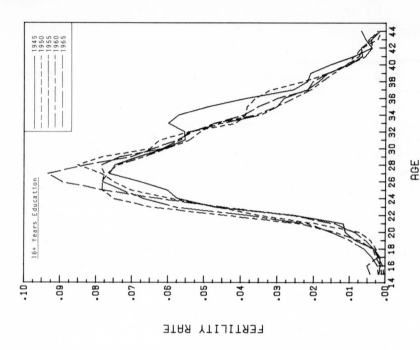

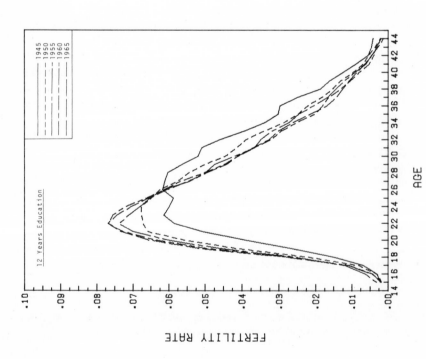

FIGURE 3-8   Standardized fertility schedules for five education groups: 1945, 1950, 1955, 1960 and 1965. Parts (C) and (D) are on page 53: Part (E) is on page 54.

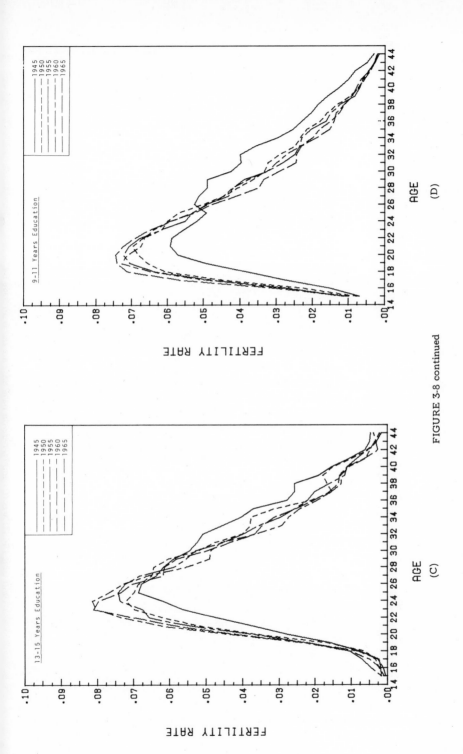

FIGURE 3-8 continued

53

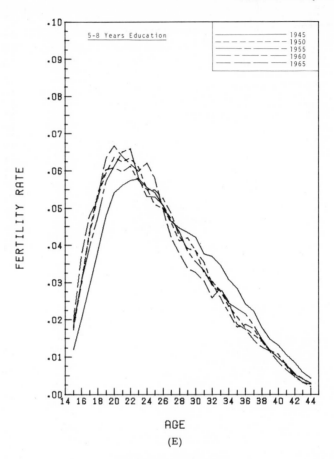

FIGURE 3-8 continued

The changes that have occurred did not take place evenly throughout the 20-year span. In fact, most of the change took place between 1945 and 1950, specifically between 1945 and 1947. After 1950, changes in the age pattern of fertility occurred more slowly. During the 2 years following World War II, the mean age of fertility declined by approximately 1 year for each education group except the highest (Table 3-8). Similar large shifts were recorded for other parameters of the fertility distribution. Such large changes in a short time period suggest that 1945 might be unique and that changes in relation to 1945 should be interpreted with the greatest care. Perhaps 1945 had an unusual fertility schedule because a large proportion of the male population in the prime fertility

TABLE 3-7

Mean Age and Standard Deviation of Fertility Schedule and Percent of Total Fertility Occurring before Age 25 and before Age 30 by Education Group: 1945-1965, Total Population.

Year	Education (in years)				
	5-8	9-11	12	13-15	16+

	Mean Age				
1945	26.72	26.76	27.96	28.74	29.76
1950	25.41	25.19	26.91	27.87	29.31
1955	25.62	24.87	26.45	27.43	28.67
1960	25.47	24.78	26.21	27.04	28.60
1965	25.05	24.48	26.21	27.28	28.95

	Standard Deviation				
1945	6.72	6.55	5.93	5.76	5.30
1950	6.49	6.27	5.85	5.59	5.05
1955	6.59	6.25	5.86	5.59	5.22
1960	6.55	6.19	5.74	5.48	5.19
1965	6.48	6.24	5.78	5.46	5.02

	Percent of Total Fertility Occurring before Age 25				
1945	43	42	32	26	17
1950	51	53	40	32	18
1955	50	55	44	34	22
1960	50	55	45	38	24
1965	54	58	46	36	18

	Percent of Total Fertility Occurring before Age 30				
1945	67	67	62	58	52
1950	74	76	69	65	56
1955	73	77	71	67	60
1960	74	78	73	70	61
1965	76	79	73	69	59

years was still overseas. Unfortunately, the education series cannot be extended back beyond 1945.

Some perspective can be gained from vital statistics data and from earlier age-specific fertility rate estimates prepared by Whelpton and used in Table 3-9. This table shows the percentage of total fertility occurring before ages 25 and 30 for the period 1930 through 1969. Although the proportions tended to be slightly lower in 1945 than in earlier years, the proportions in the 1930s and

TABLE 3-8

Mean Age and Standard Deviation of Fertility Schedule, and Percent of Total Fertility Occurring before Age 25 and before Age 30 by Education Group: 1945-1947, Total Population.

Year	Education (in years)				
	5–8	9–11	12	13–15	16+
Mean Age					
1945	26.72	26.76	27.96	28.74	29.76
1946	26.23	26.17	27.39	28.48	29.97
1957	25.67	25.57	27.00	27.95	29.37
Standard Deviation					
1945	6.72	6.55	5.93	5.76	5.30
1946	6.59	6.45	5.81	5.61	5.27
1947	6.53	6.28	5.74	5.51	5.17
Percent of Total Fertility Occurring before Age 25					
1945	43	42	32	26	17
1946	46	47	36	27	16
1947	50	50	39	30	18
Percent of Total Fertility Occurring before Age 30					
1945	67	67	62	58	52
1946	70	71	66	60	49
1947	72	74	69	63	54

1940s are clearly lower than the comparable proportions in the 1950s and 1960s. This suggests that, while the postwar trend toward earlier childbearing is somewhat exaggerated, it does indeed represent a real change in the age pattern of fertility. The consequence is that the effective span of fertility has decreased.[3]

Various parameters of the fertility schedule are shown in Table 3-10 for racial and education groups for the years 1945, 1950, 1955, 1960, and 1965. Because of restrictions on sample size, it is not possible to compare all education groups for the entire period; rather, it is only possible to use the following three groups: those with 5–8, 9–11, and 12 years of education. To minimize the effect of sampling variability, fertility schedules and parameters from adjacent years have

---

[3] This is assuming, of course, that these period changes reflect changes in cohort fertility patterns.

TABLE 3-9

Percent of Total Fertility Occurring before Age 25 and before Age 30: White Women, 1930-1969.

	Percent of Total Fertility Occurring	
Year	Before Age 25	Before Age 30
1930[a]	38	64
1935[a]	38	65
1940	40	68
1945	37	65
1950	44	72
1955	46	73
1960	47	75
1965	45	74
1969	46	76

[a]Native white women only.
Sources: National Office of Vital Statistics, Selected Studies, Births and Birth Rates in the Entire United States, 1909-1948, Vol. 33, No. 8, September 29, 1950. National Office of Vital Statistics, Vital Statistics of the United States: Vol. I, 1950. Center for Health Statistics, Vital Statistics of the United States: Vol. I - Natality, 1969.

been averaged (i.e., 1945 and 1946, 1950 and 1951, etc.); this, however, has the unfortunate effect of masking some actual changes—particularly in the period 1945–1950.

It can be seen in Table 3-10 that the same basic trend is occurring among all six racial and education groups. All groups have moved toward a younger fertility schedule and, to a lesser extent, toward a more compact fertility schedule. Yet, there are differentials as well. Among women with 5–8 or 9–11 years of education, the trend toward a younger pattern of childbearing is more pronounced among whites than among blacks. For example, among high school dropouts, the mean age of fertility declined by almost 2 years among white women and by less than $1\frac{1}{2}$ years among black women. Among high school graduates, however, this pattern is reversed; that is, the mean age of the black schedule decreased slightly more than the mean age of the white schedule. In the more recent 5-year period, 1960–1965, the continued shift toward a younger fertility regime shows acceleration among blacks, but not among whites. Unfortunately, we are unable to reliably extend our series past 1965 to see whether or not this trend continues; the series cannot be extended past 1965 because of the effect of changing educational attainment on the youngest fertility rates.

TABLE 3-10

Mean Age and Standard Deviation of Fertility Schedule, and Percent of Total Fertility Occurring before Age 25 and before Age 30 by Education Group and Race: 1945-1967.

	5-8 years		9-11 years		12 years	
Year	Black	White	Black	White	Black	White

			Mean Age			
1945	26.32	26.53	25.95	26.52	27.94	27.66
1950	25.74	25.35	25.29	25.08	26.14	26.79
1955	25.75	25.48	25.36	24.73	26.16	26.44
1960	25.67	25.18	25.16	24.58	26.01	26.15
1965	25.30	24.90	24.75	24.46	25.84	26.15

			Standard Deviation			
1945	7.09	6.57	6.97	6.44	7.16	5.82
1950	7.00	6.41	6.75	6.16	6.40	5.76
1955	6.92	6.48	6.71	6.14	6.35	5.81
1960	6.81	6.47	6.62	6.09	6.20	5.67
1965	6.93	6.43	6.65	6.16	6.23	5.73

			Percent of Total Fertility Occurring before Age 25			
1945	47	44	49	44	38	34
1950	49	51	53	53	48	41
1955	49	50	52	56	47	44
1960	49	52	53	57	48	46
1965	52	55	57	59	50	46

			Percent of Total Fertility Occurring before Age 30			
1945	68	68	70	69	61	64
1950	72	75	75	77	72	70
1955	71	74	74	78	72	72
1960	72	75	75	79	73	74
1965	73	76	77	79	74	74

SUMMARY

The single most impressive finding here is that fertility increased during the 1950s and decreased during the 1960s for every group examined. Although this chapter principally focuses on differences in fertility trends, the similarity in the observed trends for all groups cannot be overemphasized.

The increase in fertility following World War II and continuing through the 1950s was greater among younger women and among better-educated women. This increase had two components: an immediate postwar increase (presumably the making up of postponed births) and a more gradual, yet sustained, increase lasting throughout most of the 1950s.

The decline in fertility that occurred after 1957 accelerated appreciably in the latter part of the 1960s; more than two-thirds of the decline occurred in the second half of the period. This decline was largest for women who attended but did not complete high school or college. It is speculated that the more rapid decline among dropouts occurred because the fact that they were dropouts brought about greater pressures on them or on their spouses from such factors as the so-called marriage squeeze, the expansion of the military draft, and the unfavorable labor market.

A trend toward a younger and a more compact fertility schedule was found for every racial and education group examined. This trend occurred throughout the entire period examined, although it appeared to be changing during the 1960s. Unfortunately, the series of fertility schedules cannot be extended past 1965 because of the effect of changing educational attainment on the youngest fertility rates.

The next chapter focuses on trends and differentials in *marital* fertility during the 1960s in considerably greater detail than is possible with the annual age-specific fertility rates. The declines in marital fertility were the most important component of fertility change during the 1960s (Gibson, 1975) and thus deserve to be explored in greater detail. A secondary reason for dealing separately with marital fertility is that several of the characteristics important for the investigation of fertility differentials are defined for the husband or for the couple rather than for an individual woman. These include such things as the income of the husband and the duration of the marriage.

4

Differentials:
Persistence and Change

This chapter examines in detail the pattern of differentials in recent fertility in the late 1950s and the late 1960s for the U.S. population as a whole. Trends and differentials are examined for three categories of variables: demographic, such as parity or marriage duration; social, such as ethnicity or education; and residential, such as region or metropolitan/nonmetropolitan. The relationship between income and recent fertility receives extended discussion because of its complexity and its policy relevance.

In order to examine trends and differentials in greater detail than was possible in the previous chapter, it is necessary to shift from estimates of annual age-specific fertility rates to estimates of the level of recent fertility prevailing before the census. The measure, for currently married women, is the number of own children under 3 years of age. As noted in Chapter 2, this measure is more suitable when using statuses that are changeable and reversible; it is more readily adapted to the use of multivariate analyses; and, because it is restricted to currently married women, the amount of the underestimate introduced because of using unadjusted own-children data is minimized. However, because the measure is restricted to periods just prior to the census, and because Public Use Samples are available only from the 1960 and 1970 censuses, the analysis is limited to the late 1950s and the late 1960s.

Two differentials that are frequently discussed in the literature and that can be observed in decennial census data are considered: fertility differences in relation to current or recent labor force characteristics of the woman, and fertility differences in relation to poverty status. The reason labor-force participation is not examined involves the uncertainty about direction of causation. A case as good or better can be made for causation flowing from fertility to current labor-force status than the reverse. And, as Mason has noted, the ambiguity of the causal direction produces an analytical quagmire when cross-sectional data are used:

> Inferences about causal relationships between women's work and fertility simply
> cannot be made when the time periods for which work and fertility are measured are
> the same (most commonly a problem when cumulative fertility is related to cumula-
> tive labor-force experience). So long as the period in which couples are exposed to
> the risk of fertility is the same as the period in which women are "available" for
> working, the sequencing of decisions in each area is unknown and inferences about
> whether decisions in one area influence those in the others are consequently difficult.
> [Marson, 1974:5]

For these reasons, the labor-force/fertility relationship is not examined. In fact, the labor-force/fertility issue is one that deserves to have a data set collected expressly for that purpose—preferably a longitudinal data set.

POVERTY AND FERTILITY

The relationship between poverty status and fertility also is not examined, but the reasons are somewhat different. In several widely cited papers, Orshan-sky (1965, 1968) described the differential prevalence of "poverty" within the United States population. She showed that the incidence of "poverty" increases very markedly with the number of children under 18 years of age in the family (Orshansky, 1968: Table 16):

	Percentage of Families with Incomes below:	
Number of Children under Age 18	"Economy Level"	"Low-Cost Level"
1	12.1	17.7
2	11.3	17.5
3	17.4	26.8
4	22.8	34.8
5	35.8	53.0
6+	49.3	63.5

On the basis of these data, and the well-documented historical association of high fertility and low socioeconomic status, discussions of poverty and poverty policy seem increasingly to focus attention on fertility and family-planning programs for the poor. Poor people, it is often argued, have more babies than nonpoor people, and their greater number of children puts a greater strain on family economic resources, thus aggravating their poverty. For these reasons, public policy ought to facilitate control of fertility by the poor.

Although this and related policy implications seem straightforward, there is a fundamental problem affecting the underlying analyses. The principal difficulty in examining the poverty/fertility relationship is that it is, in part at least, a mechanical relationship arising out of the definition of poverty. A poor family is a family whose aggregate family income falls below a "poverty line." The poverty line varies among families, depending on their size. This concept of poverty rests on the reasonable assumption that, in order to achieve an adequate standard of living, a larger family needs a higher income than a smaller family. For each additional family member, the poverty line, as developed and used by Orshansky, increases by about $500. A family might not be poor at the beginning of a year but may become poor later in the year with the birth of an additional child, with no change in income. At any low or moderate income level, the larger the family, the greater the incidence of poverty. From the point of view of family economic welfare, this is as it should be; but the mechanical relationship precludes meaningful analysis of fertility.

Not only is fertility a determinant of the family-size component of poverty status, but it is also complexly involved in the determination of the family-income component. Family income is the sum of husband's earnings, wife's earnings, and other components of family income. In approximately half of American husband/wife families, the wife's earnings have a nonzero value. Families with young children, however, are disproportionately families in which the wife is not working and therefore is not contributing to the family income.

Thus, because the poverty/fertility relationship is in part mechanical and in part ambiguous, we have not examined it with own-children data.

DIFFERENTIALS WITHIN THE TOTAL POPULATION

This section is concerned with the pattern of differential fertility within the total U.S. population of married women in the reproductive ages. Subsequent chapters examine differential fertility, using the same methods, for various racial and ethnic minorities and for the farm population. The dependent variable used here is the number of own children under 3 years of age. In the 1970 sample, there are 19,867 cases, while, in the 1960 sample, there are 19,419. The mean value of the dependent variable, number of own children under 3 years old, is .407 in 1970 and .546 in 1960. The multivariate procedure used is simply a dummy variable multiple regression technique (multiple classification analysis) in which differentials are presented as category deviations from the individual sample means. (In Appendix A, similar tables are presented for the urban white population. This population will serve as the basis of comparison for various racial and ethnic subpopulations in subsequent chapters.)

The samples used have been restricted to currently married women under 40 at the time of the census. The currently married restriction was used in order to minimize the effects of children not living with their mothers and of under-enumeration, as well as to permit the investigation of differentials in relation to husband's characteristics (see Chapter 2). The age restriction was used in order to limit the analysis to women at risk of having a child under 3 years old. Among married women 45 or older, the fertility rate is essentially zero; among married women 40–44 years old, the fertility rate in 1971 was less than 1% per annum (National Center for Health Statistics, 1975: Table 1-31).

However, the use of a currently married sample with any age restriction presents a problem in interpreting age or marriage-duration differentials because of the truncation with respect to age at marriage (see Ryder and Westoff, 1971; Ryder, 1973). The youngest age groups have a young age at marriage distribution because the women had to have married at a comparatively young age in order to be currently married at the census. Similarly, the oldest marriage duration groups have a young age at marriage distribution because the women had to have married at a comparatively young age in order to still be less than age 40 at the time of the census. This age at marriage truncation is of concern because of the strong relationship between age at marriage and fertility. Since we will typically be more interested in the recent groups than in the older groups, we use marriage duration rather than age in the analyses involving currently married women under 40. The most recent marriage-duration groups are essentially unbiased with respect to age at marriage.

Since we are examining the recent fertility of women who are currently married at the time of the census, the differentials found here need not be the same as those found for the entire population (Chapter 3). Furthermore, the fertility of these currently married women may include a small amount of nonmarital fertility, and this is likely to vary across groups. This latter point can best be illustrated by considering the comparison of the fertility of black and white women. Both illegitimacy rates and rates of marital disruption are known to be higher for black women. A sample of black women who are married for less than 3 years[1] probably includes a larger proportion of women who recently bore an illegitimate child prior to the current marriage. If that child is living with its mother and her husband, it would be included in the recent marital fertility measure. Consequently, the recent marital fertility of black women would be inflated relative to that of white women. Another consequence is that the "marital" in "recent marital fertility" is slightly misleading.

---

[1] Marriage duration is defined as the absolute interval between the time of enumeration and the date that the woman reported as the date of her first marriage.

The higher rate of marital disruption of black women in comparison to white women may affect both the numerator and the denominator of the marital fertility measure. Women who have experienced a marital disruption within the past 3 years have been exposed to the risk of a marital birth in that period and should be included in the denominator of our measure. Similarly, the births to women no longer married that occurred in the last 3 years prior to their marital disruption, that is, when they were married and when their spouse was present, should be included in the numerator of our fertility measure. With available data, it is not possible to take into account the adjustments necessary for marital disruption, since we have no dates of disruption or dates of remarriage.

Social Characteristics

The results of the regression analyses of recent marital fertility are shown in Table 4-1. The first panel of the table presents differences in recent fertility by education. The column labeled "gross deviation" expresses the education-specific mean as a deviation from the sample mean without controlling for any of the other variables included in the table. Thus, we see that, without controlling for other factors, there is rather little variation in recent fertility by education. In 1970, women with less than 5 years of education had a fertility level that was .002 above the mean of .407. Women with 5–8 years and 13–15 years of education had rates that were about two-hundredths of a child below the mean, while those with 9–11, 12, and 16+ years of education had a rate of about one-hundredth above the mean.

The net deviation columns present deviations from the grand mean adjusted for differences in composition with respect to the other variables included in the analysis. Once such factors are controlled, we find, in 1970, as well as in 1960, a very sharp inverse relationship between fertility and education. Two net or adjusted comparisons are shown in Table 4-1, one in which all of the variables examined are included, and one in which the occupation of the husband is not included—in order to avoid confounding income differences with occupation differences. In general, the differences between the two models are small and we will usually refer to the first model. In 1970, women with less than 12 years of schooling have rates .050 to .078 above the mean, which is about 13% to 20% greater than the average. Women with 12 years of schooling have a rate that is approximately at the mean. Those with college educations have rates .040 to .054 points below the mean, which is 10% to 13% below the mean. In 1960, there was also an inverse relationship between fertility and education. However, only the two extreme categories (women with less than 5 years of schooling and women with college degrees) departed very substantially from the sample mean.

In an attempt to further explore differences in fertility by education, we have examined such differentials by husband's education as well as by wife's educa-

TABLE 4-1

Gross and Net Deviations from Mean Number of Children under 3 Years of Age for Currently Married Women under 40, for Various Characteristics: 1970 and 1960.

	1970				1960			
	N	Gross	Net$_1$	Net$_2$	N	Gross	Net$_1$	Net$_2$
Education								
<5 years	223	.002	.078	.062	361	.100	.134	.129
5-8 years	1541	-.024	.056	.050	2846	-.027	.025	.023
9-11 years	3955	.010	.050	.048	4705	.009	.004	.005
12 years	9561	.006	-.008	-.007	8351	.002	-.009	-.007
13-15 years	2650	-.027	-.054	-.052	2010	-.005	-.011	-.012
16+ years	1937	.007	-.040	-.041	1146	-.005	-.038	-.042
Racial & Ethnic Status								
White – Spanish surname	430	.140	.167	.161	392	.194	.155	.146
White – Other	17531	-.005	-.008	-.007	17237	-.020	-.017	-.017
Black	1639	.018	.044	.038	1586	.152	.147	.139
Other races	267	.005	.024	.023	204	.092	.036	.037
Husband's Occupation								
Professional	3252	.024		.012	2369	.038		.012
Manager	2069	-.065		-.031	1878	-.102		-.029
Sales	1252	-.003		-.002	1181	-.030		-.007
Clerical	1268	-.056		-.059	1240	-.004		-.031
Craftsman	4444	-.008		-.005	3971	-.044		-.014
Operative	4099	.035		.015	4304	.015		-.006
Laborer	1033	.053		.050	1256	.110		.042
Farmer	338	-.007		.053	703	.006		.075
Farm laborer	248	.102		.105	305	.228		.138
Service	1019	-.037		-.021	848	-.004		.001
Armed forces	734	-.018		-.019	663	.067		.017

continued

	N				N			
Unemployed or not in labor force	111	-.037		.036	59	-.139		-.161
Not ascertained	0	*	*	*	642	.010		-.022
Marriage Duration								
<3 years	3598	.023	-.022	-.024	2735	.030	.080	.080
3-5.9 years	3310	.369	.321	.319	3129	.496	.527	.526
6-8.9	3097	.173	.186	.186	2878	.212	.241	.239
9-11.9 years	2853	-.050	-.010	-.009	3116	-.044	-.042	-.041
12-14.9 years	2625	-.177	-.136	-.135	3398	-.219	-.233	-.232
15-17.9 years	2275	-.262	-.235	-.233	2188	-.286	-.330	-.329
18-20.9 years	1591	-.298	-.297	-.294	1486	-.367	-.444	-.443
21-23.9 years	469	-.315	-.327	-.324	451	-.397	-.523	-.523
24+ years	49	-.304	-.321	-.318	38	-.335	-.481	-.469
Age at Marriage								
<18	4183	-.028	.043	.042	4188	.034	.085	.086
18-19	6167	.021	.036	.036	5385	.007	.026	.026
20-21	4802	.008	-.004	-.004	4537	-.013	-.002	-.002
22-24	3211	-.010	-.056	-.055	3371	-.022	-.045	-.045
25-29	1234	-.010	-.120	-.120	1577	-.021	-.145	-.144
30+	270	-.018	-.199	-.198	361	-.028	-.303	-.305
Initial Parity								
0	6338	.149	.106	.107	5701	.133	-.014	-.014
1	3556	.176	.054	.054	3869	.110	-.004	.005
2	4006	-.116	-.104	-.106	4617	-.133	-.059	-.059
3	2925	-.192	-.104	-.105	2808	-.154	-.004	-.004
4+	2982	-.180	-.043	-.044	2424	-.057	.145	.143
Region								
Northeast	4392	.016	.024	.024	4566	-.006	.016	.017
North Central	5558	.024	.024	.022	5629	.017	.023	.023
South	6388	-.021	-.023	-.021	6071	-.013	-.034	-.033
West	3529	-.020	-.026	-.026	3153	.002	.002	-.001

TABLE 4-1 continued

		1970				1960		
	N	Gross	Net$_1$	Net$_2$	N	Gross	Net$_1$	Net$_2$
Type of Place of Residence								
Metropolitan								
Urban	10918	-.008	-.015	-.012	9589	-.017	-.026	-.022
Rural nonfarm	1421	.033	.025	.023	1639	.041	.048	.051
Rural farm	102	-.024	.008	-.009	173	-.043	-.003	-.024
Nonmetropolitan								
Urban	3088	-.023	-.017	-.018	2683	-.010	-.008	-.005
Rural nonfarm	1426	.037	.028	.022	1711	.001	.013	.013
Rural farm	274	-.012	.082	.054	648	.012	.045	.008
Not ascertained								
Urban	1620	.019	.028	.030	1512	.025	.020	.024
Rural nonfarm	743	.046	.070	.061	856	.061	.071	.070
Rural farm	275	-.010	.093	.061	608	.045	.083	.033
Constant Dollar Husband's Income								
<$1,000	737	-.058	-.097	-.106	899	.004	-.070	-.076
$1,000-1,999	817	-.007	-.061	-.069	1142	.047	-.058	-.069
$2,000-2,999	1054	.016	-.060	-.065	1881	.077	-.022	-.028
$3,000-3,999	1997	.019	-.045	-.048	2525	.046	-.019	-.020
$4,000-4,999	1896	.043	-.005	-.004	3090	.002	-.025	-.023
$5,000-7,499	6208	.015	-.011	-.009	6647	-.018	.016	.019
$7,500-9,999	4098	-.002	.037	.039	1886	-.043	.058	.060
$10,000-14,999	2174	-.055	.050	.051	} 1349	-.090	.062	.075
$15,000+	886	-.057	.100	.103				
	Grand Mean = .407					Grand Mean = .546		

^{1}Net of all other variables in the model except husband's occupation.

^{2}Net of all other variables in the model.

*N less than 20.

68

tion. The multiple regression analyses were rerun including an interaction variable which cross-classifies husband's and wife's educations. These results are shown in Table 4-2. It can be seen that the effect of the wife's education is the dominating one. There are, however, some deviations from the general pattern. For wives with less than 12 years of schooling, there are strong effects of husband's education: the higher the education, the lower the level of fertility within each wife's education category. For women who have completed high school but have not gone to college, there is no difference in fertility by husband's education.

The second panel of Table 4-1 shows differentials in recent marital fertility among various racial and ethnic groups. Ethnicity is of interest for several reasons. First, even though ethnic status is ascribed, the degree to which it is ascribed has been changing. During the 1950s, the prevailing tendency was for

TABLE 4-2

Gross and Net Deviations from Mean Number of Children under 3 Years of Age for Currently Married Women under 40, by Education Levels of the Woman and Her Husband: 1970.

Wife's Education	Husband's Education				
	<9	9-11	12	13-15	16+
Gross Effects					
<9 years	-.019	-.017	-.009	-.087	-.107
9-11 years	.001	.019	.024	-.026	-.151
12 years	-.075	-.013	.017	.013	.023
13-15 years	-.171	-.000	-.023	-.054	-.000
16+ years	-.234	-.273	-.009	-.035	.031
Net Effects[1]					
<9 years	.098	.040	.026	.006	-.120
9-11 years	.093	.056	.036	.036	-.113
12 years	-.014	-.012	-.010	-.018	.019
13-15 years	-.059	.044	-.065	-.102	-.029
16+ years	-.120	-.220	-.029	-.091	-.029
Number of Cases					
<9 years	912	418	332	72	30
9-11 years	857	1339	1400	273	86
12 years	691	1519	4880	1456	1015
13-15 years	68	165	660	799	958
16+ years	29	45	191	272	1400

[1]Model includes woman's age at first marriage, region, ethnicity, initial parity, and type of residence.

people to work hard at losing their ethnic identity as part of the process of social mobility. During the past decade or so, this has changed; people have been maintaining and, in some cases, creating their ethnic identities. Ethnicity is also of interest because it tends to cut across social class (see Gorden, 1963).

In this first analysis in this chapter, the population has been divided into four racial and ethnic groupings: Spanish-surname white, white other than Spanish surname, black, and other races. The Spanish-surname designation applies only to the five Southwestern states (Texas, California, Arizona, New Mexico, and Colorado). The "other races" category includes both high- and low-fertility groups: American Indians, Chinese Americans, Japanese Americans, Filipino Americans, and various Alaskan and Hawaiian racial groups as well. Race and ethnic status here are race and ethnic status of the wife. In 1970, net of other factors, blacks had a fertility rate that was .044 above the mean, or .052 above the white rate. Spanish-surname persons had fertility levels considerably higher than the white population, .167 above the mean, or .173 above the majority white population. A comparison of the figures for 1960 with those for 1970 suggests a convergence of black/white fertility, but there is essentially no convergence among white, other, and white Spanish-surname fertility levels. This issue of convergence is treated in detail in Chapter 5.

The next panel of Table 4-1 shows fertility differentials in relation to husband's occupation. In the previous chapter, such variables as occupation, income, or residence are not analyzed with annual fertility rates because such variables are subject to considerable fluctuation. However, this problem is minimized here by restricting the attention to marital fertility in a 3-year time span. Couples have been classified by the most recent occupation of the husband. This classifies persons who are currently unemployed or not in the labor force into their most recent occupation if they have been employed at any time in the last 10 years.[2]

The question to be addressed is whether or not there are differentials in fertility by occupation of husband, independent of the effects of husband's income, wife's education, and other characteristics. We conclude that there are some differences that are of sufficient magnitude to note. In 1970, the lowest fertility level, net of other characteristics, is found for women married to men in clerical occupations. Wives of managers and of service workers were also found to have lower than average fertility in 1970. The highest level of fertility is found for wives of farm laborers. Wives of professionals, sales workers, craftsmen, foremen, and operatives have rates that are very close to the mean. A generally similar pattern is found in 1960.

---

[2] This seemed to be more reasonable than placing any substantive significance on current unemployment or current absence from the labor force, as it might affect fertility in the previous 3 years, although we admit that a case might be made for the alternative measurement.

Several points deserve explicit comment here. First, fertility levels vary more widely within the white-collar occupations than we would have expected, with wives of professionals having the highest level and persons married to managers and clerical workers having the lowest level. Similarly, within the blue-collar occupations, wives of service workers have lower than average fertility, while wives of laborers and operatives have quite high fertility levels. Wives of craftsmen are intermediate. Second, farmers' wives, net of their farm residence[3] and other characteristics, have a rate considerably above the mean and slightly higher than that for laborers' wives (the highest blue-color group). Farm laborers' wives have very high fertility. Thus, it appears that both farm residence and farm occupation have a considerable impact on fertility levels.

We place no particular substantive importance on the fertility differentials shown for wives of men who are unemployed or not in the labor force in this classification, since this group is a very unusual group of men who have not been employed in the past 10 years.

Demographic Characteristics

Three variables have been included in the analysis as demographic controls: marriage duration, age at marriage, and initial parity. Initial parity is included in an attempt to control for the parity of the woman prior to the 3-year period under consideration. It is obtained by subtracting the number of own children under 3 years from the total number of children ever born. In the great majority of cases, this would be the woman's parity 3 years prior to the census. In some cases, however, this is clearly not the case. For example, we find that less than 1% of the women have a negative value of initial parity. That is to say, they have more children under 3 years than children ever born. Such cases were assigned zero parity. We have experimented with models including and excluding initial parity to see whether or not its inclusion changes the pattern of effects of other variables. It does not.

The fourth panel of Table 4-1 shows differentials by marriage duration. In both 1960 and 1970, there is the very steep inverse relationship between marriage duration and fertility. The exception is for women with marriage duration of less than 3 years, and this exception is due to two factors. The average marriage duration of such women is something around $1\frac{1}{2}$ years. The reference period for births is a 3-year period. Hence, only very few women have been married for the entire 3-year period, while some have only recently married. Thus, there is considerably less "exposure to risk" of a marital birth for

---

[3] It may seem, at first glance, inappropriate to consider fertility differentials by farm occupation and farm residence within the same model. The rationale for doing this becomes much clearer when we consider that only a minority of all farm residents have farming as their primary occupation.

such women. Second, of course, is the fact that there is time between conception and the birth of a child. So, in the absence of premarital pregnancies or premarital births, even women who have been married for nearly the full 3-year period have less than 3 years of "exposure to risk" of giving birth within the first 3 years of marriage.

It would be possible to eliminate from the denominator the person-years of exposure prior to marriage since the date of first marriage is available. We have not done this because, although we know the date of first marriage, we do not know when "exposure" began. The inclusion of a small segment of exposure prior to marriage should not produce a serious bias because, for those with 0–2.9-year marriage duration, there is relatively little difference in duration of marriage among the subgroups being considered.

The age at which women marry is correlated with their educational attainment, although the correlation is by no means a perfect one. Age at marriage has very little zero-order effect on fertility (see the fifth panel of Table 4-1). However, as in the case of education, when marriage duration and other factors are controlled, there emerges a very strong inverse relationship. In 1960, this relationship is almost linear. By 1970, there is no difference between the fertility level of women marrying at ages less than 18 and those marrying at ages 18 and 19. Both groups have a rate about .04 above the rate for women marrying at ages 20–21. Women marrying at the three oldest age levels have rates .06, .12, and .20 below the mean, respectively.

We have also done regression analyses for 1960 and 1970, entering age at marriage as a set of single year of age dummy variables.[4] This analysis is shown in Figure 4-1. Ignoring the small minority of women who marry before their fifteenth birthday, there is an almost linear relationship between age at marriage and fertility in 1960. Three things changed between 1960 and 1970. First, the level of fertility at every marriage age has declined. Every point in 1970 is below the corresponding point in 1960. Second, the slope of the line for 1970 is less steep than for 1960. In 1960, a weighted regression line fitted through these points has a slope of −.0225 and, in 1970, it has a slope of −.0156, Third, by 1970, what originally was a continuous linear relationship has turned into what appears to be a step relationship, with women who marry at ages 19 and younger having a high but almost equal level of fertility, then a decline in the range 19–22, and then women who marry at ages 22–25 having more or less equal fertility levels. Beyond age 25, there is a very steep decline, although the numbers of women in each single year age-at-marriage group in this range become quite small.

---

[4] This model also includes education, husband's income, marriage duration, initial parity, region, ethnic status, and type of place of residence.

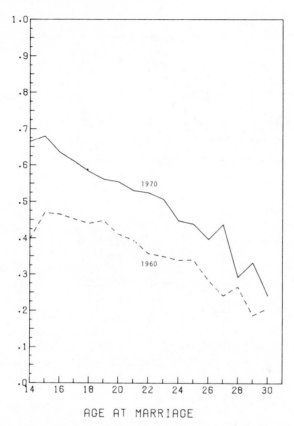

FIGURE 4-1 *Fertility differences by single year of age at first marriage: Total population,
1960 and 1970 (adjusted means).*

In order to see the effects of both husband's age at marriage and wife's age at
marriage, we have rerun the regression including an interaction variable that
cross-classifies husband's and wife's age at marriage. This is shown in Table 4-3.
It can be seen that both husband's and wife's age at marriage have effects on
recent fertility, but the effect of the wife's age at marriage is clearly the stronger
of the two.

Differentials in recent marital fertility by initial parity are shown in the sixth
panel of Table 4-1. This initial parity variable is included here and in subsequent
analyses primarily as a control variable. In 1960, there was very little relationship between initial parity and the probability of having a birth in the past 3
years, with the exception that women with an initial parity of 4 or higher had a
higher rate than women with lower initial parities. This latter group probably

TABLE 4-3

Gross and Net Deviations from Mean Number of Children under 3
Years of Age for Currently Married Women under 40, by Age at First
Marriage of the Woman and Her Husband: 1970.

Wife's Age at Marriage	Husband's Age at Marriage				
	<20	20-21	22-24	25-29	30+
	Gross Effects				
<18	.013	-.040	-.064	-.073	-.158
18-19	.058	.037	-.003	-.066	.049
20-21	.058	.009	-.002	-.000	.024
22-24	.001	-.051	-.001	-.007	-.017
25+	-.004	-.005	-.040	.001	-.015
	Net Effects[1]				
<18	.059	.024	.036	.038	-.001
18-19	.046	.039	.020	.006	.111
20-21	.066	-.004	-.024	-.003	.036
22-24	-.006	-.064	-.053	-.057	-.059
25+	-.072	-.086	-.125	-.107	-.161
	Number of Cases				
<18	1885	1027	759	351	161
18-19	1504	2141	1711	644	167
20-21	433	1412	1905	871	181
22-24	157	360	1308	1096	290
25+	82	112	254	591	465

[1] Model includes woman's age at first marriage, region, ethnicity,
initial parity, and type of residence.

represents the high-fertility segment of the population. By 1970, the relationship
is a strong inverse one with a high probability of a birth for women of initial
parity 0, is somewhat lower for women of initial parity 1, and is considerably
lower for initial parities 2 or 3. Women with initial parity 4 or more have a
higher rate than women with initial parity 2 or 3.

Residential Characteristics

The seventh and eighth panels of Table 4-1 show fertility differentials by
geographic region and type of place of residence. It is always difficult to explain
why one is interested in regional differences in fertility because, in essence,
region is an imperfect indicator of a variety of diverse variables ranging from
ethnic group membership to life style to cost of housing. The social, economic,
and demographic variables used in the regression analysis do not explain the

regional variation in the crude rates. In 1960, as well as in 1970, couples living in the Northeast and North Central states had higher fertility than couples living in the other regions. Women living in the South had lower fertility than those in any other region.

Type of place of residence here is a cross-classification of metropolitan/ nonmetropolitan residence and urban/rural-nonfarm/rural-farm residence. Because of the confidentiality requirements—no area of less than 250,000 population can be identified—metropolitan/nonmetropolitan residence cannot be distinguished in every state. In 1970, there are 12 states in which metropolitan residence is not ascertained for either the rural or the urban population, an additional 13 states in which the metropolitan residence of the rural population is not ascertained, and 2 other states in which the metropolitan residence of the urban population is not ascertained. Of the total sample of nearly 20,000, metropolitan residence is available for all but about 2700 of our cases. In general, the "not ascertained" category with respect to metropolitan status represents a population that is primarily *non*metropolitan. However, there is some slippage; some of the residents in the "not ascertained" states are residents of highly metropolitan states, such as Delaware, Connecticut, and Maryland.

In both 1960 and 1970, the fertility of the rural farm population tends to be higher than that of the rural nonfarm or urban population, within any category of metropolitan status. The fertility of the rural nonfarm population tends to be intermediate between that of the urban and rural farm population, while the fertility level of the urban population tends to be the lowest. This rural/urban difference in fertility is very pronounced in the states in which metropolitan residence is not ascertained, that is, those states that are predominantly nonmetropolitan. This farm/nonfarm differential is also large among persons designated as nonmetropolitan residents. However, within the metropolitan residence category, the rural-farm/rural-nonfarm/urban fertility differential is small and, within this metropolitan population, rural nonfarm residents have *higher* fertility than rural farm residents. Looked at in another way, we see that, within the urban population, there is higher fertility in states in which metropolitan residence is not ascertained than in nonmetropolitan or metropolitan states. There is no difference between the metropolitan and nonmetropolitan urban populations. Similarly, there is no metropolitan/nonmetropolitan difference in the rural nonfarm population's fertility rates. There is, however, a large difference between the fertility of the metropolitan and nonmetropolitan rural farm population, a difference of more than .07.

Income

The final panel of Table 4-1 shows the relationship between husband's income and fertility. The income/fertility relationship has been the subject of considerable interest recently, both because of its policy relevance and because aggregate changes in income appear to be related to changes in period fertility rates. Income, unlike most other variables in the social sciences, is subject to a certain degree of manipulability by governmental action. Since income is routinely affected by governmental actions, it is important to know what effects income has on fertility. For example, in a series of papers, Easterlin (1962, 1966, 1973) has shown that swings in the aggregate income of young adults relative to the aggregate income of their parents some 5 to 10 years earlier are related to fluctuations in period fertility rates. Although the relationship has not been found at the micro level (see MacDonald and Rindfuss, 1976), the possibility of being able to predict turning points in period fertility trends has aroused justifiable interest in this Easterlin fertility hypothesis.

In this section, we do not test any particular income/fertility hypothesis; rather, we examine the relationship between husband's current income and recent fertility. The results, however, are provocative with respect to the general family of relative income hypotheses (in addition to Easterlin, see Freedman, 1963).

The decision as to which income variable to use in the analysis of fertility is always problematic. This is particularly true when measures of cumulative fertility are used for women who have essentially completed their fertility, because, while income is being measured contemporaneously, the fertility decisions occurred 20 or more years earlier. Since we are using a measure of recent fertility, this problem is minimized but not entirely eliminated. There are, however, a variety of current income measures available for examining the income/current-fertility issue: husband's income, family income, and wife's income. We have not used the latter two because both of them are related to the labor-force participation of the wife and, as noted earlier, the labor-force-participation/fertility relationship cannot be adequately analyzed with census data. To avoid the labor-force-participation problem, Cho, Grabill, and Bogue (1970) compared fertility levels by family income, restricting their analysis to families in which the wife was not in the labor force. This procedure, unfortunately, tends to disproportionately eliminate low-income families, low-fertility families, and families with well-educated wives from the analysis.

To avoid confounding income effects with female labor-force-participation effects, we examined the relationship between husband's income and fertility. The question remains, however, as to what should be done to "standardize" income for changes in the income distribution over time. We have used two alternative measures of income to try to take into account, on the one hand, the declining value of the dollar and, on the other hand, the growth in real income through time. We used constant dollars as one of the measures. The purchasing power of the dollar declined by 26% between 1957 and 1960 and between 1967 and 1970. We have routinely deflated 1970 incomes to 1960 dollars by dividing them by 1.26. In the comparisons of income differentials and relative rates of change in fertility, the income variable is expressed in 1960 constant dollars.

The bottom panel of Table 4-1 shows differentials in recent marital fertility by husband's income. For both 1960 and 1970, there is a comparatively strong positive effect of husband's income on recent fertility, after controlling for education, age at marriage, marriage duration, and the other factors considered in this analysis.

As an alternative to constant dollars, we have also done the same analysis using income decile values. We have determined approximate decile values for both 1960 and 1970. Use of this measurement implies that what is important is not the absolute amount of income or the real value of the absolute income level, but the relative position within the income distribution. When the husband's income deciles are included in a multivariate analysis of recent fertility for urban white couples (not shown), we also find a strong positive relationship between income deciles and fertility when other factors such as education and age at marriage are controlled. This is the case in both 1960 and 1970.

Traditionally, income and cumulative fertility have had either an inverse relationship or no relationship at all; but demographers have expected a positive relationship to emerge as contraceptive control became universally practiced. A strong positive income effect on recent fertility was first found by Cho, Grabill, and Bogue (1970) in their earlier analysis of 1960 own-children data. They interpreted this positive effect on recent fertility as part of the expected transition to a positive income effect, and it was expected that a positive income effect would be found for cumulative fertility as well. But a strong positive effect on cumulative fertility has yet to be found (for example, see Bean and Wood, 1974).[5]

An alternative explanation for part or all of the income/current-fertility relationship involves the effect of income on the timing of fertility. If a couple knows that the husband's income will increase in the near future, they might postpone fertility until the higher income is realized (graduate students provide the archetypical example). If this were happening, current income could be positively related to current fertility, even though permanent income might not be related to children ever born. In order to explore this possibility, we examined a number of interactions between income and other characteristics of the couple. The remainder of this section deals with such interactions. In each case, the model includes the following variables, either in the interaction or included additively with the income variable: (1) marriage duration, (2) wife's education, (3) initial parity, (4) wife's age at first marriage, (5) region, (6) metro-

---

[5] However, until income changes over time are available, studies of the relationship between income and cumulative fertility will be plagued by the fact that income at time of measurement might be different from income at time of childbearing.

politan/nonmetropolitan residence by farm, urban, and rural nonfarm residence, and (7) ethnicity.

Looking first at the interaction between husband's income and marriage duration, in Figure 4-2, we plot the results of this analysis, showing the effect of income within each of five marriage-duration categories. We have divided marriage duration into four 4-year intervals for the first 16 years of marriage and then a terminal interval of 16 or more years. Income is expressed in quintiles.[6] In 1970, there was a positive effect of income within each of these marriage-duration intervals. The slope, however, varies from one duration interval to another, with the steepest positive slope within the first 8 years of marriage. The slope for the second 8-year interval is much less steep, while that for the last interval (16 or more years) is very small and close to zero. Similar patterns are found for 1960 (not shown). To provide a convenient summary, we have fitted regression lines (weighted) through each of these sets of five points (using values of 1, 2, 3, 4, and 5 for the quintiles), with the following results.

	Slope	
Marriage Duration	1970	1960
<4 years	.055	.062
4–7.9 years	.044	.050
8–11.9 years	.025	.022
12–15.9 years	.016	.013
16+ years	.013	.008

[6] The income categories are defined by the value of quintiles of husband's income within the urban white population of married couples with wife under 40. This sample is a total sample of couples with wife under 40. Thus, the "quintiles" do not divide the distribution precisely into five equal size groups. They are not very unequal in size, however.

	Quintiles	Number of Cases
Low	1	5006
	2	4087
	3	3948
	4	3544
High	5	3282

The distribution of income of the total population is lower than that of the urban white population.

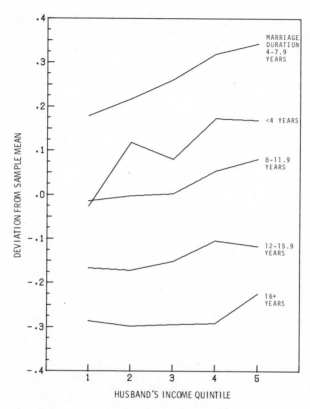

FIGURE 4-2 *Net effect of husband's income (in quintiles) on recent fertility, within marriage-duration categories, for currently married women under age 40: 1970.*

The fact that the income effect is stronger at the short marriage durations than at the longer marriage durations is suggestive of a childspacing phenomenon; spacing considerations are important in the early years of marriage, while number considerations become important after the first few years of marriage.

The interaction effect between husband's income and wife's education is shown in Figure 4-3. Again, husband's income is divided into quintiles, and the difference in income effects within the five education groups is examined. Five education groups are used here, rather than the usual six, because of the small number of cases of women with less than 5 years of schooling (see Chapter 3). It can be seen that, in 1970, the higher the level of wife's education, the greater the positive income slope. For wives with a college education, there is a steep positive income slope. For wives who are college dropouts, the slope is somewhat less steep. High school graduates show a modest positive effect of income on fertility, while high school dropouts or women who terminated their education before entering high school show essentially no effect or perhaps a slight inverse relationship. In 1960, there seems to be little systematic variation in the slope of fertility on income among education groups, except that there was a noticeable positive slope for college graduates in 1960 (not shown in the figures). The slopes of these lines (again using scores of 1, 2, 3, 4, and 5 for the quintiles) are as follows.

	Slope	
Education	1970	1960
<9 years	.001	−.014
9–11 years	−.016	.024
12 years	.025	.029
13–15 years	.055	.014
16+ years	.084	.081

Complementing the 1970 results are the results that have been found in relation to female labor force participation. The net inverse effect of husband's income on the labor-force participation of the wife becomes greater the higher the educational attainment of the wife (Sweet, 1973b: Ch. 5).

In 1970, the effect of income on recent births is strongly positive for women of zero and first parity (see Figure 4-4). There is a slight positive slope at second parity, except for women whose husbands' earnings are in the first quintile. There is very little difference in fertility by income for women of third and higher parity. Similar results are found for 1960 (not shown). Thus, again it appears that the positive income effect observed in the aggregate is, in part at least, a timing phenomenon. Young couples of relatively high income are likely to accelerate childbearing. In addition, it may be that couples with high upward income mobility are disproportionately those with low fertility early in marriage, thus producing the positive relationship in the cross section and little relationship in completed fertility. The hypothesis that the relationship between fertility and income is in the process of changing cannot be easily examined with these data, but most of the interactions with income observed in 1970 were also observed in the 1960 data.

To summarize, a strong positive relationship between income and recent marital fertility has been found; this relationship appears to be at least partly the result of the effect of the timing of income changes on the timing of fertility. It is possible that couples plan their early marital reproduction in accord with their expected income profile. Couples in which the husband is temporarily earning

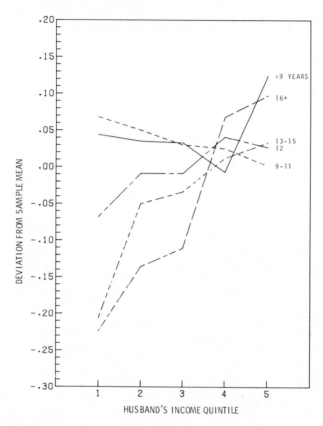

FIGURE 4-3 *Net effects of husband's income (in quintiles) on recent fertility, within education groups, for currently married women under age 40: 1970.*

relatively little, but expects to earn more, will delay their reproduction until their earnings are greater. A part of this process may involve the work life of wives. Many couples with temporarily low husband's income attain a higher standard of living by the work of the wife. This is more difficult if there are children. When the husband's income rises, the couple has its children, and the wife temporarily ceases employment. This suggests that the relationship between current income and current fertility need not be the same as the relationship between permanent income and cumulative fertility.

This is an area that needs to be explored in future research. The empirical problem is to identify young couples with relatively depressed incomes early in marriage. One approach would be to classify occupations of husbands by the ratio of peak life cycle earnings to earnings early in the life cycle. However, this

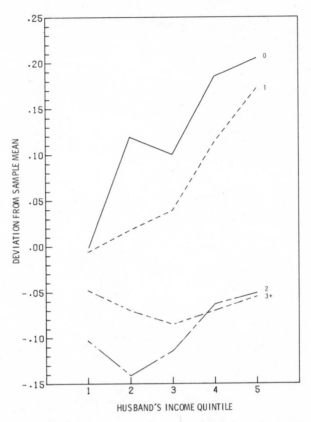

FIGURE 4-4 *Net effect of husband's income (in quintiles) on recent fertility, within initial parity groups, for currently married women under age 40: 1970.*

approach is problematic because of occupational mobility, including mobility from student or armed forces status to an occupation.

Number of Times Married

With census data, married persons can be classified by whether they are in their first marriage or in a second or later marriage. Couples can thus be classified into a fourfold division, depending on whether the husband was married once or more than once and whether the wife was married once or more than once. In 1970, 84% of the couples with wife under age 40 consist of two spouses in a first marriage. Table 4-4 shows this fourfold classification in relation to recent fertility. Data are shown for both 1960 and 1970. Irrespective of whether or not they have been married before, women wed to previously

TABLE 4-4.

Gross and Net Deviations from Mean Number of Children under 3
Years for Currently Married Women under Age 40, by Marital
History: 1970 and 1960.

Marital History	1970			1960		
	N	Gross	Net$_1$	N	Gross	Net$_1$
Wife married once, husband once	16682	.012	.006	16436	.015	.002
Wife married once, husband more than once	1246	-.033	-.067	1212	-.027	-.045
Wife married more than once, husband once	952	-.036	.023	968	-.097	.025
Wife married more than once, husband more than once	987	-.127	-.032	803	-.160	-.011
	Grand mean = .407			Grand mean = .546		

[1] The following variables are included in the model: education,
age at marriage, region, race and ethnic group, metropolitan
residence by rural nonfarm, rural farm, urban residence,
husband's income in quintiles, marriage duration and initial
parity.

married men have lower fertility than those wed to men not previously married.
The lowest fertility level is found for couples in which the wife has been married
once and the husband has been married more than once. The highest fertility
levels are found for wives who have been married more than once with husbands
who have been married only once. The same general pattern prevailed in 1960,
although the differentials were somewhat lower. An interpretation of the relatively high fertility of the wife-married-more-than-once/husband-married-once
group is suggested by earlier work of Lauriat (1969), Carter and Glick (1970),
Cohen and Sweet (1974), and Sweet (1973a). Many of the women whose first
marriage was terminated have lost some potential reproductive time. A recent
fertility measure includes the births that are being made up at a relatively
advanced duration since first marriage, births that would probably have occurred
earlier if a first marriage had not been terminated. Another possible interpretation is that women in a second marriage desire to have children in that marriage,
irrespective of their prior fertility.

TABLE 4-5

Percent Decline in Recent Fertility between 1960 and 1970 for Urban White Couples, Wife under Age 40.

	N		Percent Decline	
	1960	1970	Crude	Standard-ized[1]
Education				
<5 years	144	129	36.4	31.7
5-8 years	1409	860	18.9	22.3
9-11 years	2887	2310	20.0	17.4
12 years	5622	6255	25.5	26.5
13-15 years	1449	1933	31.6	33.6
16+ years	875	1460	26.0	22.9
Husband's Occupation				
Professional	1803	2409	28.1	26.9
Manager	1399	1504	21.1	25.4
Sales	934	956	22.2	25.7
Clerical	878	882	36.9	33.8
Craftsman	2600	2705	20.8	26.1
Operative	2333	2110	18.9	21.5
Laborer	489	446	24.4	23.0
Service	499	605	19.4	24.5
Unemployed	323	263	31.8	33.2
Armed forces	451	585	35.6	33.9
Not in labor force	254	428	43.6	43.7
Constant Dollar Husband's Income				
<$1,000	312	383	37.6	32.3
$1,000-1,999	474	452	29.0	27.4
$2,000-2,999	822	555	39.7	38.5
$3,000-3,999	1399	1031	26.6	28.6
$4,000-4,999	1916	1078	21.0	24.1
$5,000-7,499	4892	4018	19.4	28.3
$7,500-9,999	1489	3017	18.2	26.5
$10,000+	1082	2413	21.3	25.5
Husband's Income - Deciles				
1 (low)	1314	1310	36.1	33.0
2	1190	1345	26.0	28.8
3	1197	1226	25.2	27.1
4	1222	1201	20.5	21.5
5	1306	1431	21.0	27.5
6	1078	1246	22.8	27.0
7	1395	1230	22.3	22.6
8	1283	1366	17.8	22.2
9	1179	1280	28.1	30.5
10 (high)	1222	1312	26.0	25.8

continued

TABLE 4-5 continued

	N		Percent Decline	
	1960	1970	Crude	Standardized[1]
Region				
Northeast	3319	3096	21.5	22.9
North Central	3590	3553	24.0	26.6
South	3143	3537	23.8	25.5
West	2334	2761	29.3	32.6
Metropolitan Residence				
In SMSA	9054	9674	22.9	24.8
Outside SMSA	2292	2194	27.6	30.7
Not ascertained	1040	1079	33.6	34.4
Marriage Duration				
<3 years	1849	2514	27.5	
3-5.9 years	2007	2162	26.2	
6-8.9 years	1813	1998	22.8	
9-11.9 years	1981	1869	27.3	
12-14.9 years	2226	1711	27.0	
15-17.9 years	1360	1468	36.9	
18-20.9 years	899	951	40.1	
21-23.9 years	233	248	37.2	
24+ years	18	26	*	
Age at Marriage				
<18	2243	2365	30.9	27.7
18-19	3320	3916	23.6	25.8
20-21	3154	3357	22.5	28.2
22-24	2302	2282	25.0	28.9
25-29	1105	848	22.9	25.4
30+	262	179	16.3	10.7
Initial Parity				
0	3816	4435	20.8	20.5
1	2564	2297	10.3	19.2
2	3064	2675	24.9	29.8
3	1719	1868	48.0	46.4
4+	1223	1672	52.3	49.4
Total	12386	12947	24.8	26.8

[1]
Standardized on the 1960 marriage duration distribution of that group, i.e., the percent decline that would have occurred if the group's marriage duration distribution had not changed.

*
N less than 20.

85

The depressed fertility of once-married women with husbands married more than once is puzzling. One can conjecture that such husbands have probably fathered children in their first marriages. They may be financially responsible for those children. They may even view their current marriage as a possibly temporary relationship and be less likely to want to have children in it. It is easy to speculate on a process consistent with this result, although we must emphasize that there are, to our knowledge, no data to support any speculation.

DIFFERENTIALS IN TRENDS: URBAN WHITES

The pervasiveness of postwar fertility fluctuations was seen in Chapter 3; this section further examines that pervasiveness for the fertility decline of the 1960s. By contrasting the level of recent marital fertility prior to the 1960 census with the level of recent marital fertility prior to the 1970 census, it is possible to examine rates of decline in greater detail. The restrictions to currently married couples and to the time just prior to the census allow comparisons for a greater variety of social and economic groups than was possible in Chapter 3 and thus permit finer examination of the pervasiveness of these trends.

Table 4-5 shows crude and marriage-duration standardized rates of fertility decline for subgroups within the urban white population. Similar analyses for minorities and for the rural population are presented in Chapters 5 and 7. The standardized rates reported here are marriage-duration standardized rates, in which the 1960 marriage-duration distribution of the particular subpopulation is used as the standard.

The most notable conclusion from Table 4-5 is that fertility declined during the 1960s for every subgroup within the urban white population. Although there are differentials in the rates of decline, the fact that all groups experienced a decline is striking. All groups experienced a decline of at least 10%, and all but three experienced a decline of at least 20%.

As was the case for the total fertility rates for all white women (Table 3-6), the greatest decline in marital fertility is found for women who attended but did not complete college. High school dropouts, however, have a comparatively small decline in marital fertility—in comparison to their large decline in overall fertility. This suggests that different explanations are needed for the two groups of dropouts. High school dropouts probably experienced considerable declines in the proportion marrying or in nonmarital fertility.

Of interest are the patterns of decline by initial parity and marriage duration. There was a decline of about 50% for women of fourth and higher initial parity, continuing the long-term decline among this group. This rapid decline among women with comparatively high initial parities suggests that a reduction in completed fertility is occurring. It further suggests an increased concentration of completed fertility at the two-child level. The smallest declines are found among women whose initial parity was 0 or 1.[7]

Similarly, the greatest declines in fertility are found at the longest marriage-duration intervals. The rates for women whose duration was 15 or more years declined by 40%. Fertility in these intervals has been relatively rare, and now it is virtually nonexistent.

In the third panel of Table 4-5, married women are classified by the income of their husbands. The 1970 income measure is in 1960 constant dollars. Using this measure, it can be seen that fertility declined substantially at every income level. There is a tendency for the greatest declines to have occurred in the lowest income categories. For the other income categories, the rates of decline are essentially similar. When husband's income is classified by decile (fourth panel of Table 4-5), we find no systematic variation in standardized rate of fertility decline, with the exception that couples in the lowest decile have the highest rate of decline.

SUMMARY

This chapter examined the persistence and change in fertility differentials and the extent to which the trend in fertility during the 1960s pervaded all groups examined. The dependent variable throughout was the number of children under 3 years of age among currently married women under 40. Education had the expected inverse relationship to recent fertility. Although both husband's and wife's educations exert influences, the wife's effect appears to be stronger.

The Spanish-surname population had higher levels of fertility than either blacks or whites. The urban population had levels of fertility lower than either the rural farm or the rural nonfarm populations, and the rural nonfarm population had lower levels than the rural farm population. Both marriage duration and age at marriage had the expected inverse relationship to recent fertility. When the effects of both husband's and wife's age at marriage were examined, it was found that the wife's effect tends to predominate.

Husband's income is positively related to recent fertility. While it is possible that this positive income effect is the one that some demographers have been expecting to emerge, it appears to be related, in part, to temporal changes in income and the timing of fertility. If couples tend to postpone their fertility until an anticipated increase in the husband's income is realized, then it is possible for husband's current income to be related to current fertility even if it

---

[7] It should be noted that the sample here consists of currently married women and that these findings do not show possible declines in first-order fertility resulting from increases in the age at marriage.

has no relationship to completed fertility. The fact that, in 1960 and 1970, the positive effect is stronger among the shorter-marriage-duration groups, the better educated, and the early parities suggests that the relationship may be a timing phenomenon.

Although there were numerous changes in the pattern of differential fertility, the persistent cross-sectional effect of the variables examined is noteworthy. That these variables persistently differentiate in the cross section and do not differentiate with respect to the basic trend—all groups experienced a fertility decline during the 1960s—is somewhat puzzling. Similar results are found when trends and differentials are examined for minority groups in the next two chapters.

5

Fertility Trends
among Minority Groups

This is the first of two chapters dealing with the fertility of racial and ethnic minorities in the United States. This chapter examines changing fertility during the period 1955–1969. The next chapter examines differential fertility within each minority group. Fertility as of 1960 for these racial and ethnic minority groups ranges from very high levels for Southern rural blacks, American Indians, and Mexican Americans, to moderate levels for Southern urban blacks and blacks living outside the South, to low levels for Japanese and Chinese Americans. This chapter will use both types of own-children fertility measures: annual age-specific rates and recent marital fertility.

Unfortunately, analysis of minority group status and fertility is typically confined to whites and blacks; this has been noted by Roberts and Lee (1974). Because of the small populations and the geographical concentration of American Indians, Chinese Americans, and Japanese Americans, reliable data are unavailable from fertility surveys conducted in the United States. The small population size and concern about comparability in the definition of minority group status render data from the vital registration system difficult to use. Only the census provides sufficient cases for analysis, while at the same time providing comparability; but, in the past, the Census Bureau has published only limited data on the fertility of racial groups. With the release of the Public Use Samples, it is now possible to examine the relationship between minority group status and fertility for a larger number of groups.

AGGREGATE TRENDS: 1955–1969

This first section examines annual fertility rates for six racial and ethnic minorities: Mexican Americans, American Indians, Chinese Americans, Japanese

Americans, blacks, and whites. In order to ensure comparability in identification, the analysis here is restricted to rates derived from one census: the 1970 census. The stability of these estimates for whites and blacks is examined in Appendix B.

The analysis here is restricted to data from the 1970 census and, therefore, to the period 1955–1969 for an additional reason: For Chinese Americans, Japanese Americans, and American Indians, it was necessary to combine all six 1-in-a-100 Public Use Samples in order to obtain sufficiently large numbers of women to compute annual fertility rates. Even with six samples combined, a quick glance at Figures 5-1 and 5-2 indicates that large interannual fluctuations in the estimated fertility rates remain because of sampling variability. To minimize the effect of sampling variability, the trend estimates reported in Tables 5-1 and 5-3 have been computed by first averaging two adjacent years at the beginning and end points.

One final methodological note concerns Mexican Americans. There is a surfeit of techniques available from the 1970 census to identify the Mexican American population, none of which is entirely satisfactory (see Hernandez, Estrada, and Alvirez, 1973). For this initial analysis (confined to data from a single census), we have used the self-identification measure: Persons were asked to report whether their origin or descent was Mexican, Puerto Rican, Cuban, Central or South American, or other Spanish. This is the same procedure that is used to determine race and has the advantage that it probably comes closest to the social

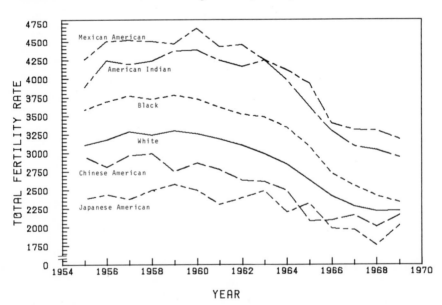

FIGURE 5-1 *Total fertility rates for six racial or ethnic groups: 1955–1969.*

concept of ethnic group membership. Throughout this section, Mexican Americans are included in the various graphs and tables twice, once by themselves and once as a component of the white population. Although ease of calculation was the reason for this admittedly unconventional procedure, its effect should be minimal because Mexican Americans are a small fraction of all whites. Three samples were combined to obtain the Mexican American rates, one sample was used for white and black rates, and six samples were used for the other rates.

Total fertility rates for the six racial and ethnic groups are shown in Figure 5-1 for the period 1955–1969. The fertility levels of all six groups declined during the period. The decline was greatest for the two largest groups: whites and blacks (see Table 5-1). The smallest rate of decline was recorded for Japanese Americans. Most of the decline occurs in the latter half of the period. This is particularly the case for American Indians. From 1957–1963, they experienced a 2% decline in fertility; but, from 1963–1969, there was a 27% decrease in fertility. Such contrasts are to be found for the other racial groups, with the exception of the Chinese Americans.

TABLE 5-1

Percent Decline in Total Fertility, Fertility 15-29, and Fertility 30-44 in Periods 1957-1969, 1957-1963, and 1963-1969, by Race or Ethnic Status.

Rate and Race or Ethnic Status	Percent Decline in Period		
	1957-1969	1957-1963	1963-1969
Total Fertility Rate			
American Indian	29	2	27
Japanese American	22	4	19
Chinese American	30	14	18
Mexican American	28	3	26
Black American	36	9	30
White American	32	11	24
Fertility 15-29			
American Indian	27	3	25
Japanese American	21	4	18
Chinese American	30	12	21
Mexican American	24	2	23
Black American	35	9	29
White American	30	10	22
Fertility 30-44			
American Indian	34	1	33
Japanese American	24	3	22
Chinese American	30	17	15
Mexican American	35	6	31
Black American	39	8	34
White American	37	11	29

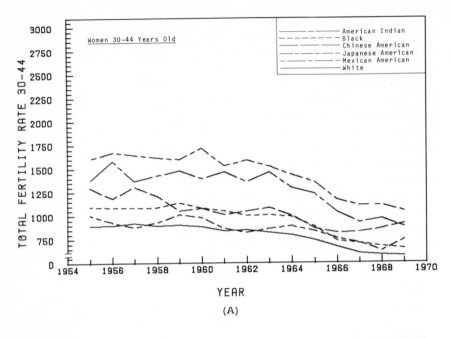

(A)

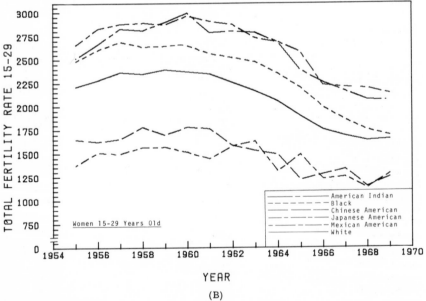

(B)

FIGURE 5-2 *Fertility rates for women 15–29 and 30–44 years old for six racial or ethnic groups: 1955–1969.*

As noted earlier (Chapter 2), annual fertility rates from own-children data tend to accurately describe *trends,* but differences in *levels* of fertility between groups should be interpreted with caution. However, the differences in the levels among the six racial groups are sufficiently large to warrant comment. The total fertility rate among American Indians or Mexican Americans is almost twice that of the Japanese Americans for most of the period. Furthermore, this difference is probably even larger, because factors leading to underestimation of the fertility rates, such as infant mortality, tend to be higher among American Indians or Mexican Americans than among other groups (for example, see Kitagawa and Hauser, 1973).

Figure 5-2 shows fertility rates for younger (15–29 years old) and older (30–44 years old) women; the expected decline in fertility is found for all groups. Among both the older and the younger women, the largest relative rate of decline was recorded for blacks, followed by whites. Also, for all groups, the decline among older women is greater than the decline among younger women (Table 5-1).

Among all minority groups, the pervasiveness of fertility trends can be seen; we find essentially the same trend (i.e., a substantial decline in fertility) for all six racial and ethnic groups. This similarity with respect to trends suggests that the six groups are responding to the same or similar sets of stimuli that resulted in lower fertility among all groups. Unfortunately, we cannot be sure that all groups are responding to the same set factors.

The data are also somewhat ambiguous with respect to the issue of convergence, because independent evidence is not available regarding the extent to which compositional differences have been lessened or removed. In some areas, there has been limited convergence between whites and blacks (Hauser and Featherman, 1974); but little is known about the other groups. Using whites as the majority group, convergence in fertility levels has occurred if, for those

TABLE 5-2

Ratio of Various Minority Total Fertility Rates to the White Total Fertility Rate: 1957-1959 to 1967-1969.

	Ratio to White Rate			
	1957-1959	1960-1962	1963-1966	1967-1969
American Indian	1.30	1.34	1.39	1.35
Japanese American	0.76	0.75	0.83	0.86
Chinese American	0.89	0.87	0.85	0.94
Mexican American	1.37	1.42	1.44	1.46
Black American	1.15	1.14	1.16	1.09

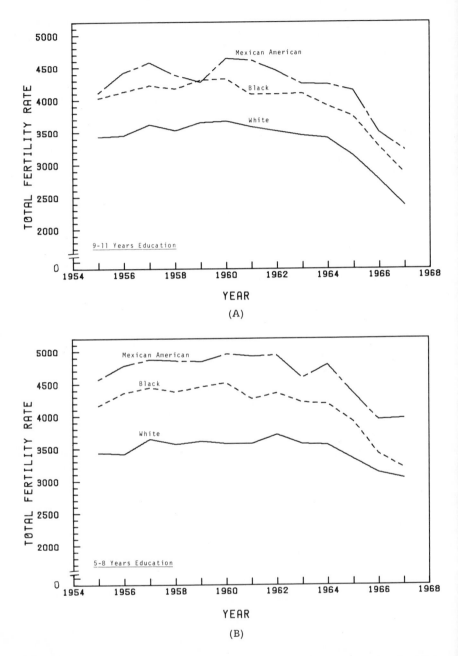

FIGURE 5-3 *Total fertility rates for whites, blacks, and Mexican Americans by education: 1955–1967. Parts (C) and (D) are on facing page.*

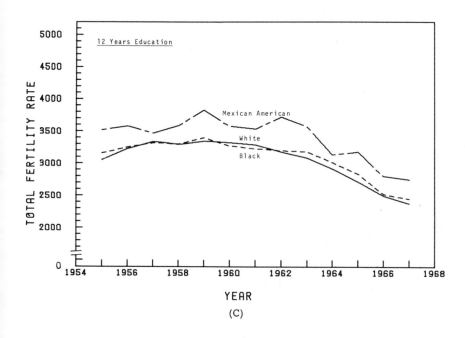

(C)

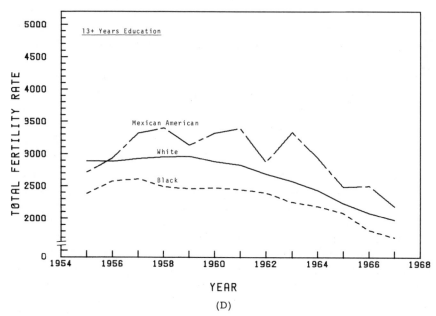

(D)

FIGURE 5-3 continued

TABLE 5-3

*Percent Decline in Total Fertility 1957-1967 by Education for
Whites, Blacks, and Mexican Americans.*

Education	White American	Black American	Mexican American
5-8 years	13	25	18
9-11 years	28	27	25
12 years	26	24	21
13+ years	30	32	25

groups with levels of fertility higher than the white level, the rate of decline was greater than that for whites, or if, for those groups with levels of fertility lower than the white level, the rate of decline was less than that for whites. Overall, there was only a slight amount of convergence for three of the five comparisons.

An alternative way of examining convergence, or lack thereof, between the majority white population and the various racial and ethnic minorities is to compare, over time, the ratio of the minority total fertility rate to the white total fertility rate. This is shown in Table 5-2. Again, there is no evidence of substantial reduction in fertility differentials. Rates for Mexican Americans and American Indians have not converged; rather, the Mexican Americans and American Indians had a less rapid decline than did whites. Those rates for blacks, Chinese Americans, and Japanese Americans have converged slightly to the white rates.

Although direct information on the convergence of independent characteristics is not available for these groups, it is possible to begin to address the issue by controlling for education of wife, that is, by examining the trend within education groups. This is not the same as controlling in a cross section, because the composition of the group is changing during the period 1955–1967. For example, the percentage of black women 25–29 years old who attended college increased from 12% in 1960 to 17% in 1970. However, even controlling for education, it is likely that the groups differ with respect to other social, demographic, and economic characteristics. Figure 5-3 shows total fertility rates for four education groups within the white, black, and Mexican American populations.[1] Because of the need for large numbers of women in order to make reliable annual estimates, we were unable to compute fertility rates by education for American Indians, Chinese Americans, and Japanese Americans. It can be seen that fertility declined for every racial–ethnic/education group (also see

[1] The series has been truncated at 1967 instead of 1969, because, for 1968 and 1969, the estimated rates for the younger women are misleading. For a detailed explanation, see Chapter 3.

Table 5-3). But, among eight possibilities, the only significant contraction occurred between whites and blacks with 5–8 years of education. For the other three black/white comparisons, the rates of decline are similar; for three of the four white/Mexican American comparisons, there is divergence rather than convergence. Thus, there is no evidence of substantial reduction in fertility differentials among these groups.

ANNUAL RATES AND RECENT MARITAL FERTILITY

Before examining detailed trends in marital fertility within the various racial and ethnic groups, this section examines aggregate trends in marital fertility. The same measure is used here as was used in earlier analyses, that is, comparison between the number of own children under 3 years old among married women in the 1960 census and the comparable number from the 1970 census. The fertility rate comparisons have again been standardized by marriage duration in order to control for this potentially important source of fertility decline.

The classification of couples by minority status differs from the classification system used in the analysis of annual fertility rates. In the analysis of marital fertility, couples are classified as being members of a group if either husband or the wife is a member of that group. Thus, some couples are included in two different ethnic analyses. The effect of homogamy on fertility is examined in the next chapter. Finally, two definitions of the Mexican American population are used: Mexican American and Spanish surname. Only the Spanish-surname population in the five Southwestern states (Arizona, California, Colorado, New Mexico, and Texas) is comparably defined in 1960 and in 1970.

In the analysis of changing marital fertility, urban white women will be used as the basis of comparison with the minority groups. (The contrast between urban and rural white trends will be shown in Chapter 7.) Also, the black population will be subdivided into three groups: Southern rural blacks, Southern urban blacks, and non-Southern blacks.

Since racial and ethnic group membership is a characteristic that ought not change, one internal check is available on the validity of the marital fertility change measures. We can compare the number of own children under 3 years old per currently married woman in 1960 with the number of own children 10–12.9 years old in 1970. The basis for the 1960 observation is all women currently married in 1960 who were, at that time, under the age of 40. The base for our 1970 measure is women 25–49 years old in 1970 whose first marriage occurred prior to April 1, 1960. This provides a comparable but not identical universe, the major difference in universe being women who were in a formerly married status, that is, who were separated, widowed, or divorced, as of April 1, 1960. There is also a slight difference in the numerator, since the children

TABLE 5-4

Comparison of Own Children under 3 Years[a] and Own Children 10-12[b]
for Urban White and Selected Racial and Ethnic Minority Women.

	N	1960 Children under 3	N	1970 Children 10-12	Ratio of 1960 and 1970 Estimates
Urban White	12386	.529	13107	.510	1.04
Black					
Non-Southern	7329	.598	6839	.560	1.07
Southern urban	5683	.644	4736	.597	1.08
Southern rural	3352	.803	2396	.770	1.04
Spanish Surname	3927	.775	3775	.724	1.07
Japanese American	777	.553	2448	.500	1.11
Chinese American	307	.550	1169	.541	1.02
American Indian	545	.881	2125	.640	1.38
Puerto Rican[c]	1418	.634	3560	.595	1.07

[a]For married women under age 40.

[b]For currently married women 25-49 who were first married prior to
April 1, 1960.

[c]Puerto Rican descent in 1970; Puerto Rican birth or parentage in
1960.

enumerated at ages 10–12 in 1970 include only the survivors of those under 3
years old in 1960. The comparisons are shown in Table 5-4. For all groups, with
the exception of American Indians, Chinese Americans, and Japanese Americans,
the ratio of these numbers is in the range of 1.04 through 1.08. The Chinese
Americans have a closer correspondence (1.02), while the Japanese Americans
have a somewhat lower level of correspondence (1.11). The American Indians,
however, have a much lower degree of correspondence than any of the other
groups. As shown in the next section, the reason for this lack of correspondence
is that, for American Indians, minority group membership is not fixed. For this
reason, marital fertility change for American Indians will not be examined.

The percentage decline in marital fertility for the decade of the 1960s is
shown in Table 5-5. This table also shows the level of marital fertility of each
subgroup relative to the urban white level of marital fertility. The decline in
marital fertility for these groups is quite similar to the overall decline in fertility
(see Table 5-1).

In the period 1957–1960, all three groups of blacks had fertility levels that
were substantially higher than the urban white rate. The rate of fertility for
blacks living outside of the South (predominantly an urban population) was 13%

TABLE 5-5

Percent Decline in Recent Marital Fertility between 1960 and 1970, and Level of Marital Fertility Relative to that of the Urban White Population, for Selected Racial and Ethnic Minorities.

| | N | | Percent Change | | Relative Level (Urban White = 1.000) | | | |
| | 1960 | 1970 | Crude | Standardized[a] | Crude | | Standardized | |
					1960	1970	1960	1970
Black								
Southern rural	3352	2545	35.9	37.4	1.52	1.29	1.56	1.33
Southern urban	5683	5930	32.8	36.3	1.22	1.09	1.20	1.05
Non-Southern	7329	8506	30.9	34.4	1.13	1.04	1.12	1.01
Japanese American	777	832	30.3	24.3	1.05	0.97	0.88	0.91
Chinese American	307	529	22.7	24.5	1.04	1.07	0.99	1.02
Puerto Rican American[b]	1418	1938	17.8	18.1	1.20	1.31	1.07	1.20
Mexican American[b]	3277	5475	28.9	29.7	1.51	1.43	1.47	1.42
Spanish Surname[c]	3927	4770	29.0	30.1	1.47	1.38	1.45	1.39
Urban White	12386	12947	24.8	26.8	1.00	1.00	1.00	1.00

[a] Standardized on 1960 urban white marriage duration distribution.

[b] Definitions differ between 1960 and 1970. Change measures are therefore not strictly correct. For 1960, these groups include first and second generation Mexican Americans and Puerto Rican Americans. For 1970, they include persons who report themselves as being of Mexican or Puerto Rican descent.

[c] Spanish surname in five Southwestern states.

greater than the rate for urban whites, while the rates for Southern urban blacks and Southern rural blacks were 22 and 52% greater than the urban white rates, respectively. The rates for all three groups of blacks declined by more than 30%, with the largest decline of 36% for Southern rural blacks. This is greater than the decline in urban white marital fertility. Thus, the differences in marital fertility between these three groups of blacks and the urban white population diminished during the decade.

CHANGING STATUS AND OWN-CHILDREN TREND ESTIMATES

Marital fertility trends will not be examined for American Indians, and no fertility trend estimates will be examined for Filipino Americans. In both cases, the effects of changing status prompted this decision. In the case of American Indians, some people "became" Indian during the 1960s; for Filipino Americans, migration is the cause of the analytical problem. We will discuss these two problems in detail because they illustrate how own-children trend estimates can be misleading if there have been considerable shifts in composition.

We observed and reported in Sweet (1974) that the rate of decline in marital fertility for American Indians has been very rapid, more rapid than for any other group (a 45% decline between 1957–1960 and 1967–1970). In an analysis subsequent to that reported in Sweet (1974), we computed annual total fertility rates, as reported earlier in this chapter. These annual rates showed a 29% decline, concentrated late in the period. All other racial and ethnic groups studied had similar rates of decline using the two methods.

There are three separate sources of potential discrepancy between the rate of decline computed from the annual rates and that computed from the marital rates. (1) The annual rates are computed for all women, while the marital rates refer to the currently married population only. (2) The annual rates are computed from a single census: the 1970 census. Thus, the 1967–1970 period makes use of children under 3 years, whereas the 1957–1960 period makes use of children 10–13 years old as enumerated in the 1970 census. The marital fertility rates are computed from two censuses. (3) The annual rates classify women in terms of their own ethnic or racial status, whereas the marital rates classify couples' racial or ethnic status in terms of the status of either the husband or the wife. To further explore the issue, we calculated the "survival ratios" implied by surviving 1960 cohorts of female American Indians to 1970 (Table 5-6). In each case, this ratio was greater than unity, which is obviously impossible. This suggests either (a) that a much better job of enumerating American Indians was done in 1970 than in 1960, or (b) that a substantial number of persons who in 1960 were enumerated as being white or other races were enumerated in 1970 as

TABLE 5-6

"Survival Ratios" Implied by Surviving 1960 Cohorts of Female American Indians to 1970.

Age in 1960	1970:1960 Ratio
0-4	1.08
5-9	1.10
10-14	1.06
15-19	1.08
20-24	1.22
25-29	1.24
30-34	1.20
35-39	1.15
40-44	1.29

Sources: U.S. Bureau of the Census, U.S. Census of Population: 1960, Subject Reports, Nonwhite Population by Race, Final Report PC(2)-1C, U.S. Government Printing Office, Washington, D.C., 1963. U.S. Bureau of the Census, Census of Population: 1970, Subject Reports, Final Report PC(2)-1F, American Indians, U.S. Government Printing Office, Washington, D.C., 1973.

American Indian. The latter explanation seems to be the more plausible of the two, since it was during the late 1960s and early 1970s that there was a more active American Indian political movement and a revival of interest and pride in the Indian heritage and culture. Presumably, people who did not formerly identify themselves as American Indians are doing so now, possibly because, as Wax (1971:33) notes, "a variety of advantages—economic, political, and even social—have begun to accrue to those classified as 'Indians'."

The fact that the 1960 fertility measure based on the persons enumerated as Indians at that time is so much higher than the 1970 measure based on persons reporting themselves as Indian in 1970 suggests that those persons who redefine themselves as Indian by 1970 had substantially lower fertility than those people who were defining themselves as Indian as of 1960. Our guess would be that the 1960 "Indian" population was predominantly a reservation population with low income and education. This population had been losing its better-educated component through migration from reservations to urban areas. By 1970, some of these individuals who had previously redefined themselves as non-Indians once again redefined themselves as American Indians.

The second group not included because of compositional changes is the Filipino American group. Annual age-specific fertility rates were originally calculated for this group. Among young Filipinos (15–29 years old), there was an actual increase in fertility during the period 1955–1969. However, this increase is artifactual rather than real.

An understanding of the increase among young Filipinos and the fact that it is artifactual begins with the realization that the composition of the Filipino American population has been changing rapidly since 1965. The Immigration Act of 1965 eliminated the national origins system; instead, immigrant visas were to be issued on a first-come, first-served basis, with the provision that no country could use more than 20,000 visas a year (Keely, 1974; Boyd, 1974). In addition, a limited number of visas have been issued in accordance with special public laws. The effect of this change can be seen by looking at the numbers of Filipinos admitted to the United States. Between 1953 and 1965, the average number of Filipinos coming to the United States was 2477. By 1968, this number had increased to 16,391 (Keely, 1971); in 1969, 23,339 were admitted (Tidalgo, 1974). Because of the initial small size of the Filipino American population, this influx of migrants has had a considerable impact—more than 33% of the Filipino women 15–44 years old enumerated by the 1970 census came to the United States since 1965.

Not only has there been a recent influx of Filipinos, but, also, these recent migrants differ from other Filipino Americans with respect to fertility and fertility-related characteristics. To illustrate these differences, we will use 1970 census data with women 30–34 years old as an example. Among Filipinos who arrived since 1965, the average number of children ever born is 1.3; among other Filipinos, the average is 2.5. If the foregoing calculation is restricted to ever-married women, the means become 1.5 and 2.8, respectively. Also, median age at first marriage is 3 years greater for those who arrived after 1965.

Contrary to what might be expected, the influx of a sizable proportion of low-fertility Filipinos has had the effect of lowering the pre-1965 rates relative to the post-1965 rates. Furthermore, the effect has been greatest on the age-specific rates of the youngest groups. Between 1957 and 1969, the age-specific rates of women 15–19 years old increased 109%, the rates for women 20–24 years old increased 8%, and the rates for women 25–29 years old declined 7%.

The effect of increased immigration can perhaps best be illustrated by contrasting the estimation of the fertility rate for women 15–19 years old in 1969 with the estimation of the same rate in 1959. The same principle applies to the rates for women 20–24 years old, as well as to the rates for women 25–29 years old—but to a diminished extent. The 1969 rate for women 15–19 years old is based on women approximately 15–19 at the 1970 census; the rate for 1959 is based on women approximately 25–29 years old at the 1970 census. In the 1970 census, the proportion of Filipino women 15–19 years old who recently migrated to the United States is 13%; again in the 1970 census, the comparable figure for women 25–29 years old is 58%. Thus, the effect of migrants will be greater on the earlier (1959) rate than on the later (1969) rate. The relative difference between the fertility of recent migrants and that of other Filipinos completes the effect. The effect of recent migrants diminishes for the older groups because the discrepancies in the proportion of recent migrants diminish and the fertility discrepancies between the two groups diminish.

Unfortunately, there are insufficient numbers of Filipino Americans to reliably construct two sets of annual fertility rates: (1) one for those who came to the United States since 1965 and (2) one for those who were here prior to 1965. Because of the synthetic nature of the Filipino American rates, they have not been analyzed in this chapter. Similar reasons precluded the analysis of marital fertility trends among Filipino Americans. This problem of migration does not affect the estimates for other groups, such as Mexican Americans or Chinese Americans, primarily because, even though there has been recent migration, the migration was not of sufficient magnitude vis-à-vis the original population to seriously affect the estimates.

FERTILITY DECLINES WITHIN TWO
HIGH-FERTILITY GROUPS

The remainder of this chapter examines patterns of decline in marital fertility within four comparatively large minority groups, using the two-census, own child under 3 years old measure of recent marital fertility. The results of these analyses will be divided into two sections: (1) changing fertility of two high-fertility minorities—the Southern rural black and Spanish-surname populations—and (2) changing fertility among Southern urban blacks and non-Southern blacks. Similar analyses for Puerto Rican Americans, Chinese Americans, and Japanese Americans will not be presented because of the small sample size for 1960, when only a single 1% sample is available.

Spanish-surname and Southern rural black women had very high rates of fertility in the period 1957–1960. Each group experienced large declines in marital fertility (37% of black and 30% for Spanish-surname women) between 1957–1960 and 1967–1970, and, by 1967–1970, their rates were about the same (.515 and .517, respectively). Tables 5-7 and 5-8 show crude and marriage-duration standardized rates of fertility decline for subgroups within the Southern rural black and Spanish-surname populations, respectively. The marriage-duration standardized rates have been standardized on the 1960 marriage-duration distribution of the subpopulation in question.

We will first examine the demography of the fertility decline: the pattern of decline among the two high-fertility minorities by marriage duration and parity. This is shown in the first two panels of Tables 5-7 and 5-8. The actual rates have also been graphed in Figures 5-4 and 5-5. The urban white rates for 1970 are also shown in these two figures for reference.

In Figure 5-4, we see that, in 1960, the marriage-duration-specific rates for Southern rural black and Spanish-surname populations were very similar in both

TABLE 5-7

Percent Decline in Recent Fertility between 1960 and 1970 for Southern Rural Black Couples, Wife under Age 40.

	N		Percent Decline	
	1960	1970	Crude	Standard-ized[1]
Duration Since First Marriage				
<3 years	510	477	13.4	
3-5.9 years	481	408	33.0	
6-8.9 years	474	342	39.0	
9-11.9 years	517	349	44.9	
12-14.9 years	533	311	45.6	
15-17.9 years	375	293	57.0	
18-20.9 years	300	221	39.6	
21-23.9 years	142	127	40.5	
Initial Parity				
0	689	533	- 2.2	4.6
1	496	397	19.8	30.2
2	501	382	33.3	34.4
3	431	307	52.2	49.9
4+	1235	926	54.4	53.1
Education				
<5 years	450	131	42.7	42.7
5-8 years	1416	639	36.2	35.0
9-11 years	898	884	42.1	39.1
12 years	460	708	28.0	27.0
13-15 years	65	99	16.4	29.8
16+ years	63	84	-33.7	-31.8
Age at Marriage				
<18	1245	902	41.7	39.8
18-19	830	682	34.0	35.6
20-21	576	450	30.4	39.4
22-24	421	300	31.5	37.4
25-29	215	166	31.4	34.1
30-39	65	45	13.5	- 6.8
Constant Dollar Husband's Income				
<$1,000	1130	330	35.3	49.3
$1,000-1,999	924	402	24.9	26.4
$2,000-2,999	701	500	33.4	31.2
$3,000-3,999	342	635	33.6	39.6
$4,000-4,999	164	279	17.6	33.8
$5,000-7,499	83	330	14.7	25.1
$7,500-9,999	5	51	*	*
$10,000+	3	18	*	*

[1] Standardized on the 1960 marriage duration distribution of that group, i.e., the percent decline that would have occurred if the group's marriage duration distribution had not changed.

* N less than 20.

shape and level. However, there are some slight differences. The Spanish-surname population had a higher fertility rate during the first 10 years or so of marriage, and then, beyond about 10 years, the Southern rural black population's fertility was considerably higher. Fertility levels fell for both groups at all marriage durations between 1960 and 1970, and the shape of the relationship remained quite similar to that observed in 1960. The rate of decline tended to be somewhat higher for the Southern rural blacks, particularly in the marriage-duration intervals 6–17.9 years. By 1970, the Spanish-surname population continued to have considerably higher fertility than the Southern rural black population in the first 9 years of marriage, but, after that time, rates of the two groups were almost identical.

Thus, it is clear that the fertility decline between 1960 and 1970 for these groups occurred throughout the entire marriage-duration range. It is not simply a matter of young, recently married women in 1970 behaving differently than young, recently married women did a decade earlier. Whatever the cause of the decline in fertility, it has affected women at all stages of the reproductive process. It is possible that the decline early in marriage is primarily a child-spacing phenomenon, while the decline after, say, the first 8 or 9 years of marriage is a termination phenomenon; but timing and number explanations cannot be differentiated with period-specific data.

Figure 5-5 shows the same type of measure for the same populations in relation to their initial parity. In 1960, the relationship for Southern rural blacks was positive, with higher fertility for women with higher initial parities. For the Spanish-surname population, the levels were very high for women with initial parities 0 and 1 and then were lower and rather constant for parities 2, 3, and 4+. The 1970 relationship for the Spanish-surname population had essentially the same shape as that for the urban white population in 1970, while the pattern for Southern rural blacks had shifted to a monotonic negative shape.

For Southern rural blacks, the fertility at initial parity 3+ declined by about 50% and the fertility level of women of first and second parity declined by about 33%. For the Spanish-surname population, the decline at initial parity 4+ was approximately 50%, and, for parities 2 and 3, the decline was somewhat more than 33% (see Tables 5-7 and 5-8).

The third panels of Tables 5-7 and 5-8 show rates of fertility decline for six education groups. For both populations, there was a substantial fertility decline for every education category with the single exception of college-educated Southern rural black women. With that exception, women in all education groups experienced a fertility decline of at least 20% for each of the minority populations.

In all of our analyses of differential fertility, we have found a persistent and large effect of age at marriage: Women marrying prior to their eighteenth or twentieth birthdays have considerably higher fertility than women marrying at

TABLE 5-8

Percent Decline in Recent Fertility between 1960 and 1970 for Spanish Surname Couples, Wife under Age 40.

	N		Percent Decline	
	1960	1970	Crude	Stan-dard-ized[1]
Duration Since First Marriage				
<3 years	659	915	13.7	
3-5.9 years	646	816	24.4	
6-8.9 years	615	702	33.3	
9-11.9 years	615	742	37.7	
12-14.9 years	575	588	31.1	
15-17.9 years	427	493	41.2	
18-20.9 years	273	386	55.6	
21-23.9 years	105	118	55.5	
Initial Parity				
0	1006	1320	15.4	16.6
1	606	728	16.0	20.8
2	754	782	34.4	34.7
3	611	706	38.0	35.6
4+	950	1234	49.7	48.3
Education				
<5 years	728	526	29.2	27.9
5-8 years	1312	1202	26.4	24.5
9-11 years	874	1200	23.3	21.7
12 years	807	1411	28.6	28.8
13-15 years	144	331	37.9	38.4
16+ years	62	100	20.8	23.0
Age at Marriage				
<18	1172	1357	31.9	30.4
18-19	1025	1315	29.0	30.5
20-21	738	947	37.4	39.0
22-24	605	734	19.1	21.9
25-29	290	340	17.1	21.5
30-39	97	77	1.2	3.7
Constant Dollar Husband's Income				
<$1,000	324	292	23.3	22.3
$1,000-1,999	474	326	34.1	34.4
$2,000-2,999	644	543	17.6	17.5
$3,000-3,999	631	839	23.9	24.1
$4,000-4,999	643	579	19.6	22.1
$5,000-7,499	937	1368	29.6	31.8
$7,500-9,999	197	540	23.0	36.4
$10,000+	77	283	35.5	35.7

continued

TABLE 5-8 continued

	N		Percent Decline	
	1960	1970	Crude	Standard-ized[1]
Place of Birth				
Both spouses born in U.S.	3028	3302	33.5	32.8
Husband U.S., wife not U.S.	257	365	28.2	27.7
Husband not U.S., wife U.S.	370	374	21.2	31.4
Neither spouse born in U.S.	272	729	14.4	15.2
Place of Residence				
Rural farm	243	76	42.2	46.4
Rural nonfarm	444	521	31.3	32.1
Urban	3240	4173	27.3	27.9

[1] Standardized on the 1960 marriage duration distribution of that group, i.e., the percent decline that would have occurred if the group's marriage duration distribution had not changed.

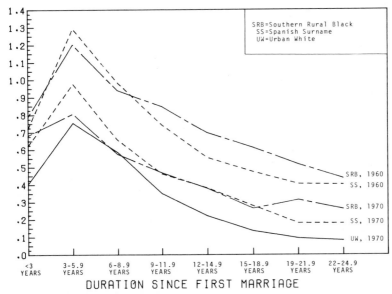

FIGURE 5-4 *Number of own children under age 3 by duration since first marriage, for three racial or ethnic groups: 1960 and 1970.*

107

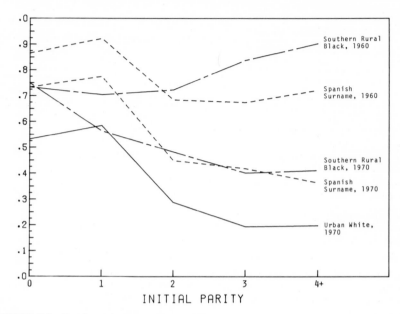

FIGURE 5-5 *Number of own children under age 3 by initial parity, for three racial or ethnic groups: 1960 and 1970.*

TABLE 5-9

Percent Decline in Recent Fertility between 1960 and 1970 for NonSouthern Black Couples, Wife under Age 40.

	N		Percent Decline	
	1960	1970	Crude	Standardized[1]
Education				
<5 years	181	116	45.9	50.7
5-8 years	1523	722	40.8	42.1
9-11 years	2428	2416	30.2	28.9
12 years	2333	3798	26.8	29.4
13-15 years	615	980	31.7	33.7
16+ years	249	474	44.2	43.7

continued

TABLE 5-9 continued

	N		Percent Decline	
	1960	1970	Crude	Standard-ized[1]
Age at Marriage				
<18	1964	2009	36.1	37.4
18-19	1719	2235	26.0	32.4
20-21	1374	1779	30.3	32.1
22-24	1266	1414	32.3	34.9
25-29	770	809	29.6	33.3
30-39	236	260	33.3	32.8
Constant Dollar Husband's Income				
<$1,000	516	524	22.4	22.6
$1,000-1,999	573	392	32.8	36.1
$2,000-2,999	993	526	13.6	18.8
$3,000-3,999	1546	1272	29.3	32.9
$4,000-4,999	1631	1216	23.6	32.6
$5,000-7,499	1836	3117	31.1	38.4
$7,500-9,999	174	1071	30.0	37.8
$10,000+	60	388	29.4	28.8
Origin of Wife				
Northeast	1119	1521	27.1	27.7
North Central	1201	1690	30.5	36.4
South	4696	4543	33.2	34.7
West	134	325	19.9	25.1
Not U.S.	179	427	34.9	34.9
Duration Since First Marriage				
<3 years	1123	1717	17.0	
3-5.9 years	1258	1510	29.9	
6-8.9 years	1138	1343	34.7	
9-11.9 years	1153	1160	47.4	
12-14.9 years	1096	1052	43.3	
15-17.9 years	815	858	46.9	
18-20.9 years	527	595	37.1	
21-23.9 years	191	232	10.4	
24+ years	28	39	16.4	
Initial Parity				
0	2240	2394	2.6	11.9
1	1567	1747	14.6	21.7
2	1321	1595	41.1	44.9
3	877	1095	44.7	44.3
4+	1324	1675	61.9	60.6

[1] Standardized on the 1960 marriage duration distribution of that group, i.e., the percent decline that would have occurred if the group's marriage duration distribution had not changed.

older ages; this is found to be true even after controlling for education and other associated factors. We have been particularly interested, therefore, to see whether or not the fertility decline that has been occurring in the United States in the past decade had included women marrying in their teens. For urban whites, we found that the rate of fertility decline between 1960 and 1970 was approximately the same for women married in their teens as for women married in their twenties. The two racial and ethnic minorities being considered here tend to marry at younger ages than does the urban white population. For all three groups, there has been a substantial reduction in fertility among women married at ages 14–17 and 18–19; the rates of decline for women marrying at these ages tend to be as high or higher than those for women marrying at older ages.

We have previously observed that the rate of fertility decline for urban white women was somewhat higher for women married to men with low incomes than for women married to men with higher incomes. For Spanish-surname women, this pattern is not observed: The largest declines tend to occur among couples in which the husband has a comparatively high income. For Southern rural blacks, the largest decline occurred for the lowest income category, but the pattern of decline is quite irregular among the other income groups.

The last two panels of Table 5-8 show differences in rate of fertility decline by place of birth and place of residence. The rate of decline for the Spanish-surname population was greater for couples in which the wife was born in the United States, whether or not the husband was born in the United States. The rate of decline for couples in which both spouses were born outside the United States was the lowest, approximately 15%. Farm residents experienced the largest rate of fertility decline and urban residents experienced the smallest.

FERTILITY DECLINES WITHIN THE SOUTHERN URBAN BLACK AND THE NON-SOUTHERN BLACK POPULATION

This section examines differential rates of fertility decline within the other two components of the black population: Southern urban blacks and non-Southern blacks. Our procedure is, again, to look at change in crude, characteristic-specific rates and then to standardize the comparison on the subgroup-specific marriage-duration distribution at the initial year. These rates of fertility decline are shown in Tables 5-9 and 5-10 for non-Southern blacks and Southern urban blacks, respectively. As in the case of white women whose rates of fertility change were discussed in an earlier chapter, fertility rates fell very rapidly and at a very similar rate for all subgroups of black women. The pervasiveness of the decline and the similar rates of decline among subgroups are again most impressive.

TABLE 5-10

Percent Decline in Recent Fertility between 1960 and 1970 for Southern Urban Black Couples, Wife under Age 40.

	N		Percent Decline	
	1960	1970	Crude	Standard-ized[1]
Education				
<5 years	337	122	50.5	55.4
5-8 years	1610	759	30.8	27.4
9-11 years	1840	1924	39.3	37.6
12 years	1325	2174	27.6	29.4
13-15 years	298	489	29.8	34.1
16+ years	273	462	24.6	28.3
Age at Marriage				
<18	1789	1680	36.9	37.6
18-19 years	1343	1569	28.0	34.9
20-21	997	1135	30.2	34.2
22-24	823	893	35.7	38.9
25-29	557	474	30.4	32.1
30-39	174	179	26.1	27.2
Constant Dollar Husband's Income				
<$1,000	548	430	37.6	41.2
$1,000-1,999	1008	521	31.8	33.7
$2,000-2,999	1760	869	25.2	27.4
$3,000-3,999	1146	1481	29.8	35.6
$4,000-4,999	706	910	18.8	27.6
$5,000-7,499	451	1334	22.9	32.9
$7,500-9,999	47	274	47.0	53.8
$10,000+	17	111	*	*
Duration Since First Marriage				
<3 years	929	1248	18.3	
3-5.9 years	979	1115	30.6	
6-8.9 years	886	874	43.0	
9-11.9 years	837	792	30.8	
12-14.9 years	812	691	50.7	
15-17.9 years	595	572	62.7	
18-20.9 years	433	432	45.7	
21-23.9 years	191	169	47.1	
24+ years	21	37	-13.4	
Initial Parity				
0	1640	1597	.7	13.0
1	1138	1205	21.1	29.0
2	907	968	30.6	32.6
3	683	705	50.0	48.8
4+	1315	1455	62.2	61.5

[1] Standardized on the 1960 marriage duration distribution of that group, i.e., the percent decline that would have occurred if the group's marriage duration distribution had not changed.

* N less than 20.

Fertility rates fell at all education levels for both Southern urban and non-Southern blacks. The decline in fertility rates (standardized) was most rapid for women in the lowest education category (less than 5 years). The differences in rates of decline for other groups were not as large, with the declines ranging from 28% to 44%. Similarly, rates fell for all age at marriage groups, but there was less variation among the age at marriage groups than among the education groups within both the Southern urban black group and the non-Southern black group. In addition, there was no systematic variation in rates of fertility decline in relation to husband's income; this was the case for both Southern urban blacks and non-Southern blacks. Among non-Southern blacks, the rate of decline for women of Southern origin is as high as for those of non-Southern origin.

Fertility declines tended to be greatest at marriage durations of 6 to 20 years, but there were substantial declines earlier in marriage as well. The rate of fertility declined more for high parities than for lower parities, although, again, there was decline at every parity. The same general pattern of change is found in both the South and the non-South.

MINORITY STATUS AND FERTILITY

The effect of minority group status on fertility has been the subject of a number of recent papers (Goldscheider and Uhlenberg, 1969; Sly, 1970; Goldscheider, 1971; Kennedy, 1973; Roberts and Lee, 1974). The primary issue is whether or not minority group status itself exerts an independent effect on fertility. There have been two principal and conflicting approaches. The first can be termed the "assimilationist" position. This position suggests that fertility differences exist between majority and minority groups because these groups differ with respect to various social, demographic, and economic characteristics. It is further argued that, as a minority *group* acquires the social, demographic, and economic characteristics of the majority, its fertility behavior will tend to resemble that of the majority group.[2] It is thus expected that, as structural assimilation takes place, fertility differentials between minority and majority groups will diminish. Unfortunately, the assimilationist perspective only addresses the issue of convergence in a series of cross-sectional differences. It does not address the possibility that reactions to outside stimuli converge such that, in any given time period, the fertility trends of minority and majority groups are identical.

An alternative approach, which can be termed the "independent effect" position, has been put forth. This position argues that, even when groups are

---

[2] It is important to note that this is not the same as saying that, when an *individual* member of a minority group acquires the social, demographic, and economic characteristics of the dominant group, his or her fertility will resemble that of the majority group.

similar socially, demographically, and economically, minority group membership will continue to exert an effect on fertility. Thus, the independent effect position does not predict convergence; rather, it predicts a continuation of differences even if compositional differences disappear.

The independent effect position has been formulated in a number of different ways; the principal difference between the various formulations is the direction of the proposed minority group effect on fertility. Goldscheider and Uhlenberg (1969) suggest that minority group status has a downward effect on fertility. They argue that

> ... the insecurities of minority group membership operate to depress fertility below majority levels when (1) acculturation of minority group members has occurred in conjunction with the desire for acculturation; (2) equalization of social and economic characteristics occurs, particularly at middle and upper social class levels, and/or there is a desire for social and economic mobility; and (3) there is no pronatalist ideology associated with the minority group and no norm discouraging the use of efficient contraceptives. [p. 372]

Kennedy (1973), on the other hand, suggests that minority group status will tend to elevate fertility. His thesis is:

> ... that minority group fertility will be higher than otherwise expected when two sets of conditions exist: (1) the group's members believe they can increase their political influence by increasing their share of the total population; and (2) the group's members believe their chances for individual upward social mobility are much less than that enjoyed by the rest of the population. [p. 86]

These two statements of the independent effects position differ because they consider different sets of mediating factors. We will consider a broader statement of the independent effects position, one that encompasses both the Kennedy and the Goldscheider and Uhlenberg formulations: Membership in a minority group can exert an influence on fertility independent of the social, economic, and demographic characteristics of that group. This minority group effect may operate either to lower or to elevate the fertility of the minority group in relation to the fertility of the dominant group. Whether or not the effect is to depress or to elevate fertility depends on a variety of intervening factors through which the influence of the minority group is accomplished.

Goldscheider and Uhlenberg have indicated some of these mediating factors, Kennedy has indicated different ones, but there are a variety of others as well. For example, a factor that would tend to lead to lower fertility is a prescription of homogamy, whether designated by the subgroup or imposed by the dominant group. The linkage of homogamy to fertility is as follows: Ceteris paribus, the necessity of finding a mate within a particular subgroup tends to lead to older ages at marriage and higher proportions never married, which in turn leads to lower fertility. Although other mediating factors could be enumerated, the point is that the minority group effect hypothesis can be "explained" in a variety of different ways. It should be noted that this is a potential problem with the independent effect hypothesis, namely, that it is simply a residual hypothesis and that any differences remaining after other factors are controlled are attributed to minority group status.

Central to both propositions—assimilationist or independent effects—is concern about what happens over time as the characteristics of the minority and majority groups change. Yet, because the required time series data have heretofore been unavailable, attempts to examine the issues empirically for the United States have relied on cross-sectional data. The use of cross-sectional data has required the assumption that changes over time can be simulated through statistical control—an assumption that is clearly dubious and that, at a minimum, requires the further questionable assumption that those members of a minority group that initially acquire the characteristics of the majority group are representative of all those who will eventually assume the characteristics of the majority group. The data that have been presented in this chapter remedy that defect by providing annual age-specific period fertility rates for a 15-year period for six groups: American Indians, Mexican Americans, Japanese Americans, Chinese Americans, blacks, and whites. The trade-off, however, has been that we have had limited control of relevant social and demographic characteristics of these groups and limited knowledge of trends in those characteristics.

When fertility rates are examined over time, as is required by both perspectives, we find confirmatory evidence for both the assimilationist perspective and the independent effects perspective. If *trends* are considered, then the fact that the same trend is found for all groups tends to support the assimilationist perspective. If *levels* of fertility in any cross section or series of cross sections are considered, then the fact that distinct and persistent differences are found tends to support the independent effects perspective, provided there have been compositional shifts. In short, if it is assumed that there has been convergence among the groups with respect to various social and economic characteristics, the evidence is ambiguous with respect to distinguishing between the two apparently conflicting perspectives.

The evidence is ambiguous because the perspectives themselves are ambiguous. Just as it was necessary to formulate a more specific yet encompassing version of the independent effect position than either the one proposed by Goldscheider and Uhlenberg (1969) or the one proposed by Kennedy (1973), perhaps it is also necessary to combine the two perspectives and consider the effects of specific mediating factors. Certain factors may affect minority/majority differences in fertility with respect to both trends and comparative levels, which other factors may only affect minority/majority differences in fertility with respect to trends or with respect to comparative levels and leave the other one unaffected. It is possible that, after a certain level of assimilation has been reached, those factors that affect secular trends in fertility operate on each racial and ethnic group; thus, all groups that have been "assimilated" experience similar trends. Yet, cross-sectional differences may remain that are due to the fact that the minority group exists and places demands on its members.

An example is in order. One factor, among others, that affected fertility trends among young people during the 1960s was the entrance into the childbearing ages of the birth cohorts born during the baby boom. The size of these cohorts in comparison with previous cohorts had a disruptive effect on a wide range of institutions: the educational system, the marriage market, and the job market. This disruption, in turn, may have tended to depress fertility. Thus, other things being equal, a trend of declining fertility would be expected for any group provided that that group was minimally integrated (assimilated) into the mainstream society such that it participated in these institutions. A group not integrated into these institutions would not be affected by such disruptive changes—the Hutterites might be an example of such a group (see Hostetler and Huntington, 1967).

The entrance of large cohorts into the childbearing ages is but one of many factors that could affect the relationship between minority group status and fertility. The point to be made is that, in future work in this area, it is necessary to specify the mediating factors thought to be operating and to specify how they affect both trends *and* cross-sectional differentials.

SUMMARY

This chapter examined fertility trends among and within various racial and ethnic subgroups. Annual age-specific fertility rates for the period 1955–1969 were constructed for six groups: Mexican Americans, American Indians, Chinese Americans, Japanese Americans, blacks and whites. Substantial declines in fertility were found for every racial or ethnic group examined. Yet there was little change in the relative positions of the various groups with respect to the level of fertility. Those groups that had comparatively low fertility in 1955 had comparatively low fertility in 1969; and those groups that had comparatively high fertility in 1955 had comparatively high fertility in 1969. Substantial declines in marital fertility were also found for every racial and ethnic group. The largest declines were found among the black population—this was the case for both marital fertility and overall fertility.

These results (i.e., similar trends and the maintenance of differences in fertility levels) tend to support two apparently conflicting hypotheses about minority group status and fertility. The two minority group status and fertility hypotheses are: (*a*) As a minority group acquires the social, demographic, and economic characteristics of the majority group, its fertility behavior will tend to resemble that of the majority group; (b) even when groups are similar socially, demographically, and economically, minority group membership will continue to exert an effect on fertility. The fact that the data support both of these hypotheses points up the inherent ambiguity involved in both.

A detailed examination of marital fertility trends was presented for four subpopulations: Spanish-surname, Southern rural black, Southern urban black, and non-Southern black. The extent of the pervasiveness of the marital fertility decline was impressive.

6

Fertility Differentials within Minority Groups

The previous chapter focused on trends in fertility, and this chapter examines differentials in fertility within and among members of various racial and ethnic minorities. Essentially, this chapter examines the extent to which those socioeconomic variables, such as education and income, that cross-sectionally differentiate the total population with respect to current fertility also differentiate within various racial and ethnic minorities. Furthermore, we examine the extent to which these relationships are similar across the various racial and ethnic groups. The first four sections of this chapter use dummy variable multiple regression analysis to examine both demographic and socioeconomic differentials in fertility, and utilize own children under 3 of currently married women under age 40. The focus will be on data from the 1970 census (the period 1967–1970), although some comparisons will be made between these 1970 patterns and those observed in the 1960 census. The analysis will resemble that reported in Chapter 4 on differential fertility for the total population. Four sets of groups are examined: (*1*) three high-fertility groups: Southern rural blacks, persons with Spanish surnames, and American Indians; (*2*) Southern urban and non-Southern blacks, both predominantly urban populations; (*3*) two racial minorities with very low fertility, Chinese and Japanese Americans; and (*4*) Puerto Ricans living in the United States. The final portion of the chapter examines differences in the age pattern of fertility, using annual age-specific fertility rates for all women.

DIFFERENTIALS WITHIN THREE HIGH-FERTILITY GROUPS

This section reports on the results of a multivariate analysis of fertility differentials within the Southern rural black, Spanish-surname, and American

117

Indian populations (Tables 6-1, 6-2, and 6-3, respectively). In each case, we are comparing fertility within the minority group itself, using 1970 census data. Three comparisons are presented: one, an unadjusted or gross effect; another, an adjusted or net effect in which we standardize for the composition with respect to each of the other variables included in the analysis; and the third, an adjusted comparison in which the occupation of the husband is not included, in order to avoid confounding income differences with occupational differences. These results can be compared with those for urban whites as reported in Appendix A.

Education differentials in fertility have persisted for the population at large, but they have become somewhat attenuated over the years. In our analysis of overall fertility differentials (Chapter 4), we found an inverse relationship between education and fertility after controlling for other variables such as age at marriage and husband's income. There was, however, no zero-order relationship between education and fertility for the total population. For the American Indian and Spanish-surname populations, there continues to be a considerable fertility differential by education. For Southern rural blacks, the relationship is smaller and less consistent. This can also be seen by looking at Figure 6-1.

These three groups marry at comparatively young ages. Early marriage is most common among Southern rural blacks: 35% marry by age 18, and 62% by age 20. For Spanish-surname women, 28% are married by age 18, and 56% by age 20. For American Indians, the figures are 29% by age 18 and 59% by age 20. Among urban whites, the comparable proportions are lower: 18% of the women have married before 18 and 49% have married before age 20.

The second panels of Tables 6-1, 6-2, and 6-3 show the relationship between age at marriage and recent marital fertility. This is also shown in Figure 6-2. Among the urban white population, age at first marriage is strongly and inversely related to recent marital fertility. After adjusting for the other factors considered here, each of the three populations has higher fertility among women marrying in their teens than among those marrying at later ages. Spanish-surname and American Indian women marrying before age 18 have rates that are .04–.05 higher than the average, while Southern rural black women have rates that are .08 above average. For all groups, the relationship is monotonic, but there is considerably greater spread in the coefficients for the Southern rural blacks than for the other two groups.

The third panels of Tables 6-1, 6-2, and 6-3 show the relationship between husband's occupation and recent marital fertility. Within the American Indian population, the effect of occupation on fertility, net of the other variables considered in this analysis, is irregular. Wives of craftsmen, managers, officials, and proprietors, and wives of men in the armed forces, have lower than average fertility. Women whose husbands are operatives, unemployed, or not in the labor force have higher than average fertility. There is not an obvious white-collar/blue-collar split, and the wives of farmers and farm laborers have slightly lower than average fertility.

TABLE 6-1

Gross and Net Deviations from Mean Number of Children under Age 3 for Currently Married Women under Age 40, for Various Characteristics: Southern Rural Black Population, 1970.

| | | Deviation from Grand Mean | | |
	N	Gross	Net$_1$	Net$_2$
Education				
<5 years	131	-.072	-.028	-.023
5-8 years	639	-.003	.024	.030
9-11 years	884	.004	-.005	-.008
12 years	708	.007	-.016	-.021
13-15 years	99	.050	.028	.026
16+ years	84	-.027	.019	.036
Age at Marriage				
14-17	902	.002	.079	.083
18-19	682	.045	.042	.041
20-21	450	.009	-.022	-.023
22-24	300	-.048	-.132	-.137
25-29	166	-.081	-.200	-.205
30-39	45	-.182	-.390	-.393
Husband's Occupation				
Professional	74	.079	.076	
Manager	35	-.201	-.134	
Sales	21	-.134	-.126	
Clerical	82	-.064	-.045	
Craftsman	381	.002	.005	
Operative	512	-.015	-.021	
Transport	266	-.053	-.009	
Laborer	395	.011	-.002	
Farmer	38	.064	.110	
Farm laborer	288	.086	.056	
Service	167	-.114	-.090	
Unemployed	63	.279	.231	
Armed forces	36	-.015	-.041	
Not in labor force	187	.004	-.005	
Constant Dollar Husband's Income				
<$1,000	330	.030	-.021	-.004
$1,000-1,999	402	.127	.079	.099
$2,000-2,999	500	.019	.026	.028
$3,000-3,999	635	-.047	-.032	-.043
$4,000-4,999	279	-.017	-.001	-.015
$5,000-7,499	330	-.073	-.037	-.048
$7,500+	69	-.168	-.078	-.075

Grand Mean = .515

[1] Variables included in the model: wife's education, age at marriage, husband's income, husband's occupation, initial parity, and duration since first marriage.

[2] Variables included in the model: same as Model 1 except that husband's occupation has been deleted.

TABLE 6-2

Gross and Net Deviations from Mean Number of Children under
Age 3 for Currently Married Women under Age 40, for Various
Characteristics: Spanish Surname Population, 1970.

| | N | Deviation from Grand Mean | | |
		Gross	Net$_1$	Net$_2$
Education				
<5 years	526	.058	.102	.115
5-8 years	1202	.044	.056	.061
9-11 years	1200	.033	.025	.024
12 years	1411	-.058	-.072	-.079
13-15 years	331	-.097	-.119	-.122
16+ years	100	-.090	-.112	-.119
Age at Marriage				
14-17	1357	.010	.046	.046
18-19	1315	-.014	.013	.013
20-21	947	-.039	-.034	-.034
22-24	734	.010	-.028	-.029
25-29	340	.079	-.044	-.044
30-39	77	.112	-.141	-.147
Husband's Occupation				
Professional	310	-.095	-.008	
Manager	239	-.061	.057	
Sales	133	-.062	-.050	
Clerical	284	-.054	-.043	
Craftsman	1008	-.040	-.002	
Operative	857	.044	.009	
Transport	345	-.017	-.022	
Laborer	441	.114	.063	
Farmer	19	*	*	
Farm laborer	282	.141	.056	
Service worker	253	-.004	-.021	
Unemployed	211	.009	-.038	
Armed forces	79	-.133	-.157	
Not in labor force	209	-.010	-.044	
Constant Dollar Husband's Income				
<$1,000	292	.080	.000	-.006
$1,000-1,999	326	.033	-.021	-.025
$2,000-2,999	543	.168	.098	.097
$3,000-3,999	839	.073	.025	.026
$4,000-4,999	579	.071	.065	.063
$5,000-7,499	1368	-.074	-.043	-.043
$7,500-9,999	540	-.124	-.051	-.046
$10,000-14,999	228	-.221	-.086	-.080
$15,000+	55	-.150	.018	.026

continued

TABLE 6-2 continued

	N	Deviation from Grand Mean		
		Gross	Net$_1$	Net$_2$
Place of Birth				
Both spouses born in U.S.	3302	-.036	-.019	-.019
Husband U.S., wife other	365	.020	.001	-.004
Husband not U.S., wife U.S.	374	.043	.008	.013
Neither spouse born in U.S.	729	.130	.081	.082

Grand Mean = .550

[1] Variables included in the model: wife's education, age at marriage, husband's income, place of birth, number of times married, husband's occupation, initial parity, and duration since first marriage.

[2] Variables included in the model: same as Model 1 except that husband's occupation has been deleted.

* N less than 20.

For Southern rural blacks, there does seem to be a tendency for wives of white-collar men to have lower than average fertility, for wives of blue-collar men to have fertility rates that are about average, and for wives of farmers and farm laborers to have higher than average fertility. Two exceptions to this pattern arise: The first is that wives of professionals have fertility that is approximately equal to that of farm laborers; the second is that wives of service workers have lower than average fertility. Wives of men who are unemployed tend to have higher fertility, while wives of those who are not in the labor force and those who are in the armed forces have rates that are very close to the mean.

Among Spanish-surname women, there is a far less consistent white-collar/blue-collar break. High rates of recent marital fertility are found among wives of managers, laborers, farmers, and farm laborers; relatively low rates of recent marital fertility are found among wives of sales workers, clerical workers, and transport workers.

For the total population, in both 1960 and 1970, there is a comparatively strong positive effect of husband's income[1] on recent fertility, after controlling for other potentially confounding variables. As discussed in Chapter 4, this positive effect of current income on current fertility probably results from the effect of the timing of income changes on the timing of fertility: Some people probably postpone their childbearing until some income growth has occurred.

[1] Throughout, all incomes are expressed in 1960 constant dollars.

TABLE 6-3

Gross and Net Deviations from Mean Number of Children under Age 3 for Currently Married Women under Age 40, for Various Characteristics: American Indian Population, 1970.

| | N | Deviation from Grand Mean | | |
		Gross	Net$_1$	Net$_2$
Education				
<5 years	142	.016	.049	.068
5-8 years	446	.038	.065	.063
9-11 years	912	.030	.029	.026
12 years	1069	-.009	-.022	-.021
13-15 years	250	-.074	-.090	-.093
16+ years	107	-.171	-.155	-.146
Age at Marriage				
14-17	844	-.021	.038	.038
18-19	890	.019	.027	.026
20-21	597	.018	-.012	-.010
22-24	357	-.011	-.054	-.050
25-29	188	-.025	-.122	-.121
30-39	50	-.018	-.141	-.161
Husband's Occupation				
Professional	228	.002	.034	
Manager	134	-.237	-.150	
Sales	78	-.024	.035	
Clerical	124	.034	-.002	
Craftsman	565	-.058	-.048	
Operative	450	.046	.034	
Transport	182	-.037	.010	
Laborer	276	.020	-.019	
Farmer	35	-.013	.003	
Farm laborer	86	-.022	-.029	
Service	184	.045	.043	
Unemployed	188	.055	.011	
Armed forces	93	-.165	-.132	
Not in labor force	303	.135	.098	
Constant Dollar Husband's Income				
<$1,000	298	.099	-.016	.020
$1,000-1,999	267	.064	-.008	.006
$2,000-2,999	318	.118	.061	.066
$3,000-3,999	475	.041	.005	.000
$4,000-4,999	343	-.041	-.024	-.027
$5,000-7,499	755	-.027	.018	.011
$7,500-9,999	306	-.100	-.018	-.031
$10,000-14,999	129	-.266	-.111	-.131
$15,000+	35	-.127	-.008	-.026

continued

TABLE 6-3 continued

	N	Gross	Net$_1$	Net$_2$
		\multicolumn{3}{Deviation from Grand Mean}		
Ethnicity				
Both spouses Indian	1297	.091	.076	.082
Wife Indian, husband other	61	.059	.115	.102
Husband Indian, wife other	49	.134	.097	.099
Wife Indian, husband white	807	-.084	-.060	-.067
Husband Indian, wife white	712	-.084	-.087	-.089

Grand Mean = .498

[1] Variables included in the model: wife's education, age at marriage, husband's income, ethnicity, husband's occupation, number of times married, initial parity, duration since first marriage, and number of times married.

[2] Variables included in the model: same as Model 1 except that husband's occupation has been deleted.

This positive effect of income on recent fertility is not found for the three groups considered here. As can be seen in the fourth panels of Tables 6-1, 6-2, and 6-3, there is a strong inverse zero-order relationship between fertility and income. Women whose husbands are earning less than $2000 or $3000 have very high fertility; there is a decline in fertility levels at each successively higher income level, with women whose husbands are earning $7500 or more having extremely low fertility. The inverse relationship between income and fertility tends to persist when other factors are controlled, although it is attenuated considerably (see Figure 6-3). Although we cannot be certain about the lack of a positive income effect among these groups, it is possible both (*a*) that there is less income growth over the life cycle among these populations than among the general population and (*b*) that the personal income growth that does occur is less predictable or more random that than which occurs in the general population.

Included in the minority population is any couple in which either the husband or the wife is a member of the minority group. Thus, we can look at differentials in fertility by the ethnic status of husbands and wives for American Indian and Spanish-surname couples.[2] This is shown in the fifth panels of Tables 6-2 and 6-3. For American Indians, we find that, for couples in which both the

[2] For Southern rural blacks, there are not a sufficient number of interracial marriages to permit analysis.

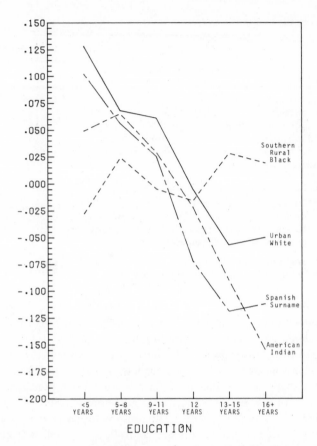

FIGURE 6-1 *Net effect of education on recent fertility for selected ethnic groups, currently married women under age 40: 1970.*

husband and the wife are classified as American Indian, the fertility rate is .08 above the mean; if the wife is American Indian and the husband is white, the fertility rate is .17 below the mean; and if the husband is American Indian and the wife is white, the rate is .09 below the mean. Evidently, the fertility level tends to be reduced somewhat more in a mixed marriage if the husband is white than if the wife is white. The fertility level of American Indians married to persons of other races (i.e., other than American Indian or white) is about as high or slightly higher than the rate for couples in which both spouses are American Indian.

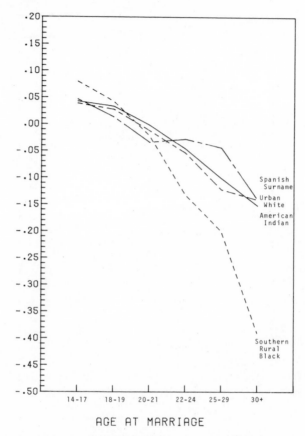

FIGURE 6-2 *Net effect of age at first marriage on recent fertility for selected ethnic groups, currently married women under age 40: 1970.*

For the Spanish-surname population, couples have been classified with respect to the place of birth of each spouse. If both spouses were born outside the United States, they have a rate about .08 points above the mean. If both were born in the United States, they have a rate about .02 points below the mean. When one spouse was born in the United States and the other was born outside the United States, the rate is approximately at the sample mean. It should be noted that this classification does not look specifically at couples born in Mexico. We have taken U.S. birth as the reference point and have classified with respect to whether the person was born inside or outside the United States. Consequently, some of the Spanish-surname people born outside the United

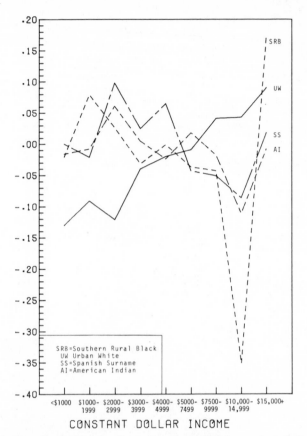

FIGURE 6-3 *Net effect of husband's income (expressed in constant dollars) on recent fertility for selected ethnic groups, currently married women under age 40: 1970.*

States may well have been born in other Latin American countries, or even, for example, in Europe.

DIFFERENTIALS WITHIN THE URBAN
BLACK POPULATION

This section considers differential fertility for two groups of black women: married women living in the non-Southern region in the United States and urban black women living in the Southern states. We will refer to both groups as urban blacks, although there are a few rural residents in the non-Southern sample (9%). Most of our analysis relates to 1970, but we will make note of important

TABLE 6-4

Gross and Net Deviations from Mean Number of Children under
Age 3 for Currently Married Women under Age 40, for Various
Characteristics: NonSouthern Black Population, 1970.

		Deviation from Grand Mean		
	Ń	Gross	Net$_1$	Net$_2$
Education				
<5 years	116	-.112	-.113	-.104
5-8 years	722	-.089	-.019	-.014
9-11 years	2416	.052	.051	.055
12 years	3798	.010	-.006	-.007
13-15 years	980	-.029	-.033	-.040
16+ years	474	-.125	-.088	-.097
Age at Marriage				
14-17	2009	.013	.088	.089
18-19	2235	.075	.077	.078
20-21	1779	-.010	-.010	-.010
22-24	1414	-.043	-.070	-.072
25-29	809	-.086	-.173	-.173
30-39	260	-.168	-.352	-.351
Husband's Occupation				
Professional	647	-.035	-.018	
Manager	283	-.085	-.040	
Sales	225	-.050	-.070	
Clerical	705	-.034	-.059	
Craftsman	1253	-.022	-.011	
Operative	1802	.038	.028	
Transport	701	.016	.023	
Laborer	776	.017	.018	
Farmer	8	*	*	
Farm laborer	25	-.014	.003	
Service	917	-.018	-.005	
Unemployed	418	.103	.041	
Armed forces	242	-.034	-.012	
Not in labor force	504	-.005	.004	
Constant Dollar Husband's Income				
<$1,000	524	.033	-.019	-.015
$1,000-1,999	392	.022	-.035	-.032
$2,000-2,999	526	.137	.063	.066
$3,000-3,999	1272	.046	.019	.020
$4,000-4,999	1216	.026	.002	.004
$5,000-7,499	3117	-.032	-.018	-.018
$7,500-9,999	1071	-.060	.005	-.000
$10,000-14,999	306	-.090	.009	-.000
$15,000+	82	.049	.165	.147

continued

TABLE 6-4 continued

		Deviation from Grand Mean		
	N	Gross	Net_1	Net_2
Region of Origin				
Northeast	1521	-.002	-.004	-.006
North Central	1690	.045	.004	.005
South	4543	-.020	.000	.001
West	325	.112	.027	.025
Not U.S.	427	-.046	-.022	-.030

Grand Mean = .414

[1] Variables included in the model: wife's education, age at marriage, husband's income, occupation, origin of husband, origin of wife, initial parity, and marriage duration.

[2] Variables included in the model: same as Model 1 except that husband's occupation has been deleted.

[*] N less than 20.

changes in patterns of differentials between 1960 and 1970. Appendix C includes a table showing differentials as of 1960. The sample includes 5930 Southern black couples and 8506 non-Southern black couples in 1970. As indicated earlier, the mean 1970 fertility levels for these two groups are very similar: .433 for the Southern urban blacks and .414 for non-Southern blacks. The analysis, like that of the previous section, will present deviations, both gross and adjusted, taken from the respective sample mean for the individual samples (see Tables 6-4 and 6-5).

If the fertility of women with less than 5 years of education is ignored (see Chapter 3), then fertility is inversely related to education. The highest fertility for the Southern urban black couples is found for women with 5-8 years of schooling. There is a monotonic decline in fertility rates with increasing education; the 5-8-year group has a rate that is about .05 above the mean, while college graduates have a rate that is about .08 below the mean. A similar pattern exists among non-Southern black couples, except that the 5-8-year group has lower fertility than the 9-11-year education group. College-educated black women living outside the South have a rate that is .10 below the average. These patterns, along with that for the urban white population, are shown in Figure 6-4.

For nonfarm blacks, there is the expected decline in fertility with increasing age at marriage, after controlling for education and other confounding variables. For both groups, the differential by age at marriage is considerably greater than it is for urban whites (see Figure 6-5).

TABLE 6-5

*Gross and Net Deviations from Mean Number of Children under
Age 3 for Currently Married Women under Age 40, for Various
Characteristics: Southern Urban Black Population, 1970.*

| | N | Deviation from Grand Mean | | |
		Gross	Net_1	Net_2
Education				
<5 years	122	-.179	-.159	-.144
5-8 years	759	-.012	.054	.060
9-11 years	1924	.017	.016	.017
12 years	2174	.031	-.000	-.003
13-15 years	489	-.028	-.031	-.039
16+ years	462	-.122	-.077	-.074
Age at Marriage				
14-17	1680	.048	.128	.127
18-19	1569	.045	.053	.051
20-21	1135	-.009	-.029	-.027
22-24	893	-.058	-.102	-.103
25-29	474	-.108	-.212	-.209
30-39	179	-.221	-.405	-.406
Husband's Occupation				
Professional	364	-.051	.015	
Manager	136	-.007	.058	
Sales	93	-.035	-.070	
Clerical	400	-.021	-.040	
Craftsman	952	.002	.000	
Operative	1052	.023	.001	
Transport	697	-.010	-.006	
Laborer	847	.038	.034	
Farmer	4	*	*	
Farm laborer	84	.126	.154	
Service	617	-.013	-.011	
Unemployed	137	-.039	-.076	
Armed forces	239	-.057	-.089	
Not in labor force	308	-.008	.029	
Constant Dollar Husband's Income				
<$1,000	430	-.024	-.073	-.064
$1,000-1,999	521	.066	.007	.013
$2,000-2,999	869	.072	.031	.035
$3,000-3,999	1481	.013	.003	.000
$4,000-4,999	910	.012	.021	.017
$5,000-7,499	1334	-.062	-.014	-.017
$7,500-9,999	274	-.083	-.016	-.017
$10,000-14,999	86	-.073	.030	.032
$15,000+	25	-.193	-.037	-.034

Grand Mean = .433

[1] Variables included in the model: wife's education, age at
marriage, husband's income, husband's occupation, initial parity,
and duration since first marriage.

[2] Variables included in the model: same as Model 1 except that
husband's occupation has been deleted.

* N less than 20.

129

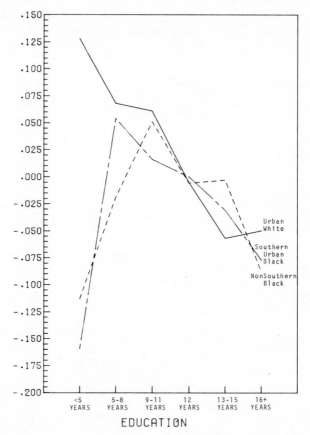

FIGURE 6-4 *Net effect of education on recent fertility for selected ethnic groups, currently married women under age 40: 1970.*

Net of other factors considered in this analysis (including husband's income), there are interesting occupational differences. For Southern urban blacks, the lowest fertility rates are found for wives of men in sales and clerical occupations and also in the unemployed and armed forces categories. Higher than average rates are found for our small sample of wives of managers, officials, and proprietors, for wives of laborers, and for wives of men who are not in the labor force. The fertility rates for wives of professionals, craftsmen, operatives (including transport operatives), and service workers are very similar to one another and very close to the average. Among non-Southern blacks, however, there seems to be a white-collar/blue-collar split. Wives of professionals, managers, and sales and

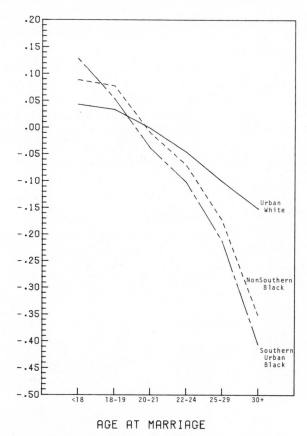

AGE AT MARRIAGE

FIGURE 6-5 *Net effect of age at first marriage on recent fertility for selected ethnic groups, currently married women under age 40: 1970.*

clerical workers have recent marital fertility rates below the mean. Wives of craftsmen are close to the mean, and the other groups are above the mean. Wives of men who were in the armed forces have a slightly lower than average rate, while the wives of men who were unemployed at the time of enumeration had higher than average rates.

Overall, there are only very small differentials in fertility by husband's income. For both Southern urban and non-Southern blacks, the lowest income groups (approximately the lowest decile) have depressed fertility. Highest fertility levels are found for women married to men earning $2000–2999 (approximately the second decile in the non-Southern category and the third decile in the Southern). Beyond that level, differentials are irregular. The consistent positive income effect that was found for urban whites is not found for these two groups (see Figure 6-6).

For non-Southern women, we have also examined the effects of wives' region of origin on recent marital fertility. The highest rate is found for women of Western origin, and the lowest rate for women whose origin is the Northeast. It is not the case, if indeed it ever was the case, that Northern black women with Southern origins have higher fertility than indigenous Northern black women.

Finally, it should be noted that we divided the sample of "urban" blacks into persons residing in the Southern region and those residing in the other regions of the country, because of a suspicion that their fertility patterns might differ. However, they did not. Both the level and the pattern of differentials in fertility were found to be very similar for Southern and non-Southern urban blacks.

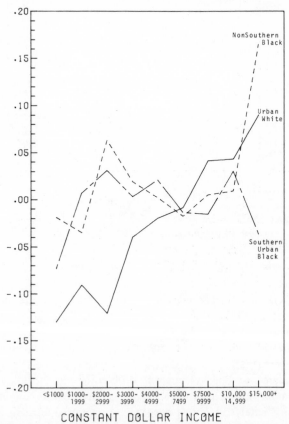

CONSTANT DOLLAR INCOME

FIGURE 6-6 *Net effect of husband's income (expressed in constant dollars) on recent fertility for selected ethnic groups, currently married women under age 40: 1970.*

DIFFERENTIALS WITHIN TWO LOW-FERTILITY POPULATIONS

This section examines fertility differentials within the Chinese American and Japanese American populations. These two groups had lower fertility than the urban white population (see Chapter 5). Tables 6-6 and 6-7 summarize the fertility differentials for these two groups using the same procedure used earlier.

For both the Chinese American and the Japanese American populations, there is the usual inverse relationship between wife's education and recent marital fertility. This is shown in the first panels of Tables 6-6 and 6-7. However, there are exceptions in both cases. For example, unusually low rates are found among Japanese American women with 5–8 years of education and among Chinese American women with less than 5 years of education.

For both groups, there is the expected age at marriage difference in recent fertility. The Chinese Americans marrying in their teens have rates that are .05 to .09 above the mean, while those marrying at ages 25–29 have a rate that is .07 below the mean. Japanese American women marrying under age 18 (only 6% of the sample) have a rate that is .17 above the mean. Among Japanese American couples first marrying at age 30 and beyond, the rate of recent marital fertility is exceptionally low.

A tendency for a positive relationship between husband's income and fertility is found for both groups. The pattern is more pronounced among the Japanese Americans than among the Chinese Americans.

For both Japanese and Chinese Americans, we have constructed a variable cross-classifying race of husband by race of wife. Of the Chinese couples, 72% are both Chinese. In 13% of the cases, the wife is Chinese and the husband is

TABLE 6-6

Gross and Net Deviations from Mean Number of Children under Age 3 for Currently Married Women under Age 40, for Various Characteristics: Japanese American Population, 1970.

| | | Deviation from Grand Mean | | |
	N	Gross	Net_1	Net_2
Education				
<5 years	20	.073	.087	.089
5-8 years	113	-.120	-.025	-.019
9-11 years	277	.002	.050	.052
12 years	1176	-.025	.003	.003
13-15 years	438	.036	-.005	-.006
16+ years	443	.056	-.033	-.033

continued

TABLE 6-6 continued

	N	Deviation from Grand Mean		
		Gross	Net$_1$	Net$_2$
Age at Marriage				
14-17	154	.045	.166	.168
18-19	330	-.001	.058	.060
20-21	493	-.018	.030	.028
22-24	792	-.015	-.019	-.019
25-29	560	.032	-.035	-.035
30-39	138	-.029	-.180	-.181
Husband's Occupation				
Professional	646	.052	.011	
Manager	235	-.037	-.062	
Sales	125	-.009	-.037	
Clerical	187	-.029	-.035	
Craftsman	466·	-.008	.003	
Operative	160	-.002	.021	
Transport	66	-.013	.015	
Laborer	112	.043	.048	
Farmer	39	-.069	.072	
Farm laborer	13	*	*	
Service	131	-.003	.044	
Unemployed	0	--	--	
Armed forces	275	-.050	-.004	
Not in labor force	12	*	*	
Constant Dollar Husband's Income				
<$1,000	79	-.086	-.127	-.123
$1,000-1,999	74	-.053	-.132	-.126
$2,000-2,999	70	.037	-.057	-.043
$3,000-3,999	176	-.002	-.045	-.038
$4,000-4,999	225	-.008	-.024	-.024
$5,000-7,499	750	-.018	-.027	-.025
$7,500-9,999	624	.014	.042	.038
$10,000-14,999	369	.030	.055	.051
$15,000+	100	.043	.112	.105
Ethnicity				
Both spouses Japanese	1200	.017	.015	.016
Wife Japanese, husband white	843	-.064	-.037	-.037
Wife Japanese, husband other	156	.033	.035	.034
Wife white, husband Japanese	184	.090	.001	.000
Wife other, husband Japanese	84	.135	.086	.089

Grand Mean = .377

[1] Variables included in the model: wife's education, age at marriage, husband's income, husband's occupation, number of times married, ethnicity, initial parity, and duration since first marriage.

[2] Variables included in the model: same as Model 1 except that husband's occupation has been deleted.

* N less than 20.

TABLE 6-7

Gross and Net Deviations from Mean Number of Children under Age 3 for Currently Married Women under Age 40, for Various Characteristics: Chinese American Population, 1970.

| | N | Deviation from Grand Mean | | |
		Gross	Net$_1$	Net$_2$
Education				
<5 years	81	-.130	.002	.007
5-8 years	161	-.017	.087	.099
9-11 years	147	-.032	.004	.015
12 years	472	.031	.044	.045
13-15 years	253	-.004	-.035	-.043
16+ years	433	.010	-.061	-.067
Age at Marriage				
14-17	163	-.114	.050	.049
18-19	233	.020	.087	.083
20-21	293	-.027	-.000	.006
22-24	461	.007	-.007	-.009
25-29	328	.037	-.069	-.068
30-39	69	.095	-.038	-.034
Husband's Occupation				
Professional	622	.032	-.010	
Manager	187	-.079	-.045	
Sales	51	-.054	-.012	
Clerical	97	-.045	-.029	
Craftsman	110	-.036	-.026	
Operative	103	-.126	-.083	
Transport	34	.073	.027	
Laborer	31	.057	.095	
Farmer	2	*	*	
Farm laborer	2	*	*	
Service	252	.050	.088	
Unemployed	0	--	--	
Armed forces	44	.142	.138	
Not in labor force	12	*	*	
Constant Dollar Husband's Income				
<$1,000	85	-.109	-.187	-.199
$1,000-1,999	56	.020	.011	-.000
$2,000-2,999	91	-.031	-.083	-.060
$3,000-3,999	184	.068	.044	.059
$4,000-4,999	162	.036	.007	.023
$5,000-7,499	322	-.045	-.065	-.066
$7,500-9,999	303	.012	.020	.014
$10,000-14,999	258	.007	.059	.049
$15,000+	86	.015	.156	.143

continued

TABLE 6-7 continued

		Deviation from Grand Mean		
	N	Gross	Net_1	Net_2
Ethnicity				
Both spouses Chinese	1112	-.012	.003	.003
Wife Chinese, husband white	141	-.037	-.095	-.088
Wife Chinese, husband other	60	.257	.202	.207
Wife white, husband Chinese	151	.017	-.032	-.029
Wife other, husband Chinese	83	.007	.029	.018

Grand Mean = .427

[1]Variables included in the model: wife's education, age at marriage, husband's income, husband's occupation, number of times married, ethnicity, initial parity, and duration since first marriage.

[2]Variables included in the model: same as Model 1 except that husband's occupation has been deleted.

* N less than 20.

some other race (in 9% of these couples, the husband is white and, in 4%, he is some other nonwhite race). In 15% of our couples, the husband is Chinese and the wife is some other race (in two-thirds of this 15%, the wife is white; in the remaining one-third, she is a member of some other racial group). This situation is somewhat different for the Japanese Americans: In only 49% of the cases are both spouses Japanese. In 40% of the cases, the wife is Japanese, married to a person of some other race. In 10% of the cases, the husband is Japanese and the wife is some other race. The comparatively high incidence of Japanese women married to non-Japanese men is undoubtedly a function of the low sex ratio among Japanese Americans, particularly among Japanese Americans 30–39 years old (computed from U.S. Bureau of the Census, 1973d: Table 1):

Age Group	Sex Ratio
15–19	1.03
20–24	92
25–29	.86
30–34	.72
35–39	.54
Total	.80

This is not the case among Chinese Americans; their sex ratio among the population 15–39 years old is 1.07.

Among the Chinese American population, lower than average fertility is found for Chinese persons married to whites, and somewhat higher than average fertility is found for Chinese persons married to persons of other nonwhite races. The fertility of the dominant group of couples, both of whom are Chinese, is very close to the average for the Chinese group. Within the Japanese American population, the lowest fertility is found for Japanese wives married to white husbands. Intermediate fertility is found for couples if both spouses are Japanese, while higher than average fertility is found for Japanese spouses married to a member of some other nonwhite race.

DIFFERENTIALS WITHIN THE PUERTO RICAN
POPULATION

This section examines differentials in recent marital fertility within the Puerto Rican population. Puerto Ricans are defined as those who report themselves as being of Puerto Rican origin or descent. The analysis here is restricted to Puerto Ricans residing in mainland United States in 1970. In Chapter 8, we contrast the recent marital fertility of mainland Puerto Ricans with the recent marital fertility of Puerto Ricans residing in Puerto Rico.

Puerto Ricans living in the United States had a fertility rate that was somewhat higher than that of urban whites (Chapter 5). Table 6-8 shows the results of the multivariate analysis of differential fertility for Puerto Ricans living in the United States in 1970. Approximately 35% of the married Puerto Rican women had less than 9 years of education. These women had a fertility level that was about .06 above the mean. An additional 29% had 9–11 years of schooling, and their fertility level was very close to the average. The 28% who were high school graduates had a fertility level .06 below the mean; those who were college dropouts and college graduates also had rates that were below the average.

Net of education and other factors, there was a very sharp inverse relationship for Puerto Ricans between age at first marriage and fertility. This is shown in the second panel of Table 6-8. The 25% of the sample who married prior to age 18 had a rate that was .12 above the average, whereas for those who married beyond age 25, the fertility level was very, very low: .15 below the mean for women marrying at ages 25–29, and .32 below the mean for women marrying at ages 30 and older.

Occupation differences are quite small, with lower than average fertility being found for wives of managers, transport workers, men in the armed forces, and

TABLE 6-8

*Gross and Net Deviations from Mean Number of Children under
Age 3 for Currently Married Women under Age 40, for Various
Characteristics: Puerto Rican American Population, 1970.*

		Deviation from Grand Mean		
	N	Gross	Net_1	Net_2
Education				
<5 years	572	-.054	.046	.051
5-8 years	1514	.028	.057	.061
9-11 years	1646	.033	.005	.006
12 years	1617	-.018	-.051	-.054
13-15 years	286	-.089	-.112	-.121
16+ years	121	-.087	-.067	-.082
Age at Marriage				
14-17	1505	.045	.120	.120
18-19	1481	.034	.038	.038
20-21	1177	-.048	-.050	-.051
22-24	913	-.004	-.053	-.052
25-29	544	-.069	-.157	-.155
30-39	136	-.155	-.327	-.326
Husband's Occupation				
Professional	313	-.042	-.012	
Manager	261	-.117	-.067	
Sales	223	.039	.010	
Clerical	536	-.014	-.029	
Craftsman	1003	.009	.020	
Operative	1445	.046	.016	
Transport	429	-.033	-.041	
Laborer	388	.007	.013	
Farmer	9	*	*	
Farm laborer	59	.051	-.003	
Service	784	.011	.039	
Unemployed	11	*	*	
Armed forces	148	-.137	-.111	
Not in labor force	147	-.093	-.081	
Constant Dollar Husband's Income				
<$1,000	369	-.042	-.055	-.071
$1,000-1,999	326	.069	.042	.033
$2,000-2,999	520	.088	.007	.007
$3,000-3,999	1272	.032	-.008	-.004
$4,000-4,999	953	.009	-.004	.000
$5,000-7,499	1534	-.021	-.002	-.000
$7,500-9,999	541	-.079	.009	.010
$10,000-14,999	189	-.080	.070	.066
$15,000+	52	-.220	.019	-.004

continued

TABLE 6-8 continued

	N	Deviation from Grand Mean		
		Gross	Net$_1$	Net$_2$
Place of Birth				
Both spouses born in U.S.	753	-.037	-.034	-.035
Husband U.S., wife not U.S.	509	.009	.030	.019
Husband not U.S., wife U.S.	795	-.026	-.049	-.050
Neither spouse born in U.S.	3699	.012	.013	.015

Grand Mean = .508

[1] Variables included in the model: wife's education, age at marriage, husband's income, husband's occupation, number of times married, place of birth, initial parity, and duration since first marriage.

[2] Variables included in the model: same as Model 1 except that husband's occupation has been deleted.

* N less than 20.

those not in the labor force. Higher than average fertility rates are found for service workers.

The relationship between income and fertility for Puerto Rican Americans is inverse if adjustment is not made for other factors. But when factors such as education, marriage duration, and age at marriage are included in the regression model, we find that the relationship between income and recent marital fertility is virtually eliminated.

Lower than average fertility is found for Puerto Rican couples if both spouses were born in the United States, or for couples in which the wife was born in the United States and the husband was born outside the United States. The highest rates are found for couples in which the wife was born outside the United States (presumably in Puerto Rico) and the husband was born within the continental United States.

DIFFERENCES IN THE TIMING OF FERTILITY

The groups considered in this chapter vary considerably with respect to fertility levels; in this section, we examine one component of that difference, namely, differences in the age pattern of fertility. To do so, we return to the annual age-specific fertility rates presented in the first part of Chapter 5, and the same six groups examined there will be contrasted here: American Indians, Mexican Americans, Chinese Americans, Japanese Americans, whites, and blacks.

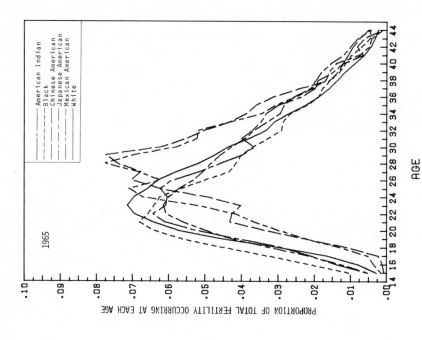

(A)

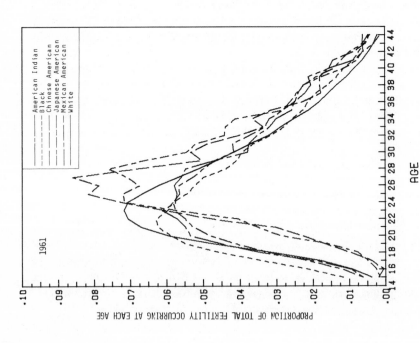

(B)

FIGURE 6-7 *Standardized fertility schedules by racial or ethnic group: 1957, 1961, 1965, and 1969. Parts (C) and (D) are on facing page.*

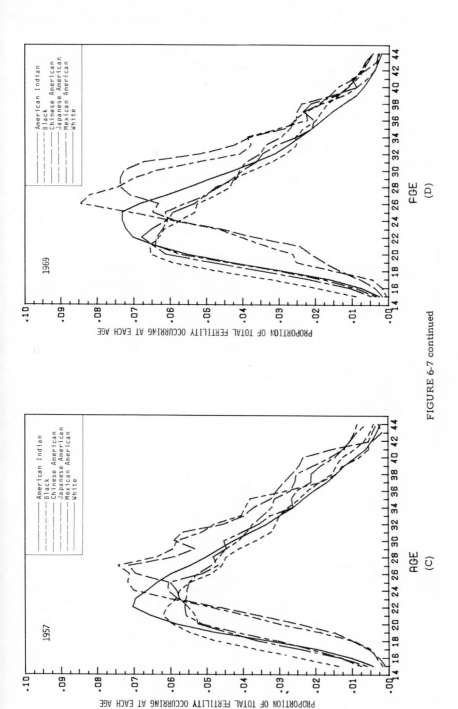

FIGURE 6-7 continued

141

However, instead of aggregating the single-year age-specific fertility rate estimates into total fertility rates, the complete fertility schedules themselves will be
examined. Since the fertility schedules to be examined are for all women and all
fertility, differences in shape can reflect both differences in the timing of
marriage and marital fertility, and differences in the timing of illegitimate
fertility.

As we noted in our consideration in Chapter 3, the issue of the timing of
fertility is essentially a cohort issue, but, unfortunately, the time series employed here is not sufficiently long to construct cohort fertility schedules. Thus,
period fertility schedules have been employed, and what is being examined is the

TABLE 6-9

Percent of Total Fertility Occurring before Age 25, 30 and 35 by
Race or Ethnic Status for 1957, 1961, 1965 and 1969.

Year and Race or Ethnic Status	Percent Occurring before Age:		
	25	30	35
1957			
American Indian	41	68	85
Japanese American	28	63	87
Chinese American	25	57	80
Mexican American	39	63	82
Black American	48	71	86
White American	45	72	89
1961			
American Indian	39	66	84
Japanese American	27	63	87
Chinese American	26	64	85
Mexican American	39	65	83
Black American	48	72	88
White American	45	74	90
1965			
American Indian	41	66	83
Japanese American	29	64	87
Chinese American	24	59	83
Mexican American	40	66	84
Black American	50	73	88
White American	43	72	89
1969			
American Indian	44	70	87
Japanese American	24	63	87
Chinese American	22	58	86
Mexican American	41	67	85
Black American	47	72	87
White American	43	74	90

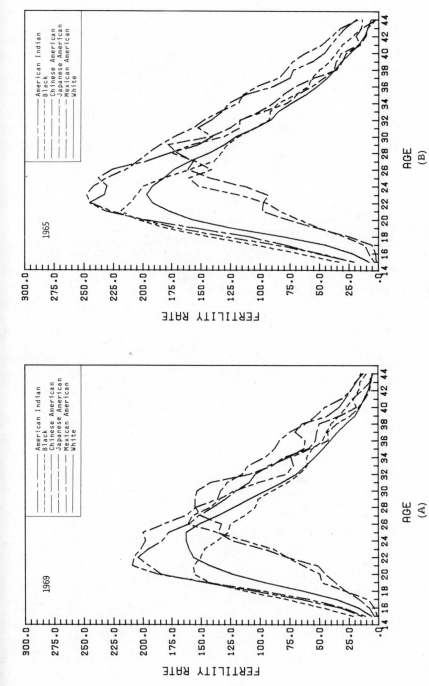

FIGURE 6-8 Fertility schedules by racial or ethnic group: 1957, 1961, 1965, and 1969. Parts (C) and (D) are on page 144.

143

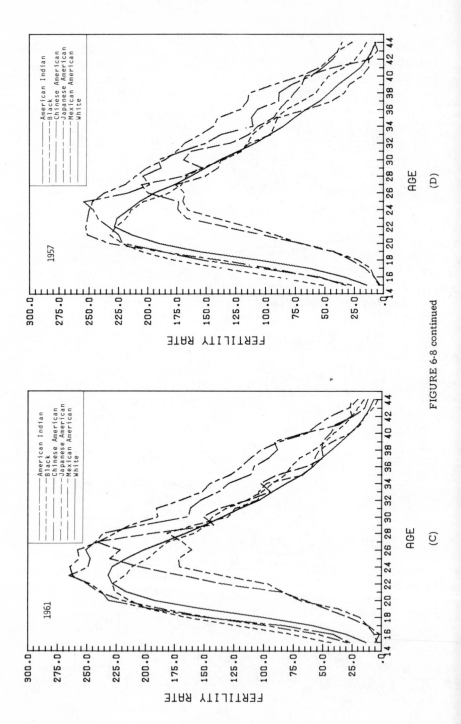

FIGURE 6-8 continued

144

proportionate contribution made to a period total fertility rate by women of various ages within the childbearing span. In an attempt to minimize the effects of relying on period fertility schedules, fertility schedules from four periods will be examined: 1957, 1961, 1965, and 1969.

Two types of fertility schedules will be graphically presented. One set of schedules will simply plot the single-year age-specific fertility rates. As such, these graphs simultaneously show differences in the age patterns of fertility and differences in the level of fertility. In order to examine differences in the age pattern of fertility without the confounding effect of differences in levels of fertility, a second set of fertility schedules has been constructed such that the total fertility rate of each group is equal to 1.0. This latter set will be labeled "standardized."

Standardized fertility schedules for the years 1957, 1961, 1965, and 1969 are shown in Figure 6-7. It can be seen that there are two distinctly different age patterns of fertility. American Indians, Mexican Americans, blacks, and whites begin their childbearing early and reach their peak level of fertility by their early twenties. Among these four groups, blacks have an earlier pattern than the other three. The Chinese Americans and Japanese Americans, on the other hand, begin their childbearing substantially later and do not reach their peak level of childbearing until their late twenties. Among the early fertility groups, between 40 and 50% of their total fertility occurs before age 25; among Chinese Americans and Japanese Americans, the comparable figure is 25% (see Table 6-9). By age 35, the six groups are fairly similar with respect to the cumulative proportion of total fertility that has occurred.

TABLE 6-10

*Median Age at First Marriage by Race or Ethnic Status and Age:
1970, Women.*

Race or Ethnic Status	Age		
	25–34	35–44	45–54
White American	20.0	20.5	21.7
Black American	19.9	20.3	21.2
Mexican American*	20.3	20.7	21.6
American Indian	19.7	20.1	20.7
Japanese American	23.1	24.3	24.4
Chinese American	23.5	21.9	22.9

* White persons of Mexican origin

Source: U.S. Bureau of the Census, Census of Population: 1970. Subject Reports, Final Report PC(2)-4D, Age at First Marriage, Tables 1, 5, and 10.

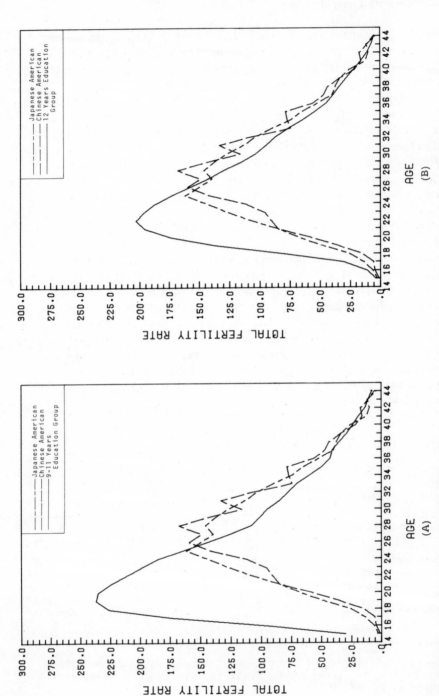

FIGURE 6-9 Fertility schedules for Chinese Americans, Japanese Americans, and four education groups: 1966. (The four education groups include all women regardless of race or ethnic group.) Parts (C) and (D) are on facing page.

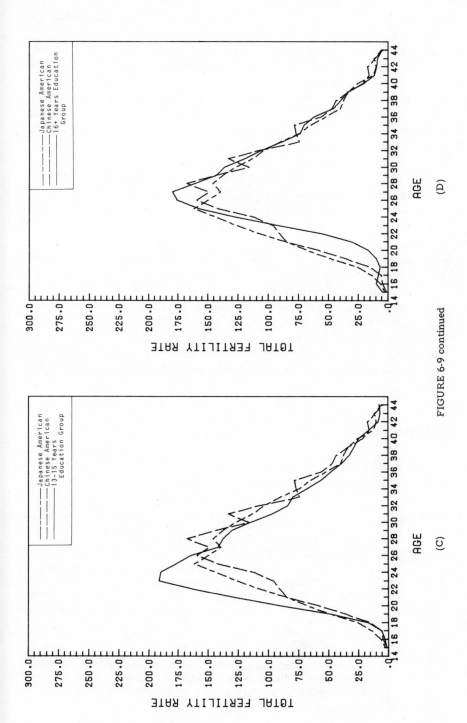

FIGURE 6-9 continued

147

Figure 6-8 shows the actual fertility schedules for the racial groups in each of the four years—that is, the schedules have not been subjected to the requirement that the total fertility rate equal unity. Thus, Figure 6-8 simultaneously shows differences in the age pattern of fertility and differences in the level of fertility. These schedules show that, with the exception of the American Indians and Mexican Americans, differences in fertility past age 27 or so are minimal. American Indians and Mexican Americans have comparatively high levels of fertility at virtually every age.

The fertility patterns shown in Figures 6-7 and 6-8 suggest that the Chinese Americans and the Japanese Americans have a later age at marriage than the other two groups, and this is indeed the case (Table 6-10). The Chinese Americans and, to an even greater extent, the Japanese Americans, marry 1 to 3 years later than the other groups. Thus, to a large extent, what must be explained is the marriage pattern of the Japanese and Chinese Americans rather than their marital fertility behavior.

To illustrate the uniqueness (in a United States perspective) of the Japanese and Chinese American age patterns of fertility, Figure 6-9 contrasts the Chinese and Japanese American fertility schedules with those of four education groups. Only the college graduates have a pattern of fertility as late as the Chinese and Japanese Americans—yet the educational attainment of the Chinese and Japanese Americans is not too dissimilar from that of the total population (Table 6-11).

SUMMARY

This chapter has examined a large number of fertility differentials for various ethnic and racial minority groups. To summarize three of these differentials, we

TABLE 6-11

Median School Years Completed by Age for Chinese Americans, Japanese Americans, and United States Total: 1970, Women.

Age	Total*	Chinese American	Japanese American
25–29	12.5	14.2	12.5
30–34	12.4	12.5	12.2
35–44	12.3	11.9	12.0
45–54	12.1	10.6	11.8

*
Source of Total: U.S. Bureau of the Census, Census of Population: 1970. Subject Reports, Final Report PC(2)-5B, Educational Attainment. Medians for the other two groups computed from a Public Use Sample.

have prepared Table 6-12. For all groups considered in this chapter, the more detailed analyses suggest that income, education, and age at marriage each has roughly linear effects on fertility. Thus, as a convenient summary measure, this table reports the zero-order and partial regression coefficient of fertility on income, education, and age at marriage. In each case, the partial regression coefficient is that from a model including all of the variables that were considered in the earlier analysis for that group. Income is coded in thousands of dollars; education and age at first marriage are coded in years.

Income does not have a consistent relationship with fertility across all groups. For urban whites, the effect of income on fertility is strongly positive. The same strong positive relationship is also found for Chinese and Japanese Americans. Income is negatively related to fertility for Southern rural blacks, the Spanish-surname population in the Southwest, and the American Indian population. There is essentially no relationship between fertility and income for non-

TABLE 6-12

Zero Order and Partial Regression Coefficients of Fertility on Income, Education, and Age at First Marriage, by Ethnicity: 1970.

	Income	Education	Age at Marriage
	Zero Order Regression Coefficients		
Urban White	-.003	-.001	.001
Black - Non-Southern	-.012	-.002	-.013
Black - Southern Urban	-.016	-.002	-.017
Black - Southern Rural	-.024	+.004	-.010
Spanish Surname	-.027	-.014	+.005
Puerto Rican American	-.013	-.003	-.011
Chinese American	+.002	+.006	+.009
Japanese American	+.005	+.013	+.001
American Indian	-.023	-.012	-.000
	Partial Regression Coefficients[*]		
Urban White	+.011	-.016	-.014
Black - Non-Southern	+.002	-.006	-.027
Black - Southern Urban	+.000	-.007	-.033
Black - Southern Rural	-.010	-.001	-.029
Spanish Surname	-.009	-.019	-.010
Puerto Rican American	+.004	-.015	-.025
Chinese American	+.010	-.010	-.011
Japanese American	+.012	-.006	-.016
American Indian	-.007	-.016	-.014

[*] The variables included in the model are those included in the analysis for the particular ethnic group as reported earlier in this chapter.

Southern blacks, Southern urban blacks, and Puerto Rican Americans. Thus, the positive income effect on recent fertility is only found among those groups that have higher aggregate income.

There is a consistent inverse relationship between education and fertility for almost all groups studied. The Spanish-surname, Puerto Rican American, American Indian, and rural farm populations all have coefficients very similar to that for the urban white population. The only exception is for Southern rural blacks, where there is a very small relationship. For other blacks, the effect is about half the level of the white rate. Chinese Americans and Japanese Americans also have a lower relationship between education and fertility than do urban whites.

Net of education, income, and the other factors considered in our analysis, age at marriage has a consistent inverse effect on fertility. Particularly strong effects were found for each of the three groups of blacks and for Puerto Ricans living in the United States.

7

Rural Fertility Trends
and Differentials

Previous chapters have examined fertility trends and differentials within the entire U.S. population, the urban white population, and various minority populations. This chapter extends this analysis to the rural population. Rural fertility is of interest because fertility has traditionally been high in rural areas and because the rural/urban differential has been one of the most persistent fertility differentials. Furthermore, as will be seen, older, less-educated rural women constitute the only major subgroup in the United States that did not participate in the baby boom of the 1950s.

DEFINITIONS OF "RURAL" AND "URBAN"

When annual fertility rates or age patterns of fertility are examined, the population of interest will be all white women of childbearing age residing in rural areas. Rural areas are basically defined as places with less than 2500 inhabitants.[1] And when the dependent variable is number of own children under 3 years old, the population of interest will be currently married women under age 40 residing on farms, that is, living on places of 10 acres or more from which sales of crops, livestock, and other farm products amounted to $50 or more during the previous calendar year, or on places of less than 10 acres (other than city or suburban lots) from which sales of farm products amounted to $250 or more. This latter group (the farm population) is a small subset of the first (the rural population) and is of interest because it is substantially more homogeneous. As noted in Chapter 2, the methodology for constructing annual fertility rates requires very large numbers of women to provide reliable estimates; for this

[1] For a more complete definition, see U.S. Bureau of the Census (1972:134).

151

TABLE 7-1

Ratio of 1960 Census Estimates to 1970 Census Estimates of Ferti-
lity Rates among Urban and Rural White Women for Five-Year Overlap
(1955-1959), by Education and Age Group.

Education Group and Years Being Compared	Age Specific Fertility Rate Comparisons					
	15-19		20-24		25-29	
	Urban	Rural	Urban	Rural	Urban	Rural
5-8 years						
1959	.87	.63	1.14	.99	1.09	.95
1958	1.14	.86	1.12	.96	1.09	1.02
1957	1.18	.88	1.16	.95	.99	.95
1956	1.17	1.03	1.14	1.09	1.03	.95
1955	1.22	1.03	1.13	.93	1.09	.96
9-11 years						
1959	.46	.40	1.02	.98	1.06	1.12
1958	.51	.49	1.13	1.06	1.03	1.12
1957	.64	.59	1.05	1.05	1.03	1.05
1956	.86	.85	1.08	1.08	1.06	1.08
1955	.97	1.00	1.00	1.03	.96	1.01
12 years						
1959	1.80	1.72	1.04	1.06	1.03	.99
1958	1.25	1.28	1.04	1.05	1.03	1.04
1957	1.01	1.14	1.06	1.07	1.00	1.02
1956	.82	1.07	1.00	1.02	1.02	1.05
1955	.89	.98	1.04	1.11	1.05	1.01
13+ years						
1959	2.17	2.09	.93	1.14	1.01	1.07
1958	1.48	1.56	.97	1.10	.98	1.02
1957	.77	1.47	.98	1.06	1.05	1.05
1956	.64	1.17	.95	1.11	1.03	1.07
1955	.57	.61	.97	1.00	.96	.89
Total*						
1959	1.09	.82	1.03	1.04	1.03	1.02
1958	1.06	.91	1.06	1.06	1.02	1.04
1957	1.03	.98	1.06	1.04	1.01	1.01
1956	.96	1.10	1.03	1.06	1.03	1.04
1955	1.01	1.07	1.03	1.05	1.01	.99

	30-34		35-39		40-44		Total Fertility Rate Comparison	
	Urban	Rural	Urban	Rural	Urban	Rural	Urban	Rural
	1.01	1.14	1.10	.87	.85	.83	1.05	.90
	1.06	1.05	.94	1.19	1.06	1.12	1.09	.99
	.94	.91	.99	.95	.94	1.14	1.07	.93
	.99	1.01	.97	.92	.85	1.09	1.07	1.02
	.98	.99	.97	.87	.79	.82	1.09	.96
	.98	.97	1.01	1.15	1.16	.90	.91	.87
	1.08	1.11	1.09	1.03	1.00	1.25	.96	.95
	.96	1.07	1.06	1.03	.99	.82	.94	.94
	1.04	1.00	.96	1.06	1.14	.94	1.01	1.01
	1.05	1.15	.92	1.10	1.01	.76	.98	1.03
	1.04	1.04	1.10	.91	.88	1.22	1.10	1.10
	1.07	1.00	1.05	.91	.99	.89	1.06	1.05
	1.02	1.01	.98	.95	.97	.95	1.02	1.04
	1.04	.95	.99	.98	.83	.97	.99	1.01
	1.07	1.02	.99	1.04	1.23	1.06	1.04	1.05
	1.06	1.06	1.10	1.13	.89	.97	1.04	1.13
	1.05	.94	1.07	.97	.88	1.23	1.01	1.05
	1.00	1.16	.90	1.23	.83	.86	.99	1.10
	.99	1.10	.96	1.17	.96	1.11	.98	1.10
	.95	1.04	1.01	.97	1.05	.80	.96	.94
	1.03	1.05	1.07	.98	.92	.94	1.04	1.00
	1.07	1.04	1.04	1.03	.97	1.14	1.05	1.03
	1.00	1.04	.97	1.02	.93	1.01	1.02	1.02
	1.01	1.01	.97	1.02	.90	1.06	1.01	1.05
	1.02	1.04	.98	1.00	1.01	.91	1.02	1.03

*
Total includes women with 0-4 years of education.

reason, the entire rural population is utilized whenever annual rates are reported. For trends during the decade of the 1960s and for differentials at the time of the 1970 census, it is possible to make reliable estimates for smaller groups, and, thus, the more homogeneous population will be used for this part of the analysis.

MIGRATION AND FERTILITY RATE ESTIMATES

The use of own-children data to estimate fertility behavior in years prior to the census assumes that the classification of women by the independent variables of interest remains constant over time or changes in a predictable manner. When using number of own children under 3 years, departures from this assumption of constancy have a minimal effect. However, departures from the constancy assumption could have a substantial effect on the annual age-specific fertility rate estimates. In previous chapters, the effects of departures from the constancy assumption were examined for education and race. Urban/rural residence presents a slightly different problem than did these other two variables; urban/rural residence is both changeable and reversible (Schnore, 1961). As before, since the fertility rate estimates are available for each of 15 years preceding the 1960 and 1970 censuses, it is possible to compare the correspondence of the two sets of estimates for the period 1955–1959. This is shown in Table 7-1.

By first examining the bottom panel of Table 7-1, it can be seen that the two sets of estimates are remarkably close for all age groups for both the total rural group and the total urban group. This suggests that, whatever change in status did take place, it was not sufficient to significantly affect our estimates of rural and urban fertility rates. Since there was a net rural to urban migration during the decade, the probable explanation for the stability of the estimates is twofold: The rural emigrants had fertility patterns similar to their contemporaries who remained in rural residences, and there were not a sufficient number of rural migrants to affect the urban rates.

An examination of the remainder of Table 7-1 reveals the effect of changes in educational status. For the older women, the two sets of rates tend to be close in every education and rural/urban category. For the younger women, changes in educational status affect the comparisons of the two rates, and this effect is the same in both the rural and the urban subgroups. This lack of agreement between the two sets of rates for younger women by education was also noted in Chapter 3. As before, in order to minimize the effect of these educational change biases, whenever fertility rates for women 15–19 or 20–24 years old have been examined, the following steps have been taken: (a) the rates for the two years closest to the census (i.e., 1968–1969 for the 1970 census and 1958–1959 for the 1960 census) have been eliminated; and (b) for each of the three years for which there are two estimates available (1955–1957), the estimates from the 1960 and 1970 censuses have been averaged. This has the unfortunate disadvantage of truncating the series at 1967 instead of 1969. Whenever fertility rates for women 15–19 and 20–24 years old are not being examined, the series will be extended the full 25 years, and, for the 5-year overlap period, the two estimates will be averaged.

AGGREGATE TRENDS

Both rural and urban white women experienced increased fertility during the 1950s, but the increase ended earlier and was substantially smaller among rural white women than among urban white women. This can be seen by examining Figure 7-1, which shows total fertility rates for rural and urban white women for the period 1945–1969. The rural total fertility rate reached its peak in 1957, whereas the urban rate continued to increase slightly for two more years. More significant than the difference in timing of peak fertility is the difference in the rate of fertility increase during the baby-boom years. Although both groups had the usual marked postwar rise in fertility, the rate of increase during the 1950s was substantially less among rural women than among urban women. Among urban women, the total fertility rate in 1957 was 64% larger than it was in 1945;

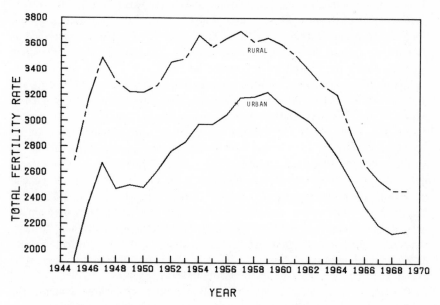

FIGURE 7-1   *Total fertility rates for white rural and urban women: 1945–1969.*

TABLE 7-2

Percent Change in Total Fertility, Fertility 15-29, and Fertility 30-44, in Period 1945-1957 and 1957-1967, by Education and Rural-Urban Residence, for White Women.

Period, and Years of Education	Total Fertility		Fertility 15-29		Fertility 30-44	
	Rural	Urban	Rural	Urban	Rural	Urban
1945-1957						
Total*	+37	+64	+ 60	+ 91	0	+22
5-8 years	+25	+64	+ 38	+ 88	- 3	+16
9-11 years	+38	+67	+ 58	+ 92	- 1	+16
12 years	+60	+76	+ 87	+107	+15	+26
13+ years	+69	+55	+109	+ 79	+22	+25
1957-1967						
Total*	-31	-31	-28	-30	-40	-33
5-8 years	-24	-14	-19	-12	-37	-22
9-11 years	-33	-33	-31	-31	-38	-38
12 years	-30	-29	-26	-27	-40	-36
13+ years	-34	-32	-31	-32	-40	-33

*
 Total includes women with 0-4 years of education.

among rural women, the comparable rate of increase was 37% (see top panel of Table 7-2). Over the next decade, both groups exhibited the same rate of decline (see bottom panel of Table 7-2). Thus, during the 25-year period, there was an overall contraction in the rural/urban fertility differential. This contraction occurred during the 1950s, but not during the 1960s.

Figure 7-2 shows the differential participation of younger and older rural and urban women in the 1950s baby boom and the subsequent fertility decline. Although the fertility rate of younger urban women increased more rapidly during the 1950s than the fertility of younger rural women, both groups experienced substantial increases. There was no *net* change, however, in the fertility rates of older rural white women from 1945 to 1957; despite some fluctuations, which can be seen in Figure 7-2, the rate in 1957 was the same as the rate in 1945. Older urban women, by contrast, experienced a 22% increase during this period. During the 1960s, the fertility rate declined by 40% among older rural women, compared to 33% among older urban women. Thus, throughout the entire period, there was a contraction of the rural/urban fertility differential among older women—to the point that, by the last few years of the 1960s, both groups were reproducing at about the same rate.

The lack of a net increase in fertility among older rural white women is the only exception that we have found to the postwar baby-boom trend. Among all

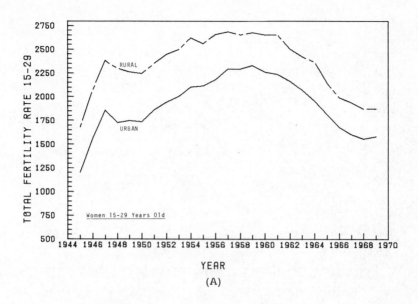

(A)

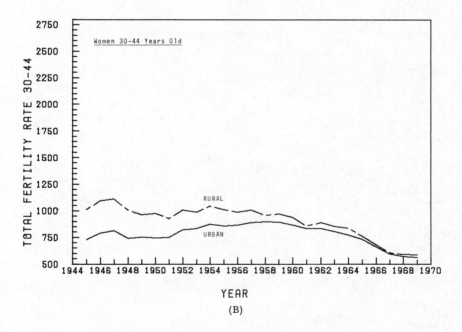

(B)

FIGURE 7-2 *Fertility rates for white women 15–29 and 30–44 years old for rural and urban residents: 1945–1969.*

157

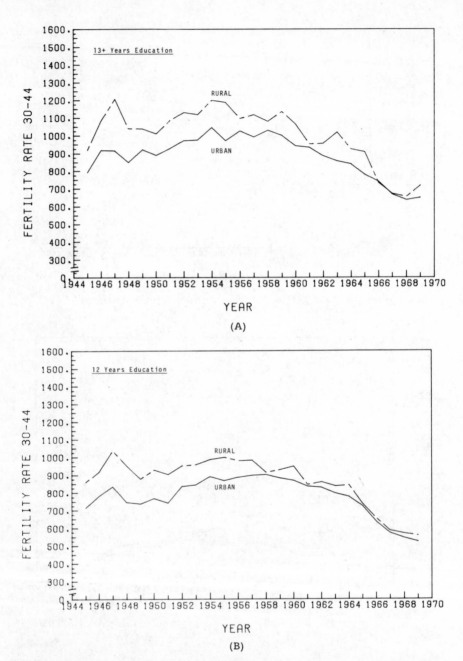

FIGURE 7-3 *Fertility rates for white rural and urban women 30–44 years old by education: 1945–1969. Parts (C) and (D) are on facing page.*

158

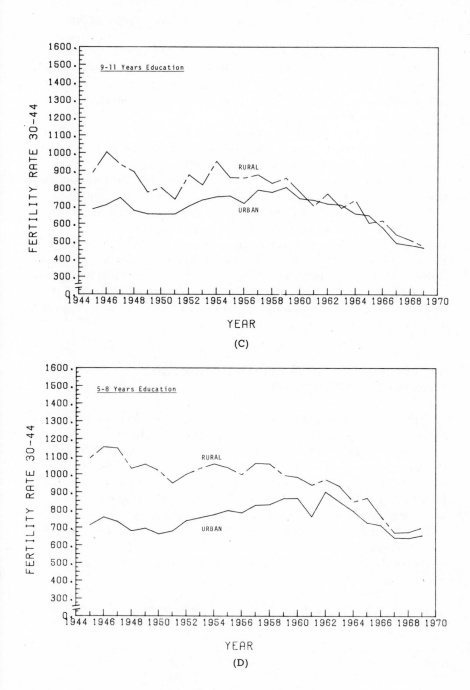

FIGURE 7-3 continued

159

other social groups examined, fertility increased substantially during the 1950s (see Chapter 3). Indeed, as can be seen in Figure 7-3 and in the top panel of Table 7-2, the fertility of older rural women with only a grade school education and of older rural women who attended but did not complete high school actually declined between 1945 and 1957.[2]

Rural women with limited education traditionally have had the highest rates of fertility in the United States. They also might be expected to be among the last to adopt moderately effective methods of birth control, such as the condom and diaphragm.[3] However, it is quite possible that, among these women, there were increased awareness and utilization of contraception—especially the condom—as a result of education about prophylactics during World War II. Increased use of contraception should lead to lower fertility rates, but this may have been offset by the counterbalancing forces leading to the baby boom of the 1950s, resulting in moderate fertility declines among older rural women with limited education.[4] Whatever the explanation, these two groups of rural women are the only exceptions that we have found to the generalized pattern of the baby boom; it also should be noted that both groups participated in the fertility decline of the 1960s (see bottom panel of Table 7-2).

DIFFERENTIAL FERTILITY DECLINES WITHIN THE FARM POPULATION: 1960–1970

This section examines the extent to which various subgroups within the farm population have participated in these aggregate fertility trends. In order to do this, it is necessary to shift our focus from estimates of annual fertility rates to estimates of the level of recent fertility prevailing before the census; the measure, for currently married women, is the number of own children under 3 years from the 1960 and 1970 censuses. To obtain a somewhat more homogeneous universe, the population being considered is restricted to rural farm-resident women. To permit an explicit contrast between whites and blacks, this section is not restricted to whites.

The standardized and crude rates of decline for the decade of the 1960s based

---

[2] In Figure 7-3, education groups 13–15 and 16+ years were collapsed in order to obtain a sufficiently large number of women for analysis. The 0–4-years education group is not shown (see Chapter 3).

[3] Unfortunately, fertility surveys were not conducted during the 1940s. However, an indication of this possibility may be gained by looking at the 1955 Growth of American Families Study (Freedman, Welpton, and Campbell, 1959).

[4] Lindert (1974) provides a different, though complementary, explanation for the same phenomenon.

on a measure of recent marital fertility are shown in Table 7-3 for various socioeconomic and demographic subgroups within the farm-resident population. Before examining this table in detail, it should be noted that, as has been consistently found in previous chapters, the decline in fertility during the past decade was universal, with the trivial exception of women first married at age 30 or older.

Since the definition of farm used here is residential, it is not necessary that the husbands of these women be primarily employed in farming. Approximately half of the husbands of farm-resident wives are primarily engaged in nonfarming activities. For the analysis of occupation in this chapter, the nonfarming occupations have been classified by the usual major occupation groups (e.g., "professionals"). The two farm major occupation groups ("farmers and farm managers" and "farm laborers and farm foremen") have been classified by the more detailed occupation groups. The "farmer" group was then further subdivided into three groups: those who own their place of residence, those who pay cash rent for their place of residence, and those who are not owners but pay no cash rent.

In terms of the percentage decline, there was a substantially more rapid decline in fertility of wives of farm laborers and farmers who paid no cash rent than for wives of farmers who lived on property that they either owned themselves or cash rented. Among farm-resident wives of men in nonfarm occupations, the rate for wives of professionals or managers and service workers declined vary rapidly, while rates for wives of sales and clerical workers declined very little. Wives of men whose primary occupation was craftsman, operative, or laborer had a decline of 23–28%, while (consistent with findings for urban whites and blacks) wives of service workers had a particularly large decline (47%).

For the purpose of computing changes in recent fertility by income group, women in 1970 were classified by the total income of their husbands in terms of 1960 constant dollars. The fertility decline was somewhat larger for wives of men with less than $2000, or more than $7500, of income than for the other groups, but, again, the similarity in the rate of decline is more impressive than the difference.

Fertility rates fell rapidly at every education level. The standardized decline was about 25% for women with high school diplomas and above. It was slightly more rapid (31%) for high school dropouts, but was considerably slower (16%) for women with 5–8 years of education.

In contrast to the urban white population (see Chapter 4), the rate of decline in recent marital fertility during the 1960s is greatest among those who married at relatively young ages. Those who married while they were still teenagers had rates of decline of about 33%; for the other groups, the comparable figure is closer to 20%.

TABLE 7-3

Change in Recent Fertility between 1960 and 1970 for Rural Farm
Couples, Wife under Age 40, for Various Socioeconomic, Racial,
Regional, and Demographic Groups.

	Number of Women		Percent Decline	
	1960	1970	Crude	Standard-ized[a]
Husband's Occupation				
Professional	522	285	29.6	30.1
Manager	552	285	51.6	39.7
Sales	341	133	19.9	12.4
Clerical	324	152	29.8	14.4
Craftsman	1480	876	24.9	23.1
Operative[b]	1976	923	31.2	26.7
Laborer	592	232	25.1	28.3
Service	190	126	47.8	47.1
Farmer--Owns	3391	1594	24.3	20.8
Cash rents	655	184	23.4	21.4
Pays no cash rent	1944	599	35.7	32.2
Farm laborer	1309	392	37.6	34.1
Unemployed	299	121	36.1	27.9
Not in labor force	380	230	37.0	37.4
Constant Dollar Husband's Income				
<$1,000	2177	473	37.8	37.8
$1,000-1,999	1937	504	33.5	29.2
$2,000-2,999	2295	583	20.1	20.8
$3,000-3,999	2157	854	31.5	25.4
$4,000-4,999	1709	662	19.1	22.8
$5,000-7,499	2662	1503	29.7	27.9
$7,500-9,999	738	905	34.3	29.9
$10,000+	661	864	30.7	26.6
Education				
<5 years	486	88	40.0	38.1
5-8 years	3123	710	17.9	16.1
9-11 years	3117	1161	40.3	30.9
12 years	5897	3320	32.0	24.3
13-15 years	1253	741	27.5	23.9
16+ years	460	328	30.2	26.0
Age at First Marriage				
14-17	3822	1640	46.0	35.4
18-19	4463	2287	34.9	30.1
20-21	3038	1392	21.8	23.8
22-24	2028	707	16.5	19.7
25-29	824	259	15.2	17.9
30-39	161	63	-2.8	-4.2

continued

TABLE 7-3 continued

	Number of Women		Percent Decline	
	1960	1970	Crude	Standardized[a]
Region of Residence				
Northeast	1064	456	23.6	17.2
North Central	5955	3131	28.1	23.1
South	5769	2079	37.5	34.7
West	1548	682	42.0	38.1
Race				
White	13079	6040	30.3	25.8
Black	1141	263	32.1	29.1
Other	116	45	44.7	45.0
Duration Since First Marriage				
<3 years	1525	623	18.0	
3-5.9 years	1861	724	20.4	
6-8.9 years	1913	784	24.2	
9-11.9 years	2288	959	29.1	
12-14.9 years	2767	1095	38.8	
15-17.9 years	1849	996	47.5	
18-20.9 years	1589	831	29.7	
21-23.9 years	502	312	48.4	
24+ years	42	24	100.0	
Initial Parity				
0	3082	1234	10.9	12.4
1	2356	836	6.4	10.3
2	3294	1409	34.8	35.0
3	2558	1211	45.2	37.7
4+	3046	1658	54.4	51.3

[a] Standardized on 1960 marriage duration distribution of that group.

[b] For 1970, includes transport operatives.

The fertility declines were much larger in the West and South than they were in the North Central or Northeastern regions. In addition, as often noted in this monograph, the rate of fertility decline was somewhat larger among blacks than among whites.

The final two panels of Table 7-3 show rates of decline in recent marital fertility for marriage-duration groups and initial parity groups. In general, the greatest rates of decline are found among the longest marriage-duration groups and the highest initial parity groups.

TRENDS IN THE PATTERN OF FERTILITY

To explore possible changes in the age patterns of fertility, we return to the annual age-specific fertility rate estimates to examine the shape of the fertility schedule itself. Again, the universe will shift from currently married rural farm women to all white women of childbearing age residing in rural areas. As was the case in earlier chapters, the fertility schedules have been constructed such that the total fertility rate of each group is equal to 1.0. Thus, the figures for this section plot the proportion of period total fertility occurring at each single year of age between 15 and 44, and differences in the plotted fertility schedules are the result of timing differences. Changes between 1945 and 1965 will be examined.

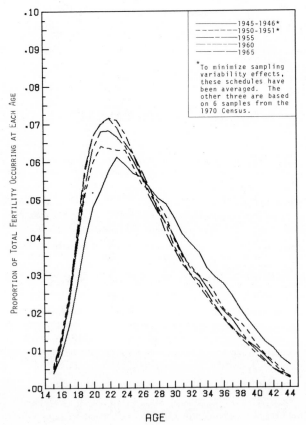

FIGURE 7-4 *Standardized fertility schedules for rural white women: 1945–1965.*

TABLE 7-4

Mean Age and Standard Deviation of Fertility Schedule, and Percent of Total Fertility Occurring before Age 25 and before Age 30 by Education Group, for Rural Women: 1945-1965.

Year	Total	Education Group			
		5-8 years	9-11 years	12 years	13+ years
			Mean Age		
1945[a]	27.56	26.73	26.76	27.45	29.18
1950[b]	26.39	25.60	24.87	26.76	28.31
1955	26.19	25.57	24.78	26.35	27.71
1960	25.87	25.14	24.41	26.00	27.42
1965	25.88	24.83	24.15	25.95	27.81
			Standard Deviation		
1945[a]	6.52	6.77	6.79	5.89	5.56
1950[b]	6.35	6.66	6.25	5.99	5.64
1955	6.23	6.64	6.40	5.94	5.62
1960	6.05	6.48	6.16	5.88	5.47
1965	6.09	6.49	6.19	5.90	5.37
		Percent of Total Fertility Occurring before Age 25			
1945[a]	37	44	44	36	22
1950[b]	45	50	55	42	29
1955	46	51	56	45	32
1960	48	53	58	48	34
1965	48	55	61	48	30
		Percent of Total Fertility Occurring before Age 30			
1945[a]	64	67	68	66	56
1950[b]	71	73	78	70	62
1955	72	73	77	72	66
1960	74	75	80	75	68
1965	74	77	81	74	66

[a]1945 and 1946 have been averaged together.

[b]1950 and 1951 have been averaged together.

The fertility schedules for rural whites for the period 1945–1965 are shown in Figure 7-4, and related parameters of these schedules are shown in Table 7-4. Two distinct trends can be seen during this 20-year period. The pattern of fertility has become more compact; that is, a greater proportion of fertility is occurring during the years closest to the mean age of fertility. Secondly, a significantly younger age pattern of fertility has been developing. The mean age of the fertility schedule has declined by almost $1\frac{3}{4}$ years, and the proportion of fertility occurring before age 25 has increased from 37 to 48%. Similar but less marked trends were occurring among the urban white population (not shown).

In general, all four rural education groups experienced similar trends with respect to patterns of fertility—trends toward a younger and a more compact fertility schedule (see Table 7-4). This change has been most dramatic among women who attended but did not complete high school. Their mean age of fertility declined by more than $2\frac{1}{2}$ years during the period, and the proportion of total fertility occurring before age 25 increased from 44 to 61%. The only exception to this pattern occurs among women who attended college. They move in the direction of a younger age pattern of fertility between 1945 and 1960; but, then, between 1960 and 1965, they register an increase in mean age of fertility. Unfortunately, because of the effect of changing education levels (see Chapter 3), we cannot extend the series past 1965 to see whether or not the other education groups also begin to move toward an older pattern of fertility. Again, although not shown, it should be noted that similar trends have been observed among comparable urban groups as well.

CURRENT DIFFERENTIALS

This section examines differentials in recent fertility levels within the resident farm population as enumerated in the 1970 census. To do this, the number of own children under 3 years is used, as is the smaller and more homogeneous universe of currently married, rural farm-resident women under 40. The analyses in this section utilize a dummy variable multiple regression approach. Table 7-5 expresses the results in terms of deviations from the overall mean. As in previous chapters, both gross and net deviations will be shown.

Of special interest in any analysis of differential fertility within the rural farm population is husband's occupation. The gross and net deviations for various occupational groups are shown in the first panel of Table 7-5. As expected, women whose husbands are actively engaged in farming tend to have higher fertility than women whose husbands are engaged in nonfarming occupations. There are exceptions, but the tendency is clearly there. Within the farming occupation group, when other factors are controlled, farm laborers have the lowest level of fertility and farm owners have the highest.

As has been consistently found for other groups, when confounding factors are controlled, education of wife is inversely related to level of fertility. Women with 5–8 years of education have a rate of recent fertility that is over 60% greater than that found for college-educated women.

Net of the effects of occupation and the other variables considered, the effect of income on fertility is small and irregular. There is a slight tendency for the

TABLE 7-5

Gross and Net Deviations from Mean Number of Children under Age 3 for Currently Married, Rural Farm Women under Age 40, by Various Characteristics: 1970.

	N	Gross	Net$_1$	Net$_2$
		\multicolumn{3}{c}{Deviations from Grand Mean}	

	N	Gross	Net$_1$	Net$_2$
Husband's Occupation[3]				
Professional	285	.028	-.029	
Manager	285	-.176	-.075	
Sales	133	.024	.042	
Clerical	152	-.027	-.014	
Craftsman	876	-.009	-.002	
Operative	647	.013	-.010	
Transport	276	.009	.018	
Laborer	232	.061	-.017	
Service	126	-.089	-.089	
Farmer--Owns	1594	-.021	.035	
Pays cash rent	184	.079	.032	
Pays no cash rent	599	.040	.008	
Farm laborer	392	.077	-.012	
Unemployed	121	.031	.034	
Not in labor force	230	-.065	-.113	
Education				
<5 years	88	.015	.071	.053
5-8 years	710	.088	.143	.137
9-11 years	1161	-.051	-.005	-.007
12 years	3320	-.007	-.018	-.016
13-15 years	741	.017	-.031	-.030
16+ years	328	.020	-.058	-.062
Husband's Constant Dollar Income				
<$1,000	473	-.006	-.036	-.041
$1,000-1,999	504	.016	-.024	-.019
$2,000-2,999	583	.093	.029	.033
$3,000-3,999	854	-.001	-.020	-.014
$4,000-4,999	662	.048	.016	.017
$5,000-7,499	1503	-.018	-.006	-.009
$7,500-9,999	905	-.029	.013	.011
$10,000-14,999	514	-.046	.019	.017
$15,000+	350	-.040	.018	.018
Race				
White	6040	-.008	-.008	-.008
Black	263	.161	.179	.167
Other	45	.084	.078	.064

continued

TABLE 7-5 continued

	N	Deviations from Grand Mean		
		Gross	Net_1	Net_2
Region of Residence				
Northeast	456	.039	.032	.032
North Central	3131	.035	.040	.044
South	2079	-.043	-.053	-.060
West	682	-.057	-.040	-.040
Age at Marriage				
<18 years	1640	-.066	.009	.008
18-19	2287	-.017	-.001	-.001
20-21	1392	.044	.012	.013
22-24	707	.059	-.023	-.023
25-29	259	.123	-.030	-.032
30+	63	.205	-.077	-.074
Initial Parity				
0	1234	.249	.120	.117
1	836	.261	.110	.109
2	1409	-.091	-.096	-.097
3	1211	-.155	-.072	-.071
4+	1658	-.127	-.010	-.007
Duration Since First Marriage				
<3 years	623	.117	.020	.015
3-5.9 years	724	.508	.431	.430
6-8.9 years	784	.237	.242	.242
9-11.9 years	959	.020	.056	.057
12-14.9 years	1095	-.130	-.095	-.093
15-17.9 years	996	-.224	-.201	-.200
18-20.9 years	831	-.226	-.208	-.209
21-23.9 years	312	-.267	-.256	-.256
24+ years	24	-.382	-.456	-.447

Grand Mean = .382

[1] Variables included in the model: wife's education, husband's income, husband's occupation, race, region of residence, age at marriage, initial parity, and duration since first marriage.

[2] Variables included in the model: same as Model 1 except that husband's occupation has been deleted.

[3] The following occupational categories are included in the analysis but are not shown separately here because the number of couples is small: farm manager, allocated farmer and farm manager, farm foreman and armed forces.

168

wives of men with very low incomes to have somewhat lower fertility than the wives of men with higher incomes, but the differentials are small and irregular. The strong positive relationship between income and fertility that was found among urban whites is not found among these women.

Whether gross or net deviations are examined, blacks have substantially higher fertility than whites. When other confounding factors are controlled, the recent fertility rate for rural farm blacks is about 50% greater than that of rural farm whites. If the analysis is further restricted to rural farm residents whose husbands are in farm occupations, the black/white differential becomes even stronger (not shown). (The Southern black rural farm population has been examined in greater detail in Chapter 6.)

The lowest fertility is found for women living in the South, with women living in the West having somewhat higher fertility, and women in the Northeast and North Central regions having the highest fertility levels. These differentials are rather substantial for regional differentials. The Southern women's rates are about .05 below the mean, while the North Central women's rates are about .04 above the mean.

There is a very little net differential in fertility by age at first marriage for marriage ages up through age 21. After age 21, there is a slight decline in fertility, but, overall, the differentials are still small. Since 84% of the sample of rural farm wives married before age 22, the differential by age at first marriage is not very significant substantively.

Couples with no children or with only one child in 1967 had rates of fertility in the next 3 years substantially greater than those who had two or three children in 1967. Women with an initial parity of four or more children have recent fertility rates close to the grand mean.

With respect to marriage duration, both the gross and net deviations are as expected. The level of recent fertility increases from the first 3 years of marriage to the third through fifth years; after the sixth year of marriage, the level of recent fertility steadily declines until it reaches a minimum for those married 24 or more years. As expected, and as consistently found in other chapters, the relationship between recent fertility and duration since first marriage is quite strong.

RURAL/URBAN DIFFERENCES IN THE AGE PATTERNS OF FERTILITY

This final section utilizes the annual age-specific fertility rates to examine rural/urban differences in the age pattern of fertility. The emphasis will be on differences that existed in 1965; but it should be noted that the same pattern of differences is found in other years as well. As before, when using the annual

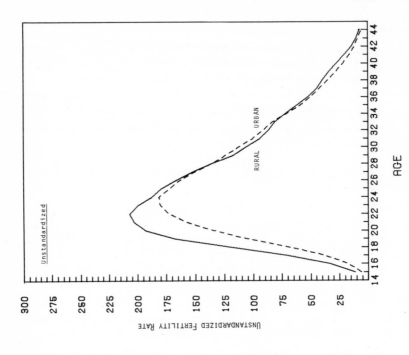

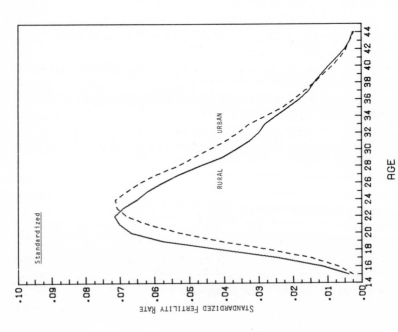

FIGURE 7-5 Standardized and unstandardized fertility schedules for rural and urban white women: 1965.

TABLE 7-6

Mean Age and Standard Deviation of Fertility Schedule, and Percent
of Total Fertility Occurring before Age 25 and before Age 30, by
Rural-Urban Status and Education Group: 1965.

Rural-Urban Status	Education (in years)				
	Total[a]	5-8	9-11	12	13+
			Mean Age		
Rural	25.88	24.83	24.15	25.95	27.81
Urban	26.57	24.89	24.57	26.36	28.15
			Standard Deviation		
Rural	6.09	6.48	6.19	5.90	5.37
Urban	5.81	6.26	6.18	5.71	5.19
	Percent of Total Fertility Occurring before Age 25				
Rural	48	55	61	48	30
Urban	42	54	57	45	27
	Percent of Total Fertility Occurring before Age 30				
Rural	74	77	81	74	66
Urban	74	77	79	73	64

[a]Total includes women with 0-4 years of education.

age-specific fertility rates, rural women are basically those who reside in places with less than 2500 inhabitants. Urban women are those who reside in places of 2500 or more.

In this section, both standardized and unstandardized fertility schedules are used. Differences in the standardized schedules are solely the result of timing differences; differences in the unstandardized schedules reflect both differences in timing and differences in levels of fertility.

The standardized and unstandardized fertility schedules for all white rural and urban women are shown in Figure 7-5. Rural women have an earlier pattern of fertility than urban women (see the standardized schedules and Table 7-6), and this is primarily the result of rural women having higher rates of fertility at the younger ages (see the unstandardized schedules). At the older ages, rural and urban women have almost identical levels of fertility. Within the various education groups, rural women consistently have a younger pattern of childbearing than urban women (not shown), but the differences are small.

SUMMARY

Overall, rural women experienced an elevation in fertility beginning after World War II and continuing through the late 1950s. A subsequent decline in fertility then began, continuing through the 1960s and, apparently, into the 1970s. However, the rural increase in fertility during the 1950s was substantially less than that experienced by urban women during the same time period. As a result, there was a contraction in the traditional rural/urban fertility differential. This contraction took place within each education subgroup except college-educated women.

Not only did rural women have a comparatively small increase in fertility during the 1950s, but also, among older, less-educated rural women, there was an actual decrease in fertility levels. Among all the racial and socioeconomic groups that have been examined, these rural women constitute the only group that registered a decrease in fertility during the so-called "baby boom." The introduction of moderately effective contraceptives probably accounts for this countervailing trend.

During the 1960s, the rates of fertility decline were virtually identical for rural and urban residents, and this is true within most education groups as well. Indeed, the pervasiveness of the decline in fertility during the 1960s is striking. With one trivial exception, every subgroup we looked at showed a decline in fertility. The pervasiveness of the decline and the similarity between the urban and rural sectors suggest that similar factors have affected both rural and urban period fertility trends, even though the differential between the two groups persists.

Within the resident farm population, a number of differentials in recent levels of fertility were found. Wives of men employed in farming have higher current fertility than wives of men who are not employed in farming. Education of wife is inversely related to recent fertility. Black farm residents have higher levels of current fertility than white farm residents, a differential that increases when the analysis is restricted to rural farm residents whose husbands are in farm occupations.

8

Fertility and Migration:
The Case of Puerto Rico

The effect of migration on fertility is primarily of interest when the areas of origin and destination differ with respect to reproductive norms and behavior. Typically, the area of origin is one of high fertility and the area of destination is one of low fertility. It is expected that migration itself and exposure to the milieu of low fertility will bring about lower fertility among migrants than among their nonmigrant contemporaries at place of origin. It is also expected that, having been socialized in an area of high reproductive norms and behavior, migrants will have higher fertility than their nonmigrant contemporaries at place of destination.

Of these two propositions, the latter has received greater research attention— for reasons of data availability. Since censuses and surveys are geographically bounded, it is quite common to have migrants and comparable nonmigrants at place of destination included in the same census or survey. However, migrants and comparable nonmigrants at place of origin are not included in the same census or survey unless the distances involved are relatively small.

Previous chapters have not explicitly treated migration, because the principal migration streams in the contemporary United States involve areas of similar fertility levels and norms. Puerto Ricans, however, provide an interesting example of migration between areas with different fertility levels: the migration of Puerto Ricans to the United States mainland. In this chapter, the fertility of Puerto Ricans who migrated to the United States is compared with the fertility of their nonmigrant counterparts who remained in Puerto Rico. We examine the effect on fertility of the migration itself and the subsequent exposure to a low-fertility milieu, rather than contrasting migrants with their neighbors. To do this, we have combined the 1-in-a-100 Public Use Sample of the 1970 census for the Commonwealth of Puerto Rico with the records of all United States-resident

Puerto Ricans from the 1-in-a-100 Public Use Sample for the 1970 United States census.

Since the 1940s, Puerto Rico has been characterized demographically by comparatively low mortality and high but persistently declining fertility rates. As a result, Puerto Rico has experienced high rates of natural increase. With the exception of the past few years, the annual rate of natural increase has been consistently above 2% since 1940. Rapid rates of natural increase, high rates of unemployment and underemployment, and the mechanization of agriculture have been the primary impetuses for migration. Industrial development in the urban areas of the island and the availability of employment on the mainland also have been contributing factors. The fact that Puerto Ricans are United States citizens and the advent of air transit between Puerto Rico and cities on the mainland have facilitated migration to the United States. Inexpensive and rapid transportation between Puerto Rico and New York (approximately $75, one way, as of this writing) has allowed for convenient return migration as well.

Previous research examining the issue of migration and fertility for Puerto Rico has been concerned with rural-to-urban migration (Myers and Morris, 1966; Macisco, Bouvier, and Renzi, 1969; Macisco, Bouvier, and Weller, 1970). However, this research has been restricted to Puerto Ricans residing on the island. This is problematic because an increasing proportion of all Puerto Ricans do not reside in Puerto Rico (Zarate and Zarate, 1974; Taeuber, 1966). As can be seen from Table 8-1, in 1970, fully 33% of all Puerto Ricans were residing in the United States.

TABLE 8-1

Percentage Distribution of Persons of Puerto Rican Birth, Parentage, or Residence, by Residence: 1950, 1960, 1970.

Residence	Percent			Numbers (in thousands)		
	1950	1960	1970	1950	1960	1970
Total	100.0	100.0	100.0	2512	3242	4103
Puerto Rico	88.0	72.5	66.1	2210	2349	2712
U.S. Mainland	12.0	27.5	33.9	301	893	1391
Puerto Rican born	9.0	19.0	19.7	226	617	810
Puerto Rican parentage	3.0	8.5	14.2	75	275	581

Source: U.S. Bureau of the Census, 1970 Census of Population, Puerto Ricans in the United States, PC(2)-1E, Table 1, p. xi; U.S. Bureau of the Census, 1970 Census of Population, Number of Inhabitants, Puerto Rico, PC(1)-A53, Table 1, pp. 53-59.

MEASURING MIGRATION STATUS

The two principal means of obtaining migration data from the 1970 census are by questions on place of birth and questions on place of residence in 1965. Both are used here, but both are unsatisfactory. Place of birth is problematic for a number of reasons. First, there is limited variation: Almost 90% of the Puerto Rican women of childbearing age residing in the United States in 1970 were born in Puerto Rico. Perhaps more critically, place of birth data do not indicate what share of a person's life was spent at the birthplace. Presumably, a large but unknown proportion of Puerto Rican women who grew up on the mainland were born in Puerto Rico. Similarly, it cannot be determined where women born in the United States and currently residing in Puerto Rico spent their formative years.

The question on place of residence in 1965 allows classification of mainland and island residents by whether they lived in Puerto Rico or the United States in 1965. As such, it provides a valuable, but limited, piece of the person's residence history. The liability of having a limited migration history is intensified because the Puerto Rican migration is so fluid. An indication of this can be gained from a question asked on the Census for the Commonwealth of Puerto Rico: All persons were asked whether or not, during the last 5 years, they had lived in the United States at any time for 6 months or more. Comparing the answers to this question with those on place of residence in 1965 shows that 40% of the current island residents who had lived in the United States for 6 months or more in the past 5 years were not living in the United States in 1965. Thus, place of residence in 1965 markedly underestimates recent migration; and, more seriously, it provides no information on migrations of longer duration.

Place of birth and place of residence in 1965 relate to migration between Puerto Rico and the mainland. Unfortunately, effective examination of the metropolitan/nonmetropolitan dimension of Puerto Rican migration is impossible. First, for Puerto Ricans who migrated to the mainland, place of origin with respect to metropolitan status was not coded. They are simply coded as missing data because they did not live within the United States in 1965.

Second, the 1970 Commonwealth Census classifies all current island residents who lived in the United States in 1965 as having a nonmetropolitan place of residence in 1965. Since the vast majority of these women were living in New York City in 1965, the code presumably is meant to indicate that the person was not living in a *Puerto Rican* metropolitan area in 1965. Nevertheless, the group of island residents classified as nonmetropolitan in 1965 contains an unusable mixture of former metropolitan island residents and former nonmetropolitan and metropolitan mainland residents. As a result of these coding practices, we cannot explicitly examine the migration and fertility relationship for rural-to-urban migration. Rather, the principal concern here will be with the influence of residence on the mainland vis-à-vis residence on the island.

OTHER METHODOLOGICAL CONCERNS

Two dependent variables will be used. The first, a measure of recent or current fertility, is the number of own children under 3 years of age, which has been used extensively in this monograph. The second measure, one of cumulative fertility, is the number of children ever born to the woman. Unless otherwise noted, the tabulations presented will be for all Puerto Rican women residing in either the United States or Puerto Rico who are currently married and under 40 years of age.

In the examination of the migration effects, other variables such as age, initial parity, education, and husband's occupation will be controlled by means of a dummy variable multiple regression technique. In the tables presented, deviations from the overall mean are shown. When the results of the various regression analyses are presented, we indicate in the tables which variables are in the model; but the effects of other predictor variables, such as age or education, are not displayed. We note here that these variables generally have the expected relationship to fertility.

The merging of the mainland and island census tapes creates a number of analytical difficulties. The first involves husband's income. The economies of Puerto Rico and the United States are sufficiently dissimilar that the income variable has different meanings in the two censuses even though the same coding procedures are used. Of the island residents, 66% earned less than $4000; the comparable figure for Puerto Rican mainland residents is 25%. For this reason, when utilizing the combined sample, husband's income has not been used; instead, husband's occupation has been relied upon.

It should also be noted that, among single Puerto Rican women, a greater proportion of those living on the mainland than of those living on the island have had children (Table 8-2).[1] For example, 20% of the never-married Puerto Rican women 20–24 years old and residing in the United States have had children, but, among comparable island residents, only 3% have had children. While it may be tempting to examine these comparisons and think about the corrupting influence of New York City, an equally plausible and less pejorative

[1] Allocation rates for the "children ever born" variable among single women are relatively high (see U.S. Bureau of the Census, 1973e: Table A-2; Rockwell, 1975). However, the allocation rates among single Puerto Ricans on the island and among single Puerto Ricans on the mainland are about 40% lower than those for all single U.S. women.

TABLE 8-2

Percentage of Never-Married Puerto Rican Women Who Have Had Children, by Age and Place of Residence: 1970.

Place of Residence	15-19	20-24	25-29
Puerto Rico	1	3	6
United States	4	20	33

explanation is that some of these "never-married" women are actually consensually married—an explicit option on the Puerto Rican census but not on the mainland census schedule. If the latter is the case, then our stateside sample is missing a number of currently married women. However, we expect that the effect of this is minimal.

MIGRATION AND CURRENT FERTILITY

This section contrasts the recent fertility of Puerto Ricans who migrated to the United States with the fertility of those who did not; it is expected that those who migrated will have lower current fertility than those who remained in Puerto Rico. The underlying hypothesis is that migration and the exposure to the reproductive norms and behavior found on the mainland result in lower

TABLE 8-3

Gross and Net Deviations from Mean Number of Children under Age Three by Current Residence and Residence in 1965 for Currently Married Puerto Rican Women under Age 40.

Residence		Gross Deviations	Net Deviations[1]	Number of Women[2]
Current	1965			
U.S.	U.S.	-.012	-.012	1328
U.S.	P.R.	.105	-.010	190
P.R.	P.R.	.013	.020	2159
P.R.	U.S.	-.114	-.074	174
	Grand Mean = .511			

[1]Controlling for age, initial parity, education, and husband's occupation.

[2]Women with missing data on place of residence have been excluded.

current fertility. However, the reverse—lower fertility facilitating migration—cannot be excluded, given the cross-sectional nature of our data.

In Table 8-3, all Puerto Rican women have been classified into four groups on the basis of their place of residence in 1965 and 1970. After the effects of age, initial parity, education of wife, and husband's occupation are accounted for, recent migrants to the mainland, as expected, have lower rates of current fertility than their contemporaries who remained in Puerto Rico. The primary reason for the large difference between the gross and net deviations for recent migrants to the United States is their age distribution; recent migrants to the United States are heavily concentrated at ages 20—29, which are the peak years of fertility.

The residence classification in Table 8-3 is based on the residence history of the wife. If the residence history of the husband is used instead (not shown), essentially the same results are found: The three groups known to have lived in the United States at some time have lower current fertility than those who resided in Puerto Rico at both time periods. If place of birth of the wife is also controlled (not shown), the same results are found.

The lowest current fertility is found among those who recently returned to Puerto Rico. For this group, it is quite possible that the low rates of recent fertility facilitated the return migration, rather than the reverse. Given the present data, we cannot distinguish between these two possibilities.

TABLE 8-4

Gross and Net Deviations from Mean Number of Children under Age 3 by Current Residence, Residence in 1965, and Rural-Urban Residence, for Currently Married Puerto Rican Women under Age 40.

Residence		Gross	Net	Number of
Current	1965	Deviations	Deviations[1]	Women[2]
U.S.	U.S.	−.012	−.013	1328
U.S.	P.R.	.105	−.009	190
Rural P.R.	P.R.	.089	.057	879
Urban P.R.	P.R.	−.039	−.004	1280
P.R.	U.S.	−.114	−.076	174
		Grand Mean = .511		

[1] Controlling for age, initial parity, education, and husband's occupation.

[2] Women with missing data on place of residence have been excluded.

TABLE 8-5

Gross and Net Deviations from Mean Number of Children under
Age 3 by Place of Birth for Currently Married Puerto Rican Women
under Age 40.

Place of Birth	Gross Deviation	Net Deviation[1]	Net Deviation[2]	Number of Women
P.R.	.012	.008	.006	3606
U.S.	-.075	-.077	-.061	328
Other[3]	-.146	-.044	-.020	118
		Grand Mean = .511		

[1] Controlling for age, initial parity, education, and husband's occupation.

[2] Controlling for age, initial parity, education, husband's occupation, and wife's residence history.

[3] "Other" includes foreign-born women as well as those born in other United States possessions.

While the differences are in the expected direction for the other groups, they are very small. Since most of the mainland residents are also currently urban residents, it is possible that what is being attributed to mainland migration might be a function of urban residence. If education, age, initial parity, and husband's occupation are controlled, there are rural/urban differentials: In the past 3 years, rural women have had an average of .54 children, and urban women have had an average of .49 children.

Since 98% of the Puerto Rican mainland residents are also urban residents, both variables should not be entered into the same equation. As an alternative, a new residence history variable has been created that further subdivides the stable island population into its rural and urban components. This is shown in Table 8-4. As before, the lowest levels of net current fertility occur among those who have recently returned to the island, and, as would be expected, the highest levels of fertility are found among stable rural residents of Puerto Rico. Among the other three groups, the net differences are exceptionally small. This suggests that the mainland effects are small.

Table 8-5 shows gross and net deviations for the place of birth categories. Women born in the United States have substantially lower current fertility than comparable women born in Puerto Rico. Even when current residence and residence in 1965 are controlled, the place of birth differential remains. Women whose place of birth was neither the United States nor Puerto Rico have lower current fertility than women who were born in Puerto Rico; a substantial proportion of these women were born in Cuba.

MIGRATION AND CHILDREN EVER BORN

To allow what may perhaps be a rather small effect of migration to the mainland to cumulate and thus become more visible, we next examine the relationship between migration and fertility, using children ever born as the dependent variable. This is done separately for currently married women 35–44 and 45–54 years old. Unfortunately, it is necessary to rely on the classification by current residence and by residence in 1965 and to assume that the overwhelming majority of mainland residents are migrants. For those who migrated in either direction in the 5 years preceding the census, the level of cumulative fertility probably has a greater influence on the migration decision than the migration has on fertility. For this reason, the two categories of recent migrants will be neglected in our discussion. Of course, the problem of fertility affecting the migration decision is a concern for the other categories as well, but, presumably, it is not as serious a concern.

The results of the multiple regression analyses for women 35–44 years old and for women 45–54 years old are shown in Table 8-6. Controlling for education of wife and occupation of husband among women 35–44 years old, long-term mainland residents have had .25 children less than their urban island counterparts. The comparable differential among women 45–54 years old is .90 children. Including place of birth in the model does not change these differentials. Thus, the expected differential between mainland residents and urban island residents is found when the dependent variable is children ever born.

That this relationship between migration and fertility is barely found for a current fertility measure, but is found for a measure of cumulative fertility, suggests two possibilities, both of which are probably partially true. First, the effect is small and thus not very visible on a current fertility measure. Second, as the island industrializes and modernizes, differences between urban sectors of the island and urban sectors of the mainland are decreasing. This reduction in differences has probably increased as the number of former mainland residents has increased. As already noted, one characteristic of the Puerto Rican migration, which began after World War II and has continued through the present, has been the high volume of return migration. Thus, differentials in children ever born probably reflect a series of differentials that have been contracting in recent years. This possibility is consistent with the fact that the differential in number of children ever born was considerably greater among women 45–54 years old than among women 35–44 years old.

TABLE 8-6

Gross and Net Deviations from Mean Number of Children Ever Born by Current Residence and Residence in 1965 for Currently Married Puerto Rican Women Age 35-44 and 45-54.

Residence		Women Age 35-44				Women Age 45-54			
Current	1965	Gross	Net$_1$	Net$_2$	Number of Women[3]	Gross	Net$_1$	Net$_2$	Number of Women[3]
U.S.	U.S.	-.558	-.389	-.412	508	-1.142	-.988	-.977	262
U.S.	P.R.	.431	.203	.204	51	*	*	*	8
Rural P.R.	P.R.	1.488	.827	.826	356	1.801	1.178	1.159	301
Urban P.R.	P.R.	-.414	-.156	-.135	557	-.395	-.089	-.085	436
P.R.	U.S.	-.570	-.315	-.312	58	-1.939	-1.446	-1.405	31
		Grand Mean = 3.984				Grand Mean - 4.455			

[1] Controlling for wife's education and husband's occupation.

[2] Controlling for wife's education, husband's occupation, and place of birth.

[3] Women with missing data on place of residence in 1965 have been excluded.

* N less than 20.

KNOWLEDGE OF ENGLISH AND CURRENT FERTILITY

Another perspective on the influence of the mainland can be gained by examining whether or not the husband or wife can speak English. This information is only available from the Commonwealth Census and not from the stateside census. Thus, the analysis in this section will be restricted to currently married women who resided in Puerto Rico in 1970. The analysis will be further restricted to urban residents in order to remove the rural/urban differences.

On the 20% questionnaire (that is, the long questionnaire given to every fifth household), the respondent was asked, for each member of the household, "Can this person speak English?" Among urban, currently married women under 40, slightly less than 60% of the wives and slightly more than 66% of their husbands can speak English. Of course, this is more than the proportion of island residents who resided in the United States for 6 months or more during the 5 years preceding the census. Presumably, this variable, the ability to speak English, reflects an unknown mix of modernization, education, having sometime resided on the mainland, and having been in contact with people who resided on the mainland. Whether or not the ability to speak English is an indicator of these latter two concepts is of primary interest here; unfortunately, it is impossible to fully separate out the effect of the former two.

When age, initial parity, education, and husband's occupation are controlled, the current fertility level of wives who speak English is .03 below the mean and the level for wives who do not speak English is .04 above the mean (Table 8-7). If the classificatory variable is the husband's ability to speak English, rather than

TABLE 8-7

Gross and Net Deviations from Mean Number of Children under Age 3 by Whether the Wife Can Speak English and by Whether the Husband Can Speak English, for Currently Married Women Residing in Urban Areas of Puerto Rico and under Age 40.

Speak English	Gross Deviation	Net Deviation[1]	Number of Women
Wife			
Yes	−.029	−.030	861
No	.038	.039	663
Husband			
Yes	−.031	−.030	1039
No	.066	.063	485
	Grand Mean = .460		

[1]Controlling for age, initial parity, education, and husband's occupation.

the wife's, somewhat larger differentials appear. These differentials are substantial and do not diminish when husband's income and residence history are entered into the regression model.

SUMMARY

This chapter has examined the relationship between migration and fertility. By combining the census records of Puerto Ricans living in the United States with the census records of Puerto Ricans living in Puerto Rico, it was possible, for the first time, to compare the fertility of migrants with the fertility of comparable nonmigrants at place of origin. The general hypothesis was that migration and residence in a place where low fertility is the norm would result in lower fertility among the migrants than among those who remained at the place of origin.

However, there is essentially no difference between the current fertility of urban island residents and of recent migrants to the mainland when age, initial parity, education, and husband's occupation are controlled. Nor do these groups differ significantly from long-term residents of the United States. There were, however, substantial differences between these three groups and rural island residents, suggesting that what might have originally been attributed to migration is a function of urban residence; thus, little if any effect was found for migration to the mainland.

To see whether or not the effect of migration might be more visible on a measure of cumulative fertility, the relationship between migration and children ever born was examined. The net differences found between long-term mainland residents and their urban island counterparts were substantial, especially among the older cohort. Part of the explanation for different sets of findings is that a comparatively small effect will be more visible on a cumulative measure than on a current measure. However, the difference between the two cohorts suggests that the effect of migration is diminishing. The reason for the diminishing effect is twofold: Puerto Rico is becoming industrialized and modernized, and an ever increasing proportion of the island population has lived on the mainland.

Finally, the relationship between the ability to speak English and current fertility was examined for urban island residents. The results of this analysis are intriguing for the questions they raise, rather than for the answers they provide. It was found that those who speak English have considerably lower levels of current fertility than those who do not, even when such variables as age, initial parity, education, husband's occupation, husband's income, and residence history are controlled. If the ability to speak English is a proxy for either having resided on the mainland or having been in contact with persons who resided on the mainland, then this would suggest that the migration to the mainland has had a somewhat more pervasive effect on the island's fertility than the migration variables themselves indicate. Unfortunately, it is not possible to identify all urban island residents who have ever resided on the mainland.

Although part of the effect of the "ability to speak English" variable is a return migration effect, the principal part of the effect is probably the result of what might be termed "modernism." That sector of the population which is most likely to have acquired the ability to speak English is also the sector most likely to have lower levels of current fertility. As such, the ability to speak English is an indicator of a whole cluster of attitudes and behaviors associated with "being modern." Furthermore, it would be expected that, if a similar measure were available for mainland Puerto Ricans, similar differentials would appear.

In addition to the substantive issues treated by this chapter, it ought to be noted that the option of combining censuses will be increasingly available to researchers examining a variety of migration-related issues. When micro data are used in migration research, the sample or census typically consists only of migrants, or migrants and their new neighbors. Without a comparable sample of the migrants' former neighbors, the analyst dealing with migration is severely limited in the number of substantive issues that can be addressed.

As additional census bureaus or statistical offices release micro census data (Rowe, 1974), it will be possible not only to more adequately address the issue of migration and fertility, but also to address a wide range of other issues. Even though combining national censuses will entail a number of methodological problems that are not ordinarily of concern, such as differential rates of underenumeration or differential patterns of age misstatement,[2] the added analytical power will outweigh the additional steps necessary to ensure comparability.

---

[2] Such problems were not a major concern here because the two censuses being combined were conducted by the same organization and subject to the same quality controls.

9

Similarity and Diversity:
Some Extensions and Implications

A persistent finding throughout this monograph, and perhaps the principal finding of this study, has been the similarity of all social and economic groups with respect to fertility trends. Every group examined, with one exception, experienced a substantial rise in fertility following World War II, continuing throughout the 1950s, and every major group examined had a substantial decline in fertility in the 1960s. Older rural women constitute the only major exception to this pervasiveness of postwar fertility trends in the United States (see Chapter 7). They did not participate in the rise in fertility of the 1950s, but they did experience a substantial decline in fertility in the 1960s.

We did not expect this pervasive participation in postwar fertility fluctuations; rather, we anticipated that some groups would have disproportionately participated in the postwar fluctuations in fertility and that some would not have participated at all. Goldberg (1974), writing on a somewhat different topic, recently noted: "Residence, education, and income typically serve as the starting point in describing the fertility process. We would be puzzled if we encountered data that failed to reveal differences in fertility associated with those variables" (p. 8). We are puzzled; the same rise and decline in fertility has been found for every group that we have been able to examine. Of course, there are differences in the timing of the peak, the amount of the increase, and the size of the decline; these differences have been reported extensively throughout this monograph. However, the same basic trend is found for every group. Previous analysts have focused attention on differences in rates of increase (or decrease); the similarity and pervasiveness of the postwar fertility trends have not received attention.

In a sense, the postwar fertility swings represent unprecedented and sweeping social change. The societal consequences of these fluctuations in period fertility rates are enormous and affect virtually every major social institution. The educational system has had to substantially expand both its physical plant and its faculty, and now, having expanded, it is faced with ever smaller entering cohorts. The marriage market has also experienced shocks. During the 1960s, there were insufficient numbers of eligible males of the appropriate age. In the future, because of the declining birth rates, we can expect the reverse to occur: an insufficient number of females of the appropriate age. Similarly, the economy, the housing market, health care facilities, and other aspects of society have had to and will have to cope with larger and then smaller cohorts. Furthermore, the sheer size of the United States population is substantially larger now than it would have been in the absence of the baby boom.

However, there is also a sense in which the postwar pattern of fertility represents minor changes. On the average, at the individual level, these fertility trends represent the difference between having two children and having three children.[1] From the perspective of the individual couple, this may be viewed as a minor difference (see Goldberg and Coombs, 1963), even though the societal consequences are substantial.

Even though there has been similarity across all social and economic groups in fertility *trends*, there has been considerable diversity in fertility *levels* in every cross section examined. The exact differences among various groups might change from period to period, but the basic cross-sectional patterns observed occur in every cross section. In the remainder of this chapter, we examine the extent to which this similarity in trends and diversity in levels persist in the early part of the 1970s with respect to recent marital fertility; we then discuss the implications and challenges that derive from this finding of the pervasiveness of trends and continuance of cross-sectional differentials.

SIMILARITY AND DIVERSITY IN THE 1970s

In our analysis of data from the 1960 and 1970 censuses, we were able to examine fertility trends and differentials during the 1950s and the 1960s, but we were not able to examine trends and differentials after 1970. The first half of the 1970s has been a period of continued and accelerated fertility decline. For example, the general fertility rate declined from 88 in 1970 to 68 in 1974. In this section, we examine the extent to which both pervasiveness and diversity continued into the 1970s. Although a complete examination of this issue will have to await the 1980 census, it is possible to obtain an indication by using data from the March Current Population Surveys (CPS).

---

[1] Note, however, that many of the changes that occurred were not a shift from two to three children but, rather, were shifts in proportion married, proportion having a first child, and other parity progressions (see Ryder, 1969).

However, before dealing directly with this seemingly straightforward question, it is necessary to discuss CPS data and their comparability with census data. In principle, the CPS and the census should be quite comparable; in practice, however, comparability is imperfect. The Current Population Survey is conducted by enumerators, while the census is largely conducted by self-enumeration. We would assume that the trained CPS enumerators can better classify ambiguous or complex cases, and their presence may exert some moral force on respondents, influencing them to report more carefully and accurately than they might in a self-enumeration.

There are also a number of important differences in the content of the March Current Population Survey and the content of the census. First, the March CPS after 1972 did not contain a question on children ever born. Because of this omission, we have had to redefine initial parity in terms of the difference between the number of own children under 18 years and the number under 3 years of age. This gives it a rather different meaning than the initial parity variable used earlier, and we have reservations about it, because high fertility and the incidence of children leaving the parental home at a young age tend to be related.

Second, the March CPS no longer includes a question on date of first marriage. Consequently, we are unable to classify persons by their age at first marriage or to control for marriage duration. Our alternative was to include age in the analysis rather than marriage duration, but this has the unfortunate consequence that the young age groups are biased toward a young age at marriage (see Chapter 2).

Furthermore, the CPS tape does not have a classification of urban and rural residence. Consequently, it is not possible to look at the urban white population alone. Rather, we have only been able to look at the entire white population.

TABLE 9-1

Number of Own Children under Age 3 per Currently Married Woman under Age 40, by Race: 1968-1975.

Year	White		Black	
	N	Rate	N	Rate
1968	13,743	.441	1,277	.487
1969	14,086	.410	1,202	.449
1970	13,542	.411	1,213	.481
1971	13,606	.414	1,177	.452
1972	12,936	.416	1,133	.452
1973	13,040	.390	1,031	.428
1974	12,635	.355	1,014	.378
1975	12,361	.335	965	.393

Finally, because of the much smaller sample size available from the CPS, it has not been possible to analyze data for the very specific subpopulations, as we did with decennial census data. Our experiences indicated that we can compute reliable estimates of character-specific fertility rates for white married women under age 40. Because of the small sample size, we are not able to compute very reliable estimates for subgroups of black women and therefore have not included the black analyses in this chapter. The tables, however, are included in Appendix D. Table 9-1 shows the number of own children under 3 years of age per currently married woman under age 40 for each year during the period 1968–1975. For white women, the rates from the 1970 CPS are very similar to those found in the 1970 census:

	1970 Census	1970 CPS	Ratio
White	.405	.411	1.01
Black	.436	.481	1.10

In order to increase the available sample sizes, we have pooled the Current Population Surveys for 1969–1971 and for 1974–1975. This gives us sample sizes that are adequate for computing rates for major population subgroups. The reason for pooling the 1974 and 1975 files and not including 1973 is that the most recent two years represent fertility of the post-1970 period, uncontaminated by the higher fertility that occurred through the end of 1970. Thus, we are comparing the experience in the late 1960s (after the decline from baby-boom levels) with that of the recent lower levels of fertility. If we included the 1973 CPS in this later period, some of the fertility measured in the number of own children under 3 years would have occurred prior to the end of 1970.

There were discussions during the early 1970s of the possibility of having a census enumeration during the middle of the decade. This idea had considerable support, but was eventually scrapped. However, Congress has recently approved a 1985 mid-decade census. This research would have greatly benefited from a census enumeration in the mid-1960s and also in the mid-1970s. There has been, in the recent past, and there will undoubtedly continue to be, rapid shifts in the level of cohort fertility and even more rapid shifts in the level and pattern of period fertility. The annual March Current Population Survey samples, which we have utilized, are simply not large enough to make stable estimates of fertility for many of the important subgroups within the population and to understand short-run fluctuations in period fertility. Additionally, the CPS does not contain the range of information available in the census. A complete enumeration, or large sample survey of 1% or 2% of the population of American households that

TABLE 9-2

Percent Decline in Recent Fertility for Currently Married White Women under Age 40: United States, 1969-1971 to 1974-1975.[1]

	N		Percent Decline	
	1969-1971	1974-1975	Crude	Standardized[2]
Age				
<20	1,699	1,141	15.2	
20-24	9,483	5,479	17.7	
25-29	10,901	6,907	16.8	
30-34	9,665	6,157	13.3	
35-39	9,486	5,312	23.4	
Education				
<9 years	3,281	1,473	2.1	4.9
9-11 years	7,488	3,829	13.8	14.4
12 years	20,999	12,523	16.2	16.0
13-15 years	5,441	3,850	20.1	22.2
16+ years	4,024	3,320	20.4	24.1
Region				
Northeast	9,050	5,312	20.0	20.2
North Central	12,071	6,885	18.7	20.1
South	12,382	8,105	12.2	12.7
West	7,730	4,695	12.3	13.3
Metropolitan Residence				
In SMSA				
Central city	9,267	5,768	15.1	16.8
Not central city	16,944	10,822	18.5	19.3
Not in SMSA	15,023	8,406	13.7	14.5
Initial Parity				
0	13,554	8,952	17.7	18.5
1	7,705	5,223	12.3	12.7
2	9,171	5,649	27.6	25.6
3	5,991	3,116	34.7	31.5
4+	4,813	2,056	32.9	30.1
Husband's Income[3]				
<$1,000	688	486	11.7	8.7
$1,000-1,999	868	489	21.7	23.1
$2,000-2,999	1,394	834	8.6	4.5
$3,000-3,999	1,954	1,237	8.1	8.8
$4,000-4,999	2,594	1,666	18.6	20.1
$5,000-7,499	10,312	5,595	14.4	17.6
$7,500-9,999	10,428	5,975	16.6	18.3
$10,000-14,999	9,457	6,138	16.5	17.3
$15,000+	3,539	2,575	16.5	18.7

[1] These rates of decline were computed from the March Current Population Surveys.

[2] Standardized on 1969-1971 age distribution of that group.

[3] Constant 1970 dollars.

TABLE 9-3

Differentials in Recent Fertility for Currently Married White Women under Age 40: United States, 1969-1971 and 1974-1975.[1]

	1969-1971			1974-1975		
		Deviations			Deviations	
	N	Gross	Net[2]	N	Gross	Net[2]
Age						
<20	1,699	.079	.055	1,141	.071	.016
20-24	9,483	.186	.142	5,479	.145	.095
25-29	10,901	.145	.131	6,907	.118	.098
30-34	9,665	-.098	-.065	6,157	-.073	-.035
35-39	9,486	-.267	-.236	5,312	-.234	-.188
Education						
<9 years	3,281	.015	.095	1,473	.073	.140
9-11 years	7,488	.007	.032	3,829	.015	.048
12 years	20,999	-.011	-.019	12,523	-.009	-.009
13-15 years	5,441	.020	-.013	3,850	-.001	-.033
16+ years	4,024	.003	-.020	3,320	-.015	-.047
Region						
Northeast	9,050	.024	.033	5,312	.003	.017
North Central	12,071	.022	.026	6,885	.007	.012
South	12,382	-.035	-.045	8,105	-.014	-.028
West	7,730	-.006	-.006	4,695	.011	.011
Metropolitan Residence						
In SMSA						
Central City	9,267	.010	-.015	5,768	.013	-.012
Not Central City	16,944	-.002	.001	10,822	-.011	-.005
Not in SMSA	15,023	-.004	.009	8,406	.006	.015
Initial Parity						
0	13,554	.129	.061	8,952	.100	.059
1	7,705	.173	.141	5,223	.167	.145
2	9,171	-.123	-.094	5,649	-.136	-.111
3	5,991	-.196	-.126	3,116	-.204	-.147
4+	4,813	-.163	-.061	2,056	-.178	-.098
Husband's Income[3]						
<$1,000	688	-.079	-.148	486	-.051	-.084
$1,000-1,999	868	-.022	-.110	489	-.040	-.121
$2,000-2,999	1,394	-.030	-.124	834	.003	-.058
$3,000-3,999	1,954	.042	-.041	1,237	.072	.002
$4,000-4,999	2,594	.065	-.006	1,666	.042	-.025
$5,000-7,499	10,312	.026	-.011	5,595	.029	-.016
$7,500-9,999	10,428	.015	.013	5,975	.010	.002
$10,000-14,999	9,457	-.024	.032	6,138	-.022	.026
$15,000+	3,539	-.091	.041	2,575	-.077	.040
	Grand Mean = .412			Grand Mean = .345		

[1] This analysis was done from the March Current Population Surveys.

[2] Net of the other variables shown.

[3] Constant 1970 dollars.

gathered complete census information, would have permitted the kind of detailed analysis presented here for the more recent period of rapid fertility decline.

The rate of decline in recent marital fertility among white wives for the period 1969–1971 to 1974–1975 is shown in Table 9-2 for a variety of subgroups. A similar table for blacks is in Appendix D. As was the case during the 1950s and 1960s, the trend in fertility during the first half of the 1970s is found among every social and economic group examined. The fertility decline during the first part of the 1970s was indeed pervasive. Although there are differences in the pace of the decline (which we do not discuss in any detail), the pervasiveness of the decline is unmistakable.

Cross-sectional differentials in levels of fertility also persisted into the 1970s. Table 9-3 shows the results of a multiple regression analysis of differential fertility among white married couples in which the wife was under age 40 for the periods 1969–1971 and 1974–1975. Similar analyses for blacks can be found in Appendix D. The same types of cross-sectional relationships found for the 1950s and the 1960s also tend to be found in the 1970s. Recent fertility is inversely related to age,[2] education, and initial parity, and is directly related to husband's current income. Fertility in the South remained lower than average, and fertility in the Northeast was the highest of the four regions. Thus, during the early part of the 1970s, there was both pervasiveness of fertility trends and persistence of cross-sectional differences.

SOME IMPLICATIONS

To summarize the findings of both this chapter and the entire study, the vast changes in fertility and fertility-related behavior since World War II and continuing through the present are both unprecedented and unpredicted, and they have had important immediate and long-range effects on American society. Furthermore, they are pervasive; that is, those social and economic variables that we have been able to examine with census data, such as race, ethnic status, education, and residence, do not indicate differences with respect to trends in fertility. Yet, these same social and economic variables do tend to differentiate current fertility levels in the cross section.

---

[2] It should be noted that the low fertility of married women under 20 years old, in comparison with married women 20–24 years old, is, in part, the result of our measurement procedure rather than a reflection of reality. We measure the fertility of married couples during the past 3 years. Most women who are under 20 years old have been married a smaller fraction of the past 3 years than those who are older. This is the same problem that was discussed in Chapter 4 with respect to the most recent marriage-duration group.

It might be asked why variables such as race, ethnic status, or education should affect fertility *trends*. The typical time series proposition is formulated as follows: A change in X implies a change in Y. Here, Y is fertility and X is race, ethnic status, or education. Since race, ethnic status, and education tend not to change, why should they be expected to affect changes in fertility? The reason is that race, ethnic status, and education (and other variables, such as income or residence, that are changeable) are "filter" variables; people tend to live their lives within groups whose boundaries are defined by these variables. We would expect that any secular change that affects fertility trends would be filtered through these groups and, therefore, fertility trends would differ among them. That this is not the case suggests that those factors responsible for changes in period fertility during the past 25 or 30 years were sufficiently powerful to permeate every group or, alternatively, that there were a number of factors operating in the same direction and that some operated on certain social groups and some operated on others. Undoubtedly, both possibilities are partially true.

It should be noted that the expected "filtering" effect of race and education is different from the more common compositional explanation to which these variables are put. The compositional explanation accounts for changes over time in some dependent variable by showing that the total population is changing with respect to the proportion of the population in each of the various categories of some predictor variable known to be related to the dependent variable. For example, education is inversely related to fertility in the cross section. Thus, an upgrading in the educational attainment of the population would be expected to bring about a reduction in fertility. This type of compositional explanation is not applicable to the fertility trends of the past 25 years, because the same *trend* is found within each group examined.

The fact that these trends were so universal suggests what the nature of the causes of these trends must be, but it does not indicate to us what those causes might be. The pervasiveness of the fertility trend suggests that the explanations needed must be of a broad and historical nature. "Broad" here refers to factors that cut across boundaries of the social structure, and "historical" implies explanations that refer to specific events or series of events. Such explanations are not uncommon in the literature; examples would include the relative prosperity of the 1950s, the introduction of the pill, or the growing impact of the women's movement.

The problem with such explanations is that they generally are ex post facto; in the short run, there is not sufficient variation to test these explanations, and they tend not to aid in the prediction of future events. (See Spilerman, 1975, for a more detailed discussion of the various problems.) However, the difficulties involved in historical explanations should not dissuade demographers from pursuing them, because, as the results of our study suggest, "historical" factors are most likely to be responsible for the recent wide fluctuations in period fertility—fluctuations that have had a substantial impact on virtually every social institution.

Because future research will have to contend with examining and testing "historical" explanations, such research would be aided considerably by the extension of the time span of fertility data available for various social and economic subgroups. The passage of time alone will partially remedy this situation, because, within 5 years, data tapes from the 1980 census ought to be available. However, the search for plausible explanations would be greatly aided by having data covering the period preceding World War II. A number of social scientists are currently preparing a proposal that would create large public use files from the 1940 and 1950 censuses.[3] Such files, in addition to data from the 1960, 1970, and 1980 censuses, would permit construction of annual fertility rates for various groups for the period 1925–1979.

We close this monograph on the somewhat pessimistic note that, since the types of explanations needed for recent fertility fluctuations must be "broad" and "historical," such explanations are very difficult to verify. But we can also be somewhat optimistic, inasmuch as it may soon be possible to have a detailed reconstruction of social fertility rates reaching back to the late 1920s. It would then be possible to put the high fertility of the baby-boom period into better historical perspective and to begin to better understand the nature of the baby boom as it occurred for subgroups within the population. It would also be possible to compare and contrast low fertility during the depression years with that of the 1970s.

---

[3] In June 1976, a conference was held in Madison, Wisconsin, to discuss the creation of public use sample tapes from the 1940 and 1950 United States Censuses. The conference organizers, William Mason, Halliman Winsborough, and Karl Taeuber, are currently preparing a research proposal for this project.

Appendix A

Urban White Recent
Marital Fertility Differentials

TABLE A-1

Gross and Net Deviations from Mean Number of Children under Age 3 for Currently Married Women under Age 40, for Various Characteristics: Urban White Population, 1960 and 1970.

	1970				1960			
	N	Gross	Net_1	Net_2	N	Gross	Net_1	Net_2
Education								
<5 years	129	.012	.140	.128	144	.117	.192	.185
5-8 years	860	-.012	.074	.068	1409	-.052	.035	.032
9-11 years	2310	.013	.062	.061	2887	-.015	-.006	-.006
12 years	6255	.005	-.006	-.005	5622	.013	-.003	-.002
13-15 years	1933	-.029	-.058	-.057	1449	.012	-.005	-.004
16+ years	1460	.003	-.051	-.050	875	.013	-.041	-.044
Husband's Occupation								
Professional	2409	.025		.017	1803	.059		.019
Manager	1504	-.051		-.022	1399	-.088		-.026
Sales	956	.008		.009	934	-.006		.012
Clerical	882	-.053		-.060	878	.019		-.022
Craftsman	2705	-.003		-.005	2600	-.029		-.005
Operative	1454	.050		.017	2333	.007		-.005
Transport	656	.006		.014				
Laborer	446	.084		.076	489	.109		.059
Farmer	18	*		*	29	-.115		-.010
Farm laborer	36	.157		.187	37	.147		.228
Service	605	.017		.024	499	-.014		.007
Unemployed	263	.000		.012	323	.057		.054
Armed forces	585	-.019		-.010	451	.061		.019
Not in labor force	428	-.125		-.080	254	-.044		-.027
Occupation not reported					357	-.050		-.068

Duration Since First Marriage								
<3 years	2514	.005	-.035	-.036	1849	.028	.071	.071
3-5.9 years	2162	.356	.298	.296	2007	.494	.510	.509
6-8.9 years	1998	.187	.189	.189	1813	.229	.248	.247
9-11.9 years	1869	-.050	-.011	-.010	1981	-.049	-.046	-.046
12-14.9 years	1711	-.176	-.131	-.130	2226	-.225	-.235	-.235
15-17.9 years	1468	-.264	-.227	-.225	1360	-.315	-.349	-.348
18-20.9 years	951	-.305	-.288	-.285	899	-.372	-.436	-.434
21-23.9 years	248	-.318	-.320	-.316	233	-.400	-.497	-.494
24+ years	26	-.245	-.241	-.237	18	*	*	*
Age at Marriage								
<18	2365	-.024	.043	.042	2243	.012	.078	.079
18-19	3916	.014	.033	.033	3320	.011	.030	.030
20-21	3357	.005	-.003	-.003	3154	-.007	.002	.002
22-24	2282	-.011	-.047	-.046	2302	-.012	-.031	-.032
25-29	848	.005	-.101	-.101	1105	-.006	-.123	-.121
30-39	179	.026	.151	-.152	262	-.021	-.279	-.280
Initial Parity								
0	4435	.133	.105	.107	3816	.144	-.001	-.001
1	2297	.186	.064	.063	2564	.123	.024	.025
2	2675	-.112	-.104	-.105	3064	-.147	-.063	-.063
3	1868	-.205	-.122	-.122	1719	-.158	.002	.002
4+	1672	-.202	-.065	-.066	1223	-.116	.108	.107
Region of Residence								
Northeast	3096	.021	.022	.021	3319	.006	.013	.014
North Central	3553	.019	.012	.010	3590	.021	.019	.019
South	3537	-.024	-.020	-.017	3143	-.038	-.039	-.038
West	2761	-.017	-.014	-.015	2334	.012	.004	.001

continued

TABLE A-1 continued

	1970				1960			
	N	Gross	Net$_1$	Net$_2$	N	Gross	Net$_1$	Net$_2$
Metropolitan Residence								
In SMSA	9674	.006	.002	.002	9054	-.005	-.008	-.008
Outside SMSA	2194	-.021	-.010	-.012	2292	-.007	.008	.007
Not ascertained**	1079	-.008	.005	.005	1040	.058	.053	.055
Constant Dollar Husband's Income								
<$1,000	383	-.124	-.151	-.130	312	-.090	-.137	-.140
$1,000-1,999	452	-.036	-.104	-.091	474	-.018	-.096	-.103
$2,000-2,999	555	-.042	-.124	-.121	822	.064	-.035	-.040
$3,000-3,999	1031	.034	-.037	-.040	1399	.062	-.015	-.018
$4,000-4,999	1078	.039	-.019	-.020	1916	.025	-.022	-.022
$5,000-7,499	4018	.025	-.007	-.009	4892	-.003	.011	.012
$7,500-9,999	3017	.014	.041	.041	1489	-.024	.055	.055
$10,000+	2413	-.056	.057	.056	1082	-.092	.044	.047
			Grand Mean =	.398			Grand Mean =	.529

[1]All variables shown in the table with the exception of husband's occupation are included in the model.

[2]All variables shown in the table, including husband's occupation, are included in the model.

*N less than 20.

**Not available for states in which the metropolitan or nonmetropolitan population is less than 250,000.

Appendix B

Stability of Racial Estimates
of Annual Fertility Rates

In Chapter 2, own-children estimates of white and black fertility rates were compared with recorded vital statistics rates. The focus was on the effect of departures from the four basic assumptions of own-children data; it was seen that departures from these four assumptions tended to affect the level of own-children estimates, but not the trend of fertility. Since two successive decennial censuses are used for blacks and whites, it is possible, for 5 calendar years (1955–1959), to compare the two estimates for each racial group (see Chapter 3). This comparison speaks to two questions: (*a*) Are the characteristics of the women stable over time, and (*b*) are departures from the four assumptions approximately constant over time. Since race is presumably fixed, by comparing the two sets of estimates for the overlap period, we can see whether or not there are substantial net departures from the constancy assumption.

Table B-1 presents the ratio of the 1960 census estimates to the 1970 census estimates for the 5-year overlap period for whites and blacks. Looking first at the upper panel, it can be seen that the ratio for each white comparison is close to unity. In only one comparison is the ratio as low as .93, and in only three cases is it as high as 1.06. For blacks (lower panel), however, two things can be noticed. In the first place, the deviations from unity tend to be greater than those found for whites, largely because of greater sampling errors. Second, and more intriguing, the ratios for women 15–19 years old are substantially below unity. And not only are they below unity, but they also tend to get progressively lower from 1955 to 1959 (the ages of the women on which the ratios are based decrease from 1955 to 1959).

TABLE B-1

Ratio of 1960 Census Estimates to 1970 Census Estimates for Five-Year Overlap (1955-1959): Whites and Blacks.

Racial Group and Years	Age Specific Fertility Rate Comparisons						Total Fertility Rate Comparison
	15-19	20-24	25-29	30-34	35-39	40-44	
White							
1959	1.00	1.03	1.03	1.04	1.05	.93	1.03
1958	1.01	1.06	1.03	1.06	1.04	1.03	1.04
1957	1.01	1.06	1.01	1.01	1.00	.97	1.02
1956	1.00	1.04	1.03	1.01	1.00	.97	1.02
1955	1.02	1.04	1.01	1.03	.99	.99	1.02
Black							
1959	.66	.96	1.09	1.03	1.08	.93	.96
1958	.81	.99	1.11	1.13	.99	.92	1.01
1957	.81	.94	1.01	1.07	.87	1.15	.96
1956	.85	1.04	.98	.97	1.00	.99	.98
1955	.87	.98	.95	1.03	.95	.96	.96

TABLE B-2

Ratio of 1960 Census Estimates to 1970 Census Estimates for Five-Year Overlap (1955-1959): Single Year Age-Specific Fertility Rate Comparisons, Black Women.

Years Being Compared	Age					
	15	16	17	18	19	20
1959	.31	.54	.67	.68	.83	.94
1958	.59	.62	.71	.95	.98	.91
1957	.57	.70	.82	.86	.90	.87
1956	.63	.83	.87	.87	.90	.99
1955	.82	.89	.82	.83	.90	.96

To further investigate this issue, we calculated the same ratios for blacks using single-year age-specific rates, instead of the usual 5-year rates (Table B-2). It can be seen that, as age increases (reading either horizontally or vertically), the ratio of the two estimates approaches unity. Our suspicion is that, in the case of illegitimate childbearing occurring to 15- and 16-year-old black women,[1] there is a tendency for the biological mother not to be recorded as the "mother" of the child until the biological mother reaches ages 18, 19, or 20. This phenomenon could take a number of different patterns, all of which stem from the fact that a 15- or 16-year-old mother is generally ill-equipped to take care of a child. One possible pattern is that the biological mother and child live with the child's maternal grandmother, forming a three-generation household—probably the biological mother is attending school and the oldest generation is responsible for the infant's care. Under such circumstances, it is quite possible that the infant is reported as the "grandmother's" child rather than as the "mother's" child (note the comparatively high ratios for black women 40–44 years old: Table B-1). As the "mother" ages (and finishes school), she may leave her parents' household (perhaps to get married), bringing her child with her. In this case, it would be expected that the child would be correctly reported as the "mother's" child. Another possible pattern is that the child might be raised for a few years by a friend or relative until the biological mother is in a position to raise the child. Again, it may be expected that the child would be reported as the "friend's" or "relative's" child rather than as the "mother's" child. The point is that there appears to be, from the point of view of the census user, a pattern of young biological mothers becoming social "non-mothers" and then, subsequently, becoming social mothers.

There is another possibility that could explain the pattern in Table B-2: Black women who become mothers at ages 15, 16, and, to some extent, 17 are likely

---

[1] Illegitimate fertility is a substantial portion of all childbearing occurring to black women 15 and 16 years old.

to be underenumerated by the census until they reach ages 18, 19, or 20. Both explanations are probably operating.

In summary, the rates from the 1970 census and the 1960 census are remarkably close, with the exception of those for young black women. The closeness of the rates suggests that departures from the four basic assumptions have not changed appreciably over time. The exception for young black women is probably the result of both their living arrangements and the census enumeration procedure. Unfortunately, it is not possible to see whether or not the same degree of correspondence holds for the minority groups examined in Chapter 5, because the requisite sample sizes are not available from the 1960 census.

Appendix C

Differentials in Recent
Marital Fertility within Various
Racial and Ethnic Groups: 1960

TABLE C-1

Gross and Net Deviations from Mean Number of Children under Age 3
for Currently Married Women under Age 40, for Various Character-
istics: Southern Rural Black Population, 1960.

		Deviation from Grand Mean		
	N	Gross	Net$_1$	Net$_2$
Education				
<5 years	450	-.029	.018	.016
5-8 years	1416	.000	-.008	-.006
9-11 years	898	.094	.045	.045
12 years	460	-.077	-.058	-.058
13-15 years	65	-.126	-.004	-.015
16+ years	63	-.438	-.171	-.170
Age at Marriage				
<18	1245	.084	.139	.139
18-19	830	.047	.042	.040
20-21	576	-.049	-.033	-.032
22-24	421	-.121	-.189	-.184
25-29	215	-.170	-.318	-.321
30+	65	-.418	-.637	-.630
Husband's Occupation				
Professional	51	-.273	.006	
Manager	15	*	*	
Sales	13	*	*	
Clerical	27	-.025	.072	
Craftsman	229	-.078	-.010	
Operative } Transport	727	.014	-.007	
Laborer	666	.011	.008	
Farmer	434	.073	.090	
Farm laborer	615	.056	.004	
Service	153	-.208	-.148	
Unemployed	147	.027	.013	
Armed forces	31	.036	.068	
Not in labor force	172	-.111	-.091	
Constant Dollar Husband's Income				
<$1,000	1130	.039	.018	.030
$1,000-1,999	924	.052	.015	.016
$2,000-2,999	701	-.001	.001	-.011
$3,000-3,999	342	-.098	-.043	-.055
$4,000-4,999	164	-.199	-.048	-.056
$5,000-7,499	83	-.285	-.137	-.139
$7,500+	8	*	*	*

Grand Mean = .803

[1] Variables included in the model: wife's education, age at
marriage, husband's income, husband's occupation, initial parity,
duration since first marriage, and times wife has been married.

[2] Variables included in the model: same as Model 1 except that
husband's occupation has been deleted.

* N less than 20.

TABLE C-2

*Gross and Net Deviations from Mean Number of Children under Age 3
for Currently Married Women under Age 40, for Various Characteristics: Non-Southern Black Population, 1960.*

| | | Deviation from Grand Mean | | |
	N	Gross	Net$_1$	Net$_2$
Education				
<5 years	181	-.040	-.000	.001
5-8 years	1523	-.050	.001	.006
9-11 years	2428	.070	.019	.020
12 years	2333	-.020	-.018	-.020
13-15 years	615	-.034	-.003	-.009
16+ years	249	-.080	-.009	-.019
Age at Marriage				
<18	1964	.070	.153	.154
18-19	1719	.063	.080	.080
20-21	1374	-.018	-.032	-.032
22-24	1266	-.050	-.086	-.088
25-29	770	-.132	-.231	-.231
30+	236	-.230	-.458	-.456
Husband's Occupation				
Professional	275	-.068	-.034	
Manager	128	-.052	.021	
Sales	91	-.016	.005	
Clerical	562	-.013	-.017	
Craftsman	792	-.083	-.050	
Operative } Transport	1991	.015	.007	
Laborer	988	.055	.045	
Farmer	12	*	*	
Farm laborer	40	.102	.053	
Service	792	-.024	-.013	
Unemployed	575	.045	.030	
Armed forces	209	.138	-.004	
Not in labor force	316	-.051	-.013	
Constant Dollar Husband's Income				
<$1,000	516	-.023	-.080	-.075
$1,000-1,999	573	.051	-.024	-.020
$2,000-2,999	993	.040	-.020	-.017
$3,000-3,999	1546	.053	.031	.031
$4,000-4,999	1631	-.023	.000	.001
$5,000-7,499	1836	-.043	.011	.008
$7,500+	234	-.094	.021	.010

Grand Mean = .598

[1]Variables included in the model: wife's education, age at
marriage, husband's income, husband's occupation, initial parity,
duration since first marriage, and times wife has been married.

[2]Variables included in the model: same as Model 1 except that
husband's occupation has been deleted.

*
 N less than 20.

TABLE C-3

Gross and Net Deviations from Mean Number of Children under Age 3 for Currently Married Women under Age 40, for Various Characteristics: Southern Urban Black Population, 1960.

| | | Deviation from Grand Mean | | |
	N	Gross	Net$_1$	Net$_2$
Education				
<5 years	337	-.130	-.029	-.028
5-8 years	1610	-.034	-.030	-.025
9-11 years	1840	.100	.041	.042
12 years	1325	-.003	-.002	-.003
13-15 years	298	-.066	-.027	-.034
16+ years	273	-.230	-.026	-.049
Age at Marriage				
<18	1789	.121	.191	.191
18-19	1343	.021	.037	.040
20-21	997	-.035	-.039	-.038
22-24	823	-.060	-.107	-.111
25-29	557	-.177	-.295	-.296
30+	174	-.356	-.572	-.579
Husband's Occupation				
Professional	222	-.166	-.056	
Manager	70	-.258	-.126	
Sales	55	-.007	.055	
Clerical	282	-.012	.044	
Craftsman	578	-.031	-.017	
Operative	1477	.056	.040	
Laborer	1203	.043	.022	
Farmer	10	*	*	
Farm laborer	84	.095	.037	
Service	745	-.050	-.051	
Unemployed	302	.006	.010	
Armed forces	144	.086	.011	
Not in labor force	217	-.100	-.085	
Constant Dollar Husband's Income				
<$1,000	548	.012	-.006	-.020
$1,000-1,999	1008	.089	.042	.040
$2,000-2,999	1760	.032	-.006	-.005
$3,000-3,999	1146	-.008	.005	.007
$4,000-4,999	706	-.095	-.043	-.038
$5,000-7,499	451	-.162	-.028	-.022
$7,500+	64	-.018	.141	.125

Grand Mean = .644

[1] Variables included in the model: wife's education, age at marriage, husband's income, husband's occupation, initial parity, duration since first marriage, and times wife has been married.

[2] Variables included in the model: same as Model 1 except that husband's occupation has been deleted.

206

TABLE C-4

Gross and Net Deviations from Mean Number of Children under Age 3 for Currently Married Women under Age 40, for Various Characteristics: Spanish Surname Population, 1960.

	N	Deviation from Grand Mean		
		Gross	Net$_1$	Net$_2$
Education				
<5 years	728	.083	.102	.120
5-8 years	1312	.032	.034	.036
9-11 years	874	-.015	-.039	-.046
12 years	807	-.087	-.084	-.095
13-15 years	144	-.046	-.048	-.059
16+ years	62	-.194	-.145	-.155
Age at Marriage				
<18	1172	.046	.076	.079
18-19	1025	-.020	.015	.015
20-21	738	.042	.039	.038
22-24	605	-.083	-.099	-.100
25-29	290	-.016	-.121	-.124
30+	97	-.105	-.397	-.407
Husband's Occupation				
Professional	188	-.068	-.004	
Manager	153	-.180	-.076	
Sales	121	-.180	-.111	
Clerical	182	-.077	-.048	
Craftsman	673	-.069	-.020	
Operative	972	.008	-.012	
Laborer	513	.069	.024	
Farmer	70	-.061	.079	
Farm laborer	323	.237	.170	
Service	210	-.113	-.087	
Unemployed	199	.114	.067	
Armed forces	81	.089	.019	
Not in labor force	113	.012	-.005	
Constant Dollar Husband's Income				
<$1,000	324	.046	-.027	-.004
$1,000-1,999	474	.109	.003	.037
$2,000-2,999	644	.096	.025	.028
$3,000-3,999	631	.044	.023	.020
$4,000-4,999	643	-.001	.020	.011
$5,000-7,499	937	-.100	-.034	-.049
$7,500+	274	-.228	-.013	-.030

Grand Mean = .775

[1]Variables included in the model: wife's education, age at marriage, husband's income, husband's occupation, initial parity, duration since first marriage, and times wife has been married.

[2]Variables included in the model: same as Model 1 except that husband's occupation has been deleted.

Appendix D

Post-1970 Fertility Trends
and Differentials within
the Black Population

TABLE D-1

Percent Decline in Recent Fertility for Currently Married Black Women under Age 40: United States, 1969-1971 to 1974-1975.[1]

	1969- 1971	1974- 1975	Percent Decline	
			Crude	Stan- dard- ized[2]
Age				
<20	199	108	17.7	
20-24	863	446	16.8	
25-29	911	521	12.9	
30-34	833	492	11.9	
35-39	786	412	24.2	
Education				
<9 years	427	178	45.4	40.9
9-11 years	1,103	453	19.2	19.0
12 years	1,511	909	6.9	8.8
13-15 years	340	289	10.5	5.9
16+ years	211	150	-11.8	-10.7
Region				
Northeast	695	355	10.8	4.6
North Central	838	410	19.6	19.1
South	1,749	1,014	16.8	18.4
West	310	199	19.1	12.4
Metropolitan Residence				
In SMSA				
Central city	2,071	1,116	11.1	10.0
Not central city	651	405	17.2	18.7
Not in SMSA	870	458	25.7	24.8
Initial Parity				
0	1,186	633	5.9	6.4
1	657	462	14.5	14.9
2	609	353	27.3	24.6
3	436	233	52.2	49.2
4+	705	297	21.7	9.3
Husband's Income[3]				
<$3,000	496	289	4.6	- 1.3
$3,000-3,999	451	174	16.3	18.9
$4,000-4,999	521	270	30.2	32.5
$5,000-7,499	1,167	574	20.1	18.1
$7,500-9,999	633	421	10.3	11.1
$10,000+	323	250	4.5	8.9

[1] These rates of decline were computed from the March Current Population Surveys.

[2] Standardized on the 1969-1971 age distribution of the group.

[3] Constant 1970 dollars.

TABLE D-2.

Differentials in Recent Fertility for Currently Married Black Women under Age 40: United States, 1969-1971 and 1974-1975.[1]

	1969-1971			1974-1975		
		Deviations			Deviations	
	N	Gross	Net[2]	N	Gross	Net[2]
Age						
<20	199	.400	.381	108	.322	.265
20-24	863	.297	.313	446	.245	.223
25-29	911	.009	.015	521	.024	.029
30-34	833	-.142	-.148	492	-.104	-.088
35-39	786	-.288	-.300	412	-.255	-.242
Education						
<9 years	427	.070	.096	178	-.096	-.043
9-11 years	1,103	.062	.051	453	.036	.038
12 years	1,511	-.029	-.035	909	.017	.003
13-15 years	340	-.052	-.067	289	-.019	-.021
16+ years	211	-.172	-.104	150	-.062	-.043
Region						
Northeast	695	-.044	-.008	355	-.014	.023
North Central	838	-.017	.007	410	-.029	-.034
South	1,749	.027	-.000	1,014	.020	.009
West	310	-.010	.002	199	-.020	-.017
Metropolitan Residence						
In SMSA						
Central City	2,071	-.038	-.035	1,116	-.010	-.006
Not Central City	651	.017	.031	405	.010	.010
Not in SMSA	870	.079	.059	458	.016	.007
Initial Parity						
0	1,186	.102	-.013	633	.145	.053
1	657	.043	.011	462	.045	.014
2	609	-.054	-.011	353	-.090	-.053
3	436	-.095	-.007	233	-.210	-.129
4+	705	-.106	.025	297	-.108	.031
Husband's Income[3]						
<$2,000	247	-.057	-.116	163	.041	-.004
$2,000-2,999	249	.042	-.051	126	.054	.002
$3,000-3,999	451	.078	.002	174	.065	.002
$4,000-4,999	521	.078	.032	270	-.010	-.051
$5,000-7,499	1,167	-.008	.000	574	-.024	-.017
$7,500-9,999	633	-.045	.019	421	-.013	.012
$10,000-14,999	278	-.086	.047	213	.008	.089
$15,000+	45	-.226	-.046	37	-.140	-.006
	Grand Mean = .461			Grand Mean = .385		

[1]This analysis was done from the March Current Population Surveys.

[2]Net of the other variables shown.

[3]Constant 1970 dollars.

References

Akers, D. S.
  1967 "On measuring the marriage squeeze." *Demography* 4:907–924.

Bean, F. D., and C. H. Wood
  1974 "Ethnic variations in the relationship between income and fertility." *Demography* 11:629–640.

Berent, J.
  1974 "Fertility and family planning in Europe around 1970: A comparative study of twelve national surveys. Some preliminary findings." Paper presented at the annual meetings of the Population Association of America, New York, April.

Blake, J.
  1974 "Can we believe recent data on birth expectations in the United States?" *Demography* 11:25–44.

Boyd, M.
  1974 "The changing nature of Central and Southeast Asian immigration to the United States: 1961–1972." *International Migration Review* 8:507–519.

Campbell, A. A.
  1974 "Beyond the demographic transition." *Demography* 11:549–561.

Carter, H., and P. C. Glick
  1970 *Marriage and Divorce: A Social and Economic Study.* Cambridge, Mass.: Harvard University Press.

Cho, L. J.
  1968 "Income and differentials in current fertility." *Demography* 5:198–211.
  1971 "On estimating annual birth rates from census data on children." Pp. 86–96 in *Proceedings from the American Statistical Association, Social Statistics Section.*
  1974 "The own-children approach to fertility estimation: An elaboration." Pp. 263–280 in *Proceedings of the International Population Conference, Liege, 1973.* Vol. 2. Liege: International Union for the Scientific Study of Population.

Cho, L. J., W. H. Grabill, and D. J. Bogue
  1970 *Differential Current Fertility in the United States.* Chicago: Community and Family Study Center.

Coale, A. J., and C. Y. Tye
   1961 "The significance of age-patterns of fertility in high fertility populations." *Milbank Memorial Fund Quarterly* 39:631–646.

Coale, A. J., and M. Zelnik
   1963 *New Estimates of Fertility and Population in the United States.* Princeton, N.J.: Princeton University Press.

Cohen, S. B., and J. A. Sweet
   1974 "The impact of marital disruption and remarriage on fertility." *Journal of Marriage and the Family* 36:87–96.

Coombs, L. C., and R. Freedman
   1966 "Childspacing and family economic position." *American Sociological Review* 31:631–648.
   1970 "Pre-marital pregnancy, childspacing, and later economic achievement." *Population Studies* 24:389–412.

Coombs, L. C., R. Freedman, J. Friedman, and W. F. Pratt
   1970 "Premarital pregnancy and status before and after marriage." *American Journal of Sociology* 75:800–820.

Davis, K., and J. Blake
   1956 "Social structure and fertility: An analytic framework." *Economic Development and Cultural Change* 4.

Davis, N. J., and L. L. Bumpass
   1976 "The continuation of education after marriage among women in the U.S.: 1970." *Demography* 13:161–174.

Easterlin, R. A.
   1962 "The American baby boom in historical perspective." National Bureau of Economic Research, Occasional Paper 79. New York.
   1966 "On the relation of economic factors to recent and projected fertility changes." *Demography* 3:131–153.
   1973 "Relative economic status and the American fertility swing." Pp. 170–223 in E. B. Sheldon (ed.), *Family Economic Behavior: Problems and Prospects.* Philadelphia: Lippincott.

Freedman, D.
   1963 "The relation of economic status to fertility." *American Economic Review* 53:414–426.

Freedman, R., P. K. Whelpton, and A. A. Campbell
   1959 *Family Planning, Sterility, and Population Growth.* New York: McGraw-Hill.

Gibson, C.
   1975 "Changes in marital status and marital fertility and their contribution to the decline in period fertility in the United States: 1961–1973." Paper presented at the annual meetings of the Population Association of America, Seattle, April.

Glass, D. V.
   1969 "Fertility trends in Europe since the Second World War." Pp. 25–74 in S. J. Behrman, L. Corsa, and R. Freedman (eds.), *Fertility and Family Planning: A World View.* Ann Arbor: University of Michigan Press.

Glick, P. C., and A. J. Norton
1973 "Perspectives on the recent upturn in divorce and remarriage." *Demography* 10:301–314.

Goldberg, D.
1974 "Modernism: The extensiveness of women's roles and attitudes." World Fertility Study, Occasional Paper 14.

Goldberg, D., and C. H. Coombs
1963 "Some applications of unfolding theory to fertility analysis." Pp. 105–129 in *Emerging Techniques in Population Research.* Proceedings of a Round Table at the 39th Annual Conference of the Milbank Memorial Fund. New York: Milbank Memorial Fund.

Goldscheider, C.
1971 *Population, Modernization, and Social Structure.* Boston: Little, Brown.

Goldscheider, C., and P. R. Uhlenberg
1969 "Minority group status and fertility." *American Journal of Sociology* 74:361–372.

Gorden, M.
1963 *Assimilation in American Life.* New York: Oxford University Press.

Grabill, W. H., and L. J. Cho
1965 "Methodology for the measurement of current fertility from population data on young children." *Demography* 2:50–73.

Grabill, W. H., C. V. Kiser, and P. K. Whelpton
1958 *The Fertility of American Women.* New York: Wiley.

Hauser, R. M., and D. L. Featherman
1974 "White–nonwhite differentials in occupational mobility among men in the United States, 1962–1972." *Demography* 11:247–265.

Hernandez, J., L. Estrada, and D. Alvirez
1973 "Census data and the problem of conceptually defining the Mexican American population." *Social Science Quarterly* 53:671–687.

Hostetler, J. A., and G. E. Huntington
1967 *The Hutterites in North America.* New York: Holt.

Jaffe, F. S., and A. F. Guttmacher
1968 "Family planning programs in the United States." *Demography* 5:910–923.

Keely, C. B.
1971 "Effects of the Immigration Act of 1965 on selected population characteristics of immigration to the United States." *Demography* 8:157–169.
1974 "Immigration composition and population policy." *Science* 185(4151):587–593.

Kennedy, R. E., Jr.
1973 "Minority group status and fertility: The Irish." *American Sociological Review* 38:85–96.

Kiser, C. V.
1969 "Educational differentials in fertility in relation to the demographic transition." Pp. 1926–1936 in *International Union for the Scientific Study of Population, General Conference: London, September 1969.* Vol. 3. London: International Union for the Scientific Study of Population.

Kiser, C. V., W. H. Grabill, and A. A. Campbell
   1968   *Trends and Variations in Fertility in the United States.* Cambridge, Mass.: Harvard
          University Press.

Kitagawa, E. M., and P. M. Hauser
   1973   *Differential Mortality in the United States.* Cambridge, Mass.: Harvard University
          Press.

Lauriat, P.
   1969   "The effect of marital dissolution on fertility." *Journal of Marriage and the
          Family* 31:484–493.

Lee, R. D.
   1974   "Forecasting births in post-transition populations: Stochastic renewal with
          serially correlated fertility." *Journal of the American Statistical Association*
          69:607–617.

Lindert, P. H.
   1974   "American fertility patterns since the Civil War." Center for Demography and
          Ecology, University of Wisconsin–Madison, Working Paper 74-27.

MacDonald, M. M., and R. R. Rindfuss
   1976   "Relative economic status and fertility: Evidence from a cross-section." Center
          for Demography and Ecology, University of Wisconsin–Madison, Working Paper
          76-1.

Macisco, J. J., Jr., L. F. Bouvier, and M. J. Renzi
   1969   "Migration status, education and fertility in Puerto Rico, 1960." *Milbank Memo-
          rial Fund Quarterly* 47:167–187.

Macisco, J. J., Jr., L. F. Bouvier, and R. H. Weller
   1970   "The effect of labor force participation on the relation between migration status
          and fertility in San Juan, Puerto Rico." *Milbank Memorial Fund Quarterly*
          48:51–70.

Mason, K. O.
   1974   *Women's Labor Force Participation and Fertility.* Final Report 21U-662, pre-
          pared for the National Institutes of Health under Contract NIH 71-2212.

Myers, G. C., and E. W. Morris
   1966   "Migration and fertility in Puerto Rico." *Population Studies* 20:85–96.

National Center for Health Statistics
   1969   *Vital Statistics of the United States.* Vol. 1. *Natality.* Washington, D.C.: Govern-
          ment Printing Office.
   1972   *Infant Mortality Rates: Socioeconomic Factors.* Washington, D.C.: Government
          Printing Office.
   1975   *Vital Statistics of the United States, 1970.* Vol. 1. *Natality.* Washington, D.C.:
          Government Printing Office.

National Office of Vital Statistics
   1950   "Births and birth rates in the entire United States, 1909–1948." *Selected Studies,*
          Vol. 33, No. 8, September 29. Washington, D.C.: U.S. Govt. Printing Office.
   1950   *Vital Statistics of the United States.* Vol. 1. Washington, D.C.: U.S. Govt.
          Printing Office.

Notestein, F. W.
   1936   "Class differences in fertility." *Annals of the American Academy of Political and
          Social Science* 188:26–36.

Orshansky, M.

1965 "Counting the poor: Another look at the poverty profile." Pp. 67–106 in L. A. Ferman, J. L. Kornbluh, and A. Haber (eds.), *Poverty in America: A Book of Readings.* Ann Arbor: University of Michigan Press.

1968 "The shape of poverty in 1966." *Social Security Bulletin* (March):3–32.

Presser, H. B.

1971 "The timing of the first birth, female roles and black fertility." *Milbank Memorial Fund Quarterly* 49:329–362.

Presser, H. B., and L. L. Bumpass

1972 "The acceptability of contraceptive sterilization among U.S. couples: 1970." *Family Planning Perspectives* 4:18–28.

Retherford, R. D., and L. J. Cho

1974 "Age-parity-specific fertility rates from census or survey data on own children." Paper presented at the annual meetings of the Population Association of America, New York, April.

Rindfuss, R. R.

1976 "Fertility rates for racial and social subpopulations within the United States: 1945–1969." Center for Demography and Ecology, University of Wisconsin–Madison, Working Paper 76-29.

Rindfuss, R. R., and L. L. Bumpass

Forth-
coming "Age and the sociology of fertility: How old is too old?" In K. E. Taeuber (ed.), *Proceedings of the Conference on Social Demography* (University of Wisconsin–Madison, July 1975).

Rindfuss, R. R., and C. F. Westoff

1974 "The initiation of contraception." *Demography* 11:75–87.

Roberts, R. E., and E. S. Lee

1974 "Minority group status and fertility revisited." *American Journal of Sociology* 80:503–523.

Rockwell, R. C.

1975 "An investigation of imputation and differential quality of data in the 1970 Census." *Journal of the American Statistical Association* 70:39–42.

Rowe, J. S.

1974 "Census data in machine-readable form." *Population Index* 40:623–635.

Ryder, N. B.

1960 "The structure and tempo of current fertility." Pp. 117–133 in *Demographic and Economic Change in Developed Countries.* Report of the National Bureau of Economic Research. Princeton, N.J.: Princeton University Press.

1969 "The emergence of a modern fertility pattern: United States, 1917–66." Pp. 99–123 in S. J. Behrman, L. Corsa, Jr., and R. Freedman (eds.), *Fertility and Family Planning: A World View.* Ann Arbor: University of Michigan Press.

1972 "Time series of pill and IUD use: United States, 1961–1970." *Studies in Family Planning* 3:233–256.

1973 "A critique of the National Fertility Study." *Demography* 10:495–506.

Ryder, N. B., and C. F. Westoff

1971 *Reproduction in the United States, 1965.* Princeton, N.J.: Princeton University Press.

1972 "Wanted and unwanted fertility in the United States: 1965 and 1970." Pp. 467–487 in C. F. Westoff and R. Parke, Jr. (eds.), *Demographic and Social Aspects of Population Growth.* Vol. 1 of research reports of U.S. Commission on Population Growth and the American Future. Washington, D.C.: Government Printing Office.

Sallume, X., and F. W. Notestein
1932 "Trends in the size of families completed prior to 1910 in various social classes." *American Journal of Sociology* 38:398–408.

Sarvis, B., and H. Rodman
1974 *The Abortion Controversy.* 2nd ed. New York: Columbia University Press.

Schnore, L. F.
1961 "Social mobility in demographic perspective." *American Sociological Review* 26:407–423 (Bobbs-Merrill Reprint S-499).

Seltzer, W.
1973 "Demographic data collection: A summary of experience." An occasional paper of the Population Council, New York.

Shryock, H. S., and J. S. Siegel
1973 *The Methods and Materials of Demography.* Washington, D.C.: Government Printing Office.

Siegel, J. S.
1974 "Estimates of coverage of the population by sex, race, and age in the 1970 Census." *Demography* 11:1–24.

Sklar, J., and B. Berkov
1975 "The American birth rate: Evidence of a coming rise." *Science* 189(4204): 693–700.

Sly, D. F.
1970 "Minority-group status and fertility: An extension of Goldscheider and Uhlenberg." *American Journal of Sociology* 76:443–459.

Spilerman, S.
1975 "Forecasting social events." Pp. 381–403 in K. C. Land and S. Spilerman (eds.), *Social Indicator Models.* New York: Russell Sage Foundation.

Sweet, J. A.
1973a "Differentials in remarriage probabilities." Center for Demography and Ecology, University of Wisconsin, Working Paper 73-29.
1973b *Women in the Labor Force.* New York: Seminar Press.
1974 "Recent fertility change among high fertility minorities in the U.S." Center for Demography and Ecology, University of Wisconsin, Working Paper 74-11.

Sydenstriker, E., and F. W. Notestein
1930 "Differential fertility according to social class." *Journal of the American Statistical Association* 25:9–32.

Taeuber, I. B.
1966 "Migration and transformation: Spanish surname populations and Puerto Rico." *Population Index* 32:3–34.

Taeuber, I. B., and C. Taeuber
1971 *People of the United States in the 20th Century* (a Census monograph). Washington, D.C.: Government Printing Office.

Teitelbaum, M. S.
   1973   "U.S. population growth in international perspective." Pp. 69–83 in C. F. Westoff
          (ed.), *Toward the End of Growth: Population in America.* Englewood Cliffs: N.J.:
          Prentice-Hall.

Tidalgo, R. L.
   1974   "Wages and the wage structure in the Philippines." Unpublished Ph.D. disserta-
          tion, Department of Economics, University of Wisconsin–Madison.

U.S. Bureau of the Census
   1963   U.S. Census of Population: 1960. Subject Reports, Final Report PC(2)-1C,
          Nonwhite Population by Race. Washington, D.C.: Government Printing Office.
   1971   "Population Characteristics." *Current Population Reports,* Series P-20, No. 211
          (January), Table 1. Washington, D.C.: Government Printing Office.
   1972   *Public Use Samples of Basic Records from the 1970 Census.* Washington, D.C.:
          Government Printing Office.
   1973a U.S. Census of Population: 1970. Subject Reports, Final Report PC(1)-A53,
          Number of Inhabitants, Puerto Rico. Washington, D.C.: Government Printing
          Office.
   1973b U.S. Census of Population: 1970. Subject Reports, Final Report PC(2)-1E, *Puerto
          Ricans in the United States.* Washington, D.C.: Government Printing Office.
   1973c U.S. Census of Population: 1970. Subject Reports, Final Report PC(2)-1F,
          American Indians. Washington, D.C.: Government Printing Office.
   1973d U.S. Census of Population: 1970. Subject Reports, Final Report PC(2)-1G,
          Japanese, Chinese, and Filipinos in the United States. Washington, D.C.: Govern-
          ment Printing Office.
   1973e U.S. Census of Population: 1970. Subject Reports, Final Report PC(2)-3A,
          Women by Number of Children Ever Born. Washington, D.C.: Government
          Printing Office.
   1973f U.S. Census of Population: 1970. Subject Reports, Final Report PC(2)-4D, *Age at
          First Marriage.* Washington, D.C.: Government Printing Office.
   1973g U.S. Census of Population: 1970. Subject Reports, Final Report PC(2)-5B,
          Educational Attainment. Washington, D.C.: Government Printing Office.
   1974a "Population Characteristics." *Current Population Reports,* Series P-20, No. 263
          (April). Washington, D.C.: Government Printing Office.
   1974b "Population Characteristics." *Current Population Reports,* Series P-20, No. 265
          (June). Washington, D.C.: Government Printing Office.
   1975   "Population Characteristics." *Current Population Reports,* Series P-20, No. 277
          (February). Washington, D.C.: Government Printing Office.

Wax, M. L.
   1971   *Indian Americans: Unity and Diversity.* Englewood Cliffs, N.J.: Prentice-Hall.

Westoff, C. F.
   1972   "The modernization of U.S. contraceptive practice." *Family Planning Perspectives*
          4:9–12.
   1974   "The population of the developed countries." *Scientific American* 231:109–120.
   1976   "The decline of unplanned births in the United States." *Science* 191(4222):38–
          41.

Whelpton, P. K.
   1928   "Industrial development and population growth." *Social Forces* 6:458–467, 629–
          638.

Zarate, A. O., and A. U. Zarate
   1974 "On the reconciliation of research findings of migrant–nonmigrant fertility differ-
         entials in urban areas." Paper presented at the annual meetings of the Population
         Association of America, New York, April.

Zelnik, M., and J. F. Kantner
   1972 "Sexuality, contraception and pregnancy among young unwed females in the
         United States." Pp. 355–374 in C. F. Westoff and R. Parke, Jr. (eds.), *Demo-
         graphic and Social Aspects of Population Growth*. Vol. 1 of research reports of
         U.S. Commission on Population Growth and the American Future. Washington,
         D.C.: Government Printing Office.

Index

A

Abortion, 4
Adoption
  age-specific fertility rates and, 31
  own-children data and, 10, 19, 50–51
Age
  annual fertility rates, by ethnicity and,
    93
  fertility trends by education and, 48–49
  first marriage, at, 3
    CPS data on, 87
    minority group differentials, 7
    recent marital fertility, by, 71–73, 87,
      105–110
      decline, 112, 161
      differentials, 118, 128, 133, 137, 150,
        169
    truncation by, 64
  missstatement in own-children data, 6
    11–12, 14, 19–20
  Puerto Rican migration by children ever
    born and, 180
  recent fertility and, 191
  rural/urban fertility rates by, 156–160
    education and, 160
American Indians, 7
  age pattern of fertility, 139–148
  annual fertility rates, 89–97, 115–116
  changing status and fertility, 100–101

  recent marital fertility, 70, 117–126,
    148–150

B

Birthplace
  husband's, by wife's, and fertility
    differentials, 139
  Puerto Rican migration and fertility
    differentials by, 179–180
  recent marital fertility by
    decline, 110, 112
    differentials, 125–126, 132
Black Americans
  age pattern of fertility, 139–148
  annual fertility rates, 89–97, 115–116
  fertility trends
    by education, 44–49
    post-1970, 209–211
  illegitimacy, 64, 201
  marital disruption, 64
  non-Southern, recent marital fertility
    decline, 110–116
    differentials, 117, 126–132, 148–150
  recent marital fertility, 70, 103–132,
    148–150
  Southern rural, recent marital fertility
    decline, 103–110
    differentials, 117–126, 148–150

221

Southern urban, recent marital fertility,
  decline, 110–116
  differentials, 117, 126–132, 148–150

C

Census data
  advantages of using, 5
  contraception reported in, 6
  disadvantages of using, 6
  migration reported in, 184
    Puerto Rican, 175–177
      husband's income and, 176
      "never-married" women and, 176–177
  period fertility, reconstruction of, and, 6
  religion reported in, 6
Children ever born, and Puerto Rican
  migration, 180, 183
Childspacing, 3
Chinese Americans
  age pattern of fertility, 139–148
    by education, 148
  annual fertility rates, 89–97, 115–116
  recent marital fertility differentials, 70,
    117, 133–137, 148–150
Contraception, 3–4, 6
  education and, 41–42
  rural women and, 172
Crude birth rate, 3
Current Population Survey, 8, 186–191

D

Demographic transition and education, 43
Divorce, see marital disruption
Draft, the, see military service

E

Easterlin fertility hypothesis, 76
Education
  demographic transition and, 43
  husband's,
    recent marital fertility by, 87
    by wife's education, 65–69
  marriage squeeze and, 42–43
  military service and, 43
  minority group fertility differentials by, 7,
    see also specific minority groups

occupation and, 43
recent fertility and, 65–69, 191
wife's
  age pattern of fertility, and
    by race, 49–59
    by rural/urban residence, 166,
      171–172
  annual fertility rates, and, 33–59
    by ethnicity, 96–97
    ultimate versus current education,
      37–38
  contraception and, 41–42
  by husband's education, 65–69
  by husband's income, 79–80
  recent marital fertility by, 65–69, 87,
    105
    declines, 86, 112, 161
    differentials, 118, 128, 133, 137, 148,
      150, 166
  total fertility rate, by age and, 160
Ethnicity, see also specific minority groups
  annual fertility rates by, 89–97
  husband's, by wife's, and fertility
    differentials, 123–124, 133–137
  recent marital fertility by, 61, 69–70, 87,
    97–116

F

Farm population, recent fertility
  differentials, 166–169, 172
  levels, 160–163
Fertility
  age pattern of, 7, 49–59
    by education and race, 49–59
    by minority group status, 139–148, see
      also specific minority groups
    rural/urban white, 164–166, 169–172
      by education, 166
  rates
    annual age-specific, 10–11, 33–59,
      89–116, 139–166, 169–172
    construction of, 11
    by education, 33–59
    fertility trends, and, 29–31
    for minority groups, 89–116, see also
      specific minority groups
    nonmarital fertility and, 30
    own-children data and, 10
    proportions currently married and, 30

by race, 33–59, 199–202
by rural/urban residence, 151–172
marital, recent, 3, 7, 11, 25–31,
61–150, 160–164, 166–169,
177–180, 182–183, 187–192,
203–207
construction of measure, 11, 25–26
definition of, 10
for minority groups, 89–116,
117–150, *see also* specific minority
groups
own-children data and, 25–29
period, 2, 5–6
total, 2, 6
by education, 38–43
by education and race, 44–49
by rural/urban residence, 155–160
timing of, 5
income changes and, 121
trends, 7
by race, 7, 33–59
by wife's education, 33–59
Filipino Americans
migration and fertility, 100–103
recent marital fertility, 70

H

Homogamy, 113

I

Illegitimacy, 64, 201
Income
family, 63
fertility differentials by, 5
husband's
Puerto Rican migration and, 176
recent marital fertility and, 75–82,
87–88, 110, 191
declines and, 87, 112, 161
differentials and, 121–123, 131–133,
139, 149–150, 166–169
minority group differentials in, 7, *see
also* specific minority groups
variability of, 29–30
Indians, *see* American Indians
Intentions, fertility, 4–5
census data on, 6

J

Japanese Americans, 7
age pattern of fertility, 139–148
annual fertility rates, 89–97, 115–116
recent marital fertility, 70, 117, 133–137,
148–150

L

Labor force participation, women's, and
recent fertility, 61–62

M

Marital disruption, 3, 64
Marriage duration
CPS data on, 187
fertility decline by, 86–87, 112, 163
fertility rates by, 61, 71–79, 87, 103–105
Marriage squeeze, 42–43, 59
Married, number of times, and recent
fertility, 82–86
Mexican Americans, 7
age pattern of fertility, 139–148
annual fertility rates, 89–97, 115–116
self-identification, 90–91
Migration and fertility, 8
Filipino American, 100–103
Puerto Rican, 173–184
rural/urban, 154–155
Military service, 43
education and, 43, 54–55, 59
Minority group status and fertility, 89–150,
173–184, 199–211
see also American Indians, Black
Americans, Chinese Americans, Filipino
Americans, Japanese Americans,
Mexican Americans, Puerto Rican
Americans, and Spanish-surname
population
age-specific fertility rates by education,
33–59
differentials within, among groups,
117–150, 203–207
Puerto Rican migration and fertility,
173–184
stability of estimates, 199–202
trends for 1955–1969, 89–116

Mortality, and own-children data, 6, 10,
13–15, 20–25
    infant, 93

O

Occupation, 3, 5
    husband's
        and education, 43, 59
        recent marital fertility by, 70–71,
            118–121, 130–131, 137–139, 161,
            166
        variability of, 29–30
Origin, region of, *see* birthplace
Own-children data, 9–31
    adjustment of, 13–25
    adoption and, 10
    advantages of using, 6
    birth history data and, 25–29, 31
    census tabulations and, 6, 10
    data requirements, 6, 9–25
    definition, 10
    disadvantages of using, 6
    recent fertility and, 25–29
    in Survey of Economic Opportunity,
        25–29
    vital registration data compared with, 13
Own children under 3, number of, *see*
    recent fertility

P

Parity, initial
    CPS data on, 187
    recent fertility by, 61, 71–74, 80, 86–87,
        103–105, 112, 163, 191
Poverty, and recent fertility, 61–63
Puerto Rican
    Americans, 8
        recent marital fertility of, 117,
            137–139, 148–150
    migrants versus nonmigrants, 173–184
Puerto Rico, Census of, 8, 173

R

Race, *see also* ethnicity, minority group
    status and fertility
    age pattern of fertility, by education and,
        49–59

annual age-specific fertility rates by,
    33–59, 199–202
CPS data on, 188
fertility differentials by, 3, 28–29
recent fertility and, 28–29, 169, 203–207
Religion, 6
Residence
    fertility differentials by, 3, 74–75
    metropolitan
        Puerto Rican migration by, 175–176
        recent marital fertility by, 61, 74–75
    region, geographic
        recent marital fertility by, 61, 74–75,
            163, 169
    rural/urban
        age pattern of fertility by, 169–172
        CPS data on, 187
        definitions, 151–154
        fertility differentials by, 3, 7–8
        Puerto Rican migration and, 154–155,
            179, 183
        recent marital fertility by, 75, 87, 110
        total fertility rate by, 155–160

S

Separation, *see* marital disruption
Spanish-surname population
    recent marital fertility, 70, 117–126
        declines in, 103–110
        differentials in, 148–150
Sterilization, 4
Survey of Economic Opportunity, 25

U

Underenumeration
    of black women, 201–202
    minimizing the effects of, 64
    own-children data and, 6, 11–12, 14–16,
        20–25

V

Vital registration data, 1, 5–6, 9
    comparison with own-children data,
        13–25

W

White Americans
    age pattern of fertility, 139–148,
        155–172
    annual age-specific fertility rates, 33–59,
    89–97, 115–116
    by rural residence, 151–172
    recent marital fertility, 70
    decline, 86–87
    differentials, 61–88, 148–150, 195–198